or

series:

egion.

c:

ania & New Jersey.

By the same autho

Watermen

Lonely Planet guidebook
Puerto Rico
The Virgin Islands
Virginia & the Capital R

National Geographic
Driving Guide to New York, Pennsylv

LOGS OF THE
DEAD PIRATES
SOCIETY

A Schooner Adventure Around Buzzards Bay

Randall S. Peffer

SHERIDAN HOUSE

First published 2000 by
Sheridan House Inc.
145 Palisade Street
Dobbs Ferry, NY 10522
www.sheridanhouse.com

Library of Congress Cataloging-in-Publication Data

Peffer, Randall S.
Logs of the Dead Pirates Society: a schooner adventure
around Buzzards Bay / Randall Peffer.
    p.   cm
ISBN 1-57409-095-X (alk. paper)
1. Marine biology—Study and teaching (Secondary)—
Massachusetts—Buzzards Bay. 2. Buzzards Bay (Mass.:Bay)—
Description and travel. I. Title

QH105.M4.P44 2000
508.3163'46—dc21   99-086721

Edited by Janine Simon
Designed by Jesse Sanchez
Map by Noah Peffer

Printed in the United States of America

ISBN   1-57409-095-X

*T*o my family
Jackie, Jake, and Noah
with love, gratitude,
and anticipation of the
voyages yet to come

The only mention the Mashpee make of former religious beliefs is that the spirits of the departed(tcipai) frequently appeared in the paths of the living, and that such ghosts required propitiation before they could be induced to clear the way.

"I wish the boy were here."
—Ernest Hemingway, *The Old Man and the Sea*

ACKNOWLEDGMENTS

This volume grew out of a complex of collaborations. Without the vision and support of Margot Rice Jay (chief scientist), Phyllis Powell (Director of Summer Session) and Don McNemar (Head of School), in 1984, the Phillips Academy *Oceans* program would never have been given license to set sail. In the wake of these founders, have come equally supportive Summer Session heads Elwin Sykes, Pam Brown, and Jan Lisiak in addition to Head of School Barbara Landis Chase. Over the years the research crew aboard the schooner SARAH ABBOT have explored the seas of coastal Massachusetts with a collection of gifted marine scientists including Neil Glickstein, Jeff Goodyear, Bruce Morehouse, Ailene Rogers, Betsy Stevens, Asha Lord, Margaret Brumsted, Jessica Hill, Sarah Hammond and John Rogers. Special recognition goes to Dr. Numi Goodyear Mitchell as the scientist aboard SARAH ABBOT who conspired with captain and crew one foggy night in Provincetown Harbor to frame the "Articles of Faith" of the Dead Pirates Society.

In a sense all of the more than 250 teenage students who have sailed aboard SARAH ABBOT are contributors to this story. Each of them has left a mark on the schooner's captain and scientists, and each has her or his name carved on "The Plank" in the forward head of the schooner. Eighteen of my shipmates contributed directly to this text. This book would simply not exist without their perceptions and words that they have permitted me to paraphrase and quote liberally. My deepest appreciation goes to Katie Tottenham, Wynne Cathcart, Roy Murillo, Craig Laws, Alex Darrow, Shin Takeda, Mark Prager, Katie Turcotte, Melanie Baker, Kathleen

Reardon, Meghan Brown, Gillian Chesney, Sarah Chung, Randy Harrell, Lew Halloway, Lia Sinoris, and Mark Kilmer.

A grant from the Keenan Trust supported the purchase of rare books on coastal Massachusetts and a computer for the ship's library. Jack Richards, John Gould, Seth Mendell, and John Rogers as well as my agent Blanche Schlessinger and publisher Lothar Simon offered thoughtful criticism on this manuscript that led to its current shape. Susan Noble and her staff of research librarians at Phillips Academy's Oliver Wendell Holmes Library aided this project with their magical ability to unearth rare and valuable sources at lightning speed.

Finally, the schooner SARAH ABBOT's safe operation over more than 45 cruises has come to no small degree as a consequence of the maritime skills of her long-time relief skipper Captain Paul Zychowicz and her first mates, my older son Noah and my wife Jackie.

Thanks to all!

Stir it up,
Randall Peffer
12/12/99

C O N T E N T S

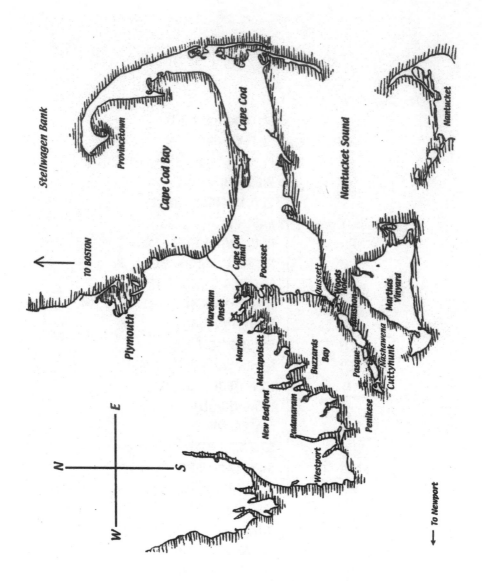

INTRODUCTION

On a morning in early July, my arms shuddered with an odd sensation as I carried my seabag aboard the research schooner SARAH ABBOT. While I stowed my gear in the hammock over the captain's quarterberth that would be my home for about the next five weeks, my breathing came fast and shallow.

It wasn't that there was anything wrong exactly, although maybe there was. But my body had never felt like this before in the two decades that I had lived in a house facing out on Buzzards Bay from the south coast of Massachusetts, nor in the fourteen years that I had been sailing south into the Bay from my home port of Marion as captain of this research schooner. Not even this mild, blue day and a fair breeze could shake the electricity from my bones. It was a tingling that I could only associate with the feelings I got almost 25 years ago, on my first day aboard the RUBY G. FORD.

I remembered the moment like it was only yesterday. RUBY G. FORD had been one of the last 20 or so working skipjacks —the graceful white sloops with long needle-like bowsprits that have been drudging oysters on Chesapeake Bay under sail since the 1860s. On the first Saturday of November 1975 the skipjacks were dressed for a ritual. The ritual was the Chesapeake Bay Appreciation Day skipjack race, which marked the beginning of the oyster season. This was to be my first season as crew aboard one of America's last working sailboats. It was a chance to call time out after graduate school and before plunging into a career as a writer and teacher. A chance to do something that seemed more important at the time than just "getting on" with academic professions.

1

Although I had been messing about in boats most of my young life, I mark this skipjack race as the beginning of my adulthood and a life forever divided between the dreamy intrigues of academia and the high-stakes challenges of seafaring. With this race I was embarking on a course that would eventually lead me from the duties of able-bodied seaman and fisherman to the responsibilities of mate and captain aboard traditional sailing vessels. But no such insights into my future crossed my mind on race day. All I knew was that joining the crew of the RUBY G. FORD as a deck hand offered me the rare chance to track down the mythology of my family's roots that ran back through the generations to a slough of mariners. One, Captain John Smith of Jamestown and Pocahontas fame, had been among the first English explorers of America. And in his wake came a tide of his relatives—and mine—to settle this eastern frontier as Chesapeake watermen and New England whalers. So the skipjack race posed a special opportunity and a challenge to me. It signified what workboat races always have to young, unseasoned sailors—a time to find oneself in the mariner's work, a rite of passage.

On the morning of the race, I was the first of the crew to arrive at the skipjack as she bobbed in the current at a wharf on Tilghman Island, Maryland. Images from *Captains Courageous* and *Moby Dick* flashed through my mind with a thousand hopes and fears. For the race, for the coming oyster season, but most of all for what I might find out about myself and the shadowy mariners who had passed this way in other generations, bearing my blood.

Now, aboard the schooner SARAH ABBOT, more than 500 miles of coastline and nearly 25 years lay between me and my youth on the Chesapeake. But today the memory of my rite of passage aboard RUBY G. FORD swam in my mind. Somehow I should have known that Buzzards Bay had set barbs in me that it had never used before, that my leave taking today was different from my hundreds of other goings to sea. I might have guessed that this summer I had no choice but to get to know this place and my relation to the waters of my own frontyard in ways I could not yet begin to imagine.

But I couldn't read the clues. Yet, looking back, I see something more. While the experience of exploring my home waters this summer aboard a research schooner held singular discoveries for me, the exploit was just the kind of thing that might happen to almost any traveler along any patch of largely-familiar coast. Occasionally time and environment can conspire to turn a routine trip into what Joseph Conrad described in his novella *Youth*, "those voyages that seem illustrations of life, that might stand for a symbol of existence." For Conrad such rites of passage from youth to adulthood or from innocence to experience inevitably took the shape of exotic adventures like working a bark off a lee shore in the Gulf of Thailand, trying to sail a burning cargo of coal from England to Bangkok, or navigating the uncharted waters of the Congo into the heart of darkness. Conrad and his cast of characters lived grand, dangerous, foreign epics. But no such thing for me. This adventure found me close to home when I was too distracted by familiar roles and obligations to see the lightning bolt of fate pointing in my direction.

Some years ago a sailing captain I know lost his ship on a reef at the entrance to his home port on a fair summer day. How does such a thing happen, I wondered aloud to another professional schooner captain. I remember him looking me in the eyes with a face that seemed to age into ledges and crows' feet as I stared.

"There but for the grace of God go you or I," he said in a quiet, hoarse voice. "It is precisely when you think you know a place, that it can give you the surprise of your life."

Before this summer I thought I had a reasonably solid handle on Buzzards Bay, myself, the mariner's life and a few pieces of America's history. Total mirage.

I OUTWARD BOUND

The wind came up for the start of our research cruise, blowing a steady 15 knots out of the north. This was a rare wind for the beginning of July, but an exceedingly lucky one. The cold front that brought us this wind had passed south of Buzzards Bay and left us with crystal sunlight, visibility to the horizon, low humidity, temperatures in the high seventies, and gentle seas. Best of all, this norther was the breeze to carry SARAH ABBOT on a fast passage down Buzzards Bay from my home and the schooner's base in Marion near the head of the Bay to Cuttyhunk Island at the mouth.

Buzzards Bay is a focal point for a high school marine science program called *Oceans*. For fourteen years students in the Summer Session of Phillips Academy at Andover, Massachusetts, have been exploring the Bay as well as the rest of coastal Massachusetts. Their vehicle, research platform, and bunkhouse is SARAH ABBOT. Except for the naturally-finished mahogany topsides that make her look a bit like a yacht, the 55-foot two-master is the very image of a Grand Banks fishing schooner like the BLUENOSE on the Canadian dime. Designed and built in 1966 by David Stevens, one of Nova Scotia's legendary schoonermen, SARAH ABBOT spent the first nineteen years of her life as a private racing and cruising vessel before I bought her and put her to work for *Oceans*.

With eighteen students in the program, *Oceans* runs three separate cruises. Each student spends about four weeks on campus in Andover with other Summer Session students and eleven days sailing on the schooner. At any given moment during the program, twelve teenagers are studying ashore with one biologist; six students are aboard SARAH ABBOT with another marine scientist.

After the scientist and the six students arrived at noon today from Andover to begin their research cruise, events rushed by me in a blur as we scrambled to load two weeks of provisions, crates of scientific equipment, and a mound of personal gear aboard the schooner. Somehow, we ran through safety drills for fire, man overboard, and abandoning ship. At some point, I oriented the crew to the schooner's deck and individual sail-handling stations. But I was so eager to get out on the Bay and catch this breeze, I really do not remember casting off the lines from Island Wharf. And only a few hazy images of setting sails lingered in my mind as the schooner began gliding through the hundreds of cruising boats and racing dinghies that were swarming around the harbor entrance at Marion on this Fourth of July holiday weekend.

At last, five miles out in the middle of Buzzards Bay, the schooner was clipping along at seven knots with a bone of spray in her teeth. We could hear the creaking of the rigging as SARAH ABBOT rolled a bit before a following sea. Our two dinghies towed easily astern like a pair of offspring. A fishing line trailed off to leeward, set to catch bluefish if we hit a school. Meanwhile, a trio of roseate terns hovered above the lure wondering if it was a wounded herring, yet suspicious that it swam too fast. The mate, my wife Jackie, coached a student in the fine art of steering a schooner running before the wind.

As the Bay changed to a sea of diamonds with the sun's descent to the west, I could not help remembering the English explorer Bartholomew Gosnold and his company who sailed into Buzzards Bay aboard the square-rigged bark CONCORD in 1602. One of Gosnold's chroniclers Gabriel Archer, "a gentleman in said voyage," described this place as "one of the stateliest sounds that ever I was in."

Seeing it for the first time, the teenagers aboard SARAH ABBOT seemed to agree with Archer. Except for the boy at the helm, the crew sat saucer-eyed on the foredeck.

Jackie saw me scrutinizing the crew, cataloging their fit bodies, their smooth faces, the rich colors their hair made in the sunlight.

"Is something the matter?" she whispered when we were alone out of earshot of the helmsman.

I shook my head "no" and said I didn't think so. But didn't the crew look really young this trip?

Meanwhile SARAH ABBOT closed with the green hills of the Elizabeth Islands and a dark mound against a pastel sky, Cuttyhunk, still more than 15 miles away. Our schooner had sailed to within two miles of the Elizabeth Island chain, and I saw the sassafras and bayberry of the uplands glowing a soft emerald. Mist gathered on the lowlands and over the tidal marshes. Meanwhile minutes passed while I stood in the bows of the schooner, tried to keep my balance in the rolling seas, stared at the coast, and felt for a moment as if I had never seen this place before in my life.

Yet I knew these waters and shores the way my mother knew her kitchen cabinets. The Europeans who sailed here in the wake of Gosnold's CONCORD called Archer's stately sound "Buzzards Bay" because they saw the black and white fishhawks—osprey—wheeling in gyres like smoke from a thousand Indian fires on the Bay shores. Approximately 228 square miles in size, Buzzards Bay is a medium-sized estuary, stretching 28 miles long, with an average width of about eight miles and an average depth of 36 feet. The coastline spans over 280 miles, including 17 municipalities where more than 236,000 people live and millions vacation and go boating each summer.

Approximately 15,000 years ago, during the last ice age, advancing and retreating glaciers gouged Buzzards Bay from the earth's crust. Glacial debris deposited by the glacier's leading edge litter the southeastern side of the Bay (Bourne, Falmouth, and the Elizabeth islands). On the northwestern side (Wareham to Westport) elongated bays and inlets developed as the glacier withdrew to the north.

Such are the facts, yet command of these details failed to comfort me as I stood in the bows of SARAH ABBOT. For me, the Bay that I brought my crew to explore was not simply a geographical phenomenon. It was the flash of a bluefish cutting through a school of bait, the screech of terns, the gyres of osprey, the silhouette of a gaff-rigged schooner against the sunset, and the howl of hurricanes.

And there was a flood of history here, too. Buzzards Bay teemed with tales about the discoverers of New England, bloody King Philip's War, bold piracy, Revolutionary War daring, and the rise and fall of the whaling industry. Captain Kidd, John Paul Jones, and the heroes of Moby Dick found adventure on these waters. Gallant women like Awashonks, the squaw sachem of the Sakonnet Wampanoags, the "witch of Wall Street" Hetty Green, and philanthropist Elizabeth Taber once ruled these shores. Here was a landscape novelist Henry James depicted as "a land of dreams, a country in a picture," a place almost designed to overwhelm.

But on the first day of our cruise, the six teenagers aboard SARAH ABBOT—and their captain—had no idea what they had come up against; we were simply primed for exploration. One boy from West Virginia, caught up in this adrenaline-pumping sail down the Bay, was teaching his shipmates to shout out rebel yells in response to every burst of spray that showered aboard. His most vigorous apprentice/practitioner of the rebel yell was a girl from Athens, Greece. A girl from Texas tiptoed into the bows of the schooner to watch the sunset. Shipmates from Atlanta and Los Angeles joined her there for a while to write in their logs. Back in the cockpit a blond surfer from Virginia Beach stood his first trick at the helm.

Phillips Academy is one of America's oldest and best known preparatory schools, but SARAH ABBOT's crew were not preppies. My new shipmates were not Phillips students during the school year, nor did many of them attend other private schools. These teenagers applied to be part of the *Oceans* program from high schools all over the globe—poor and affluent, male and female, every race. Their tickets to admission had nothing to do with wealth or privilege and much to do with an open, curious mind, and adventurous spirit.

Just like their teacher. Our scientist on this cruise was Margaret Brumsted, a red-haired dynamo. Today, Margaret had started her day with a jog and followed it up by leading her students on an exploration of the intertidal zone in Marion before permitting her charges to even set a foot aboard the schooner. Whether teaching students how to make spat bags for a scallop reseeding project, testing water quality in a harbor, or organizing the crew to tow a 100-foot beach seine net, Margaret worked side-by-side with our crew. This was the style that had won her awards at Dartmouth High School in southeastern Massachusetts, including state Science Teacher of the Year. Now, as the sun set on SARAH ABBOT's passage to Cuttyhunk, Margaret patrolled the deck in her ball cap, mirror sun glasses, and polar fleece sweater, button-holing each of her students and quizzing them about the "what," "why," and "how" of their up-coming cruise projects in marine biology. She was over 40 years old, but she still had not lost the energy of a youth right out of college. I had to wonder how she managed it.

Later, as a cool wind began sweeping the deck, my wife Jackie attracted a group of admirers into the galley for tea, cookies, and conversation about the families they left behind. Jackie and I met when the schooner sailed into Marblehead, Massachusetts, some years ago after participating in one of Boston's tall ships extravaganzas. With curly brown hair and a gymnast's commitment to fitness, Jackie had now sailed as mate on SARAH ABBOT for five years. Her unusual social intelligence, perfected in her winter job as a kindergarten teacher, had brought a new level of sensitivity and reflection into the daily lives of all of us on the schooner. And because of Jackie, SARAH ABBOT had become a kinder, gentler vessel. Often I had the sense that she understood me better than I understood myself. Marrying her four years ago was the smartest thing I had ever done. She was 13 years my junior, but in many ways my lifering.

But now, even Jackie's steady presence was not enough to rescue me from feeling disoriented. Fortunately, my shipmates seemed not to notice my uneasiness. Their thoughts lay on the adventure and the mission to come. Past research cruises had generally taken a random track around the Bay and the Massachusetts coast dictated by the needs of the scientists, the cruise projects of the students, and, of course, the weather. But this summer the *Oceans* faculty and crews had pledged to try something new. We wanted to make a thorough and coherent investigation of Buzzards Bay. Like Bartholomew Gosnold's crew aboard the CONCORD, we planned to explore from west to east, crossing and recrossing this bay that lay cupped between the Elizabeth Islands on the southeast and the Massachusetts coast on the northwest.

Jackie, the scientists, and I hoped to give our young shipmates a feel for the experience Charles Darwin had when he sailed as a young man on the BEAGLE's mapping expedition around South America. Darwin kept a log of his close encounters and observations with foreign environments, creatures and cultures. From those notes, he wrote *The Voyage of the Beagle*. So, along with pursuing their study of marine biology, SARAH ABBOT's crew kept logs like Darwin and read books—like *Moby Dick* and *A Storm Without Rain*—about Bay history as well. I was not just the captain, I was the crew's English tutor, a familiar role since I taught literature and writing at Andover during the regular school year.

To be honest, I don't remember whether the idea to make a methodical survey of the Bay this summer had come from me, Jackie, or one of the scientists; but the mission appealed. The Bay was like a jigsaw puzzle whose pieces I had been laying out in my mind for years. Now, I felt a growing urge to begin connecting the fragments, to see the big picture of this "stateliest sound." As we set out, I imagined that the effort might be a mildly entertaining diversion in the midst of this job as captain that had grown largely routine and predictable after fourteen years. I could not yet conceive how the puzzle would come together, or what events lay ahead.

II CUTTYHUNK

Cruise One's mission was to explore the western end—the mouth—of Buzzards Bay for the next eleven days. The first leg of our adventure took us to Cuttyhunk just like Gosnold and his crew. This three-mile long, a half-mile wide hilly island at the southwest end of the Elizabeth Islands on the coast of Massachusetts was our landfall. We reached it, as Gosnold did nearly 400 years ago, after a fair weather passage along the moors, cliffs, and wild rocky islands that Gosnold named for his queen in England.

Given the Bay's location along the Northeast corridor between the dense populations of New York and Boston, much of Buzzards Bay remains today surprisingly undeveloped, with slightly over 60% of the land in forest and only 14% of the shore classified as residential/commercial/industrial. So the crew of SARAH ABBOT was exploring a sanctuary of sorts. The jagged border of the Bay, bound by the glacial deposits that form the Elizabeth Islands, created diverse environments. The Bay itself features unusual biodiversity. The coastal zone hosts salt marshes, tidal streams, eelgrass beds, tidal flats, barrier beaches, and rocky shores. Buzzards Bay lies within the Virginian biological province, which means that the species in Buzzards Bay are typical of those found along the East Coast between Chesapeake Bay and Cape Cod. But because of the Cape Cod Canal (a fixture at the east end of the Bay since 1914), the Bay has a direct link to the cold water environment and species that live north of Cape Cod and, therefore, claims an unusual mix of semitropical and acadian species.

After dropping anchor outside Cuttyhunk's harbor which overflowed with visiting yachts, we spotted a pair of ospreys fishing in the evening light over Canapitsit Channel, a gut of swift water boiling between the east end of Cuttyhunk and Nashawena Island. Osprey fishing in the Bay again was a good sign. At the end of the twentieth century the ospreys were not quite so prevalent here as they had been 400 years ago, but the birds had begun repopulating the Bay shores since humans stopped using the DDT pesticide that destroyed the birds' eggs back in the 1950s-60s. The great game fish of southern New England—bluefish and striped bass—seemed to be returning to hunt the Bay, too. We would see. By the time our schooner finished her exploration of Buzzards Bay, *Oceans* students expected to have a picture of the environment, history, and people that defined one of America's richest estuaries.

The first morning of our stay at Cuttyhunk came on fair and calm. Margaret got her students up early. They made their own breakfasts from a selection of fruit and dry cereal, then headed ashore in one of the dinghies, with novice rowers splashing and laughing the whole way. Once ashore, the scientist oriented our student crew to the world of the intertidal zone while it was low tide. I could see them working in pairs with plastic buckets on the rocky beach: they collected organisms, and I knew that microscopes and taxonomy books would cover the foredeck and fill the table in the main saloon when they returned to the schooner at lunch time.

Private moments like this morning on the schooner with most of the crew ashore were rare, and the three of us who were the ship keepers relished the solitude. After organizing the vessel's provisions, Jackie slipped into a bathing suit. Now, she lay in the sun on the foredeck sipping her tea and reading a Tolstoy novel. Yankee, a Rottweiler/pointer mix who had been the ship's security force since SARAH ABBOT had sailed to the Bahamas eleven years ago, found a pool of shade for napping on the cabin roof. I had a host of maintenance chores to perform on the vessel, but I procrastinated in favor of stretching out in the cockpit to dip into the schooner's library.

Maybe it was the memory of yesterday when I suddenly felt lost as I stood in the bows of SARAH ABBOT that had rearranged my priorities, but now I felt a clear need to reorient myself. Reading the logs of other explorers and immersing myself in local history texts had sometimes been as useful

12

to me as combing nautical charts for clues about how to navigate the soul of a place.

My reading carried me into the world of the Bay's native people. For five thousand years the Wampanoag Indians built their communities on these shores. They called their homelands "Land of the First Light" after its easterly place relative to the North American continent, and "Land of the Little Turtle" for the prevalence of pond turtles. But as is often the case with peoples of the Algonquin linguistic group whose words describe places according to the features of the land, the Wampanoags probably never named this bay that gave them shoals of fish and the beloved hard-shell, quahog clams. To the Wampanoags, Buzzards Bay was simply the sea.

Before the arrival of Europeans in the early 1600s, the Wampanoags lived in at least thirty, separate tribal bands around the shores of southeastern Massachusetts, each band led by a sachem. Typically, the Wampanoags clustered together in communities numbering from a few score individuals to several hundred in the larger settlements. The large camps were in the woods some distance from the coastline of Buzzards Bay, but during the summer when the woods began to swelter with humidity and bugs, the Wampanoags loaded their family and gear aboard birchbark canoes or large dugouts and traveled to their summer camps at places like Cuttyhunk here in the Elizabeth Islands and along the Bay shores where the sea breezes cooled the air.

In the morning mist lingering over a sand spit to the west, I could imagine the Wampanoags filing down to the Bay with wicker fish traps, spears, and gorge hooks; the men fished for eels, scup, mackerel, striper, bluefish, smelt, tautog, and herring. When a pod of pilot whales ventured in sight, they launched their canoes, gave chase and used a spear to harpoon the weakest of the group. Ashore, women retreated to the island uplands to plant corn—the staple food in their diet—and they fertilized the corn fields with fish and seaweed. In the forest valleys hunters took partridges, turkeys, pheasants, and quails with their bows and arrows. As the ⸱ fell, families gathered oysters, quahogs, mussels, and lobsters. Duri⸱ afternoon, everyone picked raspberries, blueberries, grapes, stra⸱

and cranberries. Later, at a long, low campfire glowing in the lee of a sand dune, Wampanoag women smoked and dried a lot of the fresh food and stored it in baskets that they buried in the cool earth to keep for the winter.

Near the cooks the Wampanoags' wigwams clustered in a rough circle. The shelters looked a bit like domes made with mats of bark and skin spread over a framework of saplings. During cold weather the Indians built individual cooking fires in the center of their wigwams and the smoke escaped through a hole in the center of the roof. But now, during the summer on the Bay, cooking was a community event at the fire pit where corn and seafood baked between a bed of steaming rocks and a blanket of seaweed in just the same way New Englanders still practice a traditional clam and lobster bake. When it came time to rest or sleep, the Wampanoags retreated to their wigwams and beds of deer skins and woven mats. Almost all of their belongings hung from hooks on the shelter frame. For now this was home to the band, but when the cool winds of October began to blow, the Indians left these wigwams and paddled back to the woods on the north shore of the Bay until another summer.

Looking south across Vineyard Sound, I saw the bold cliffs of Gay Head at the southwest end of Martha's Vineyard Island. In the morning haze, the promontory seemed misty and far off. The Aquinnah, a Wampanoag band, once thrived at Gay Head, and one of the mystical stories that the Wampanoags told about Gay Head and the Aquinnah drifted into my head as I gazed out toward the hazy cliffs.

According to tradition, the Wampanoags had a strong mystical relationship with all the natural elements of the Bay, and they created myths to explain the presence and behavior of each element in their environment. To the Indians, everything from a boulder to a beetle has a soul and a story. And under the leadership of Cautantowwit, the beneficent God of the southwest, the Wampanoags' pantheon of Gods, called "manitous," includes women, children, sun, moon, fire, water, sea, snow, earth, compass s, seasons, winds, houses, sky, corn, and colors.

e Aquinnah's story told of Maushop, a giant whose moccasins were

Cuttyhunk and Martha's Vineyard, and whose pipe ashes were the Elizabeth Islands. According to legend, Maushop began doing everything for the Aquinnah, carrying their wood and doing other chores, until the Aquinnah began to depend on him. Fearing that Maushop would spoil the Aquinnah, the Creator told Maushop he would turn the friendly giant into a white whale.

At the Gay Head cliffs, where all the Aquinnah and every creature came to say goodbye, Maushop's best friend, a giant toad, was so overcome with grief that the Creator turned him into a huge rock. Later, the Creator turned Maushop into a white whale, called Mocha Dick. During the mid-nineteenth century, this great white whale was killed by Amos Smalley, a harpooner on a New Bedford whaler and one of the last of the Aquinnah. Many white historians saw Smalley's feat as marking the end of the whaling era; for the Aquinnah the whale's death stood for something even more profound. Now, all they had left of their connection to their past and their manitous was a huge boulder standing at the bottom of the Gay Head cliffs like a giant toad.

I knew that boulder, that "toad." Often, approaching Gay Head in fog or haze, I had looked for the huge rock at the base of the cliffs to be my landmark, to help me get my bearings and avoid shoal water.

Once, perhaps a thousand years ago, a crew of Norse explorers might easily have looked at this same boulder to point the way through a confused sea. The Norsemen left Greenland to explore the North American coast. Most prominent among these Norse explorers was Leif Ericcson who built a settlement called Straumey. Scholars have placed Straumey in a dozen sites along the New England and Nova Scotian coasts. One scholar, William Hovgard, located Straumey on Martha's Vineyard and said that Buzzards Bay is the place Ericcson called Straumfiord.

Surely then, Maushop's old friend, the great toad at the base of Gay Head cliffs, would have been a landmark for Norse navigators exploring the ancestral lands of the Wampanoags. A beacon to invaders. But the Norse were hardly alone in their endeavor to make this bay their own. In the wake of Christopher Columbus' first voyage, a flurry of explorers headed for America. Probably the Portuguese, Italian, and Spanish navigators all visited what is now southeastern Massachusetts in the sixteenth century. An inscription on the so-called Dighton Rock in the Taunton River places Miguel Corte Real in the area in 1511. Some historians have argued that Martha's Vineyard and/or the Elizabeth Islands constitute a primary landmark called "Louisa" on John Verrazano's map of North America that he made for the king of France in 1524. European fishermen came here soon after.

These European explorers had only one lasting effect on Buzzards Bay and Cape Cod—smallpox. After initial contact with European fishermen, the Wampanoags suffered a plague they called "The Great Sadness" in 1617 which reduced their numbers from about 40,000 souls to about 4,000. When the pilgrims arrived in 1620, the Wampanoags were a people laid waste.

The first European visitors—like those who brought the plague to the Wampanoags—were simply passing through. The title of European discoverer of New England falls to Bartholomew Gosnold. He arrived at Cuttyhunk on May 25, 1602, with the intention of establishing a permanent settlement. The bark CONCORD carried a crew of almost thirty men. But only eight were professional mariners. The rest were men on a lark (or was it a quest?) to fill some dearth of adventure, wealth, or self-knowledge in their lives.

As I thought about Gosnold and his crew, the sea remained a soft greenish-blue color around SARAH ABBOT, but the vessel seemed to change before my eyes. I saw a captain wearing a hat that looked like one of those tricorne affairs Lord Nelson and Napoleon used to wear. Near the captain stood a skinny, bearded man who held a telescope, shouting: "Land ahoy, sir. . . ." There was a lot of scuffling of hobnail shoes on deck and sailors in wool sweaters and knee britches began running up and down pulling thick ropes and furling sails; others were unlashing the anchor from its mountings, and still others were standing amazed, staring far into the horizon.

Someone called, "Prepare the small boats."

"Aye aye sir," came a response, and I heard more shouting as the vague shapes of Indians disappeared into the Cuttyhunk brush. . . .

Then Margaret and her students rounded a point on the beach and began rooting around among the tidal pools, filling their collection buckets with treasures. But even as the appearance of Margaret and our students brought me back to America on the verge of the twenty-first century, Gosnold continued stalking my mind. The man had changed this land forever by introducing the Wampanoags to what became a traditional Yankee enterprise—commerce. Born a gentleman in 1571 at Otley Hall in Suffolk, England, Bartholomew Gosnold attended Cambridge and moved on to seafaring by the time he was 25. British lords, looking to claim lands in North America before the Dutch, French, and Spanish, turned to Gosnold as a man with nautical experience and the social connections to raise the venture capital for a colonizing expedition. Bankrolled by William Shakespeare's patron Henry Wryothesly, Third Earl of Southampton, Gosnold gathered a crew, many of whom were gentlemen, bought a vessel, and set sail to follow the forty-second parallel across the Atlantic Ocean to a place he called "Northern Virginia."

The crew left Falmouth, England, on March 26 aboard a tired, three-masted bark called the CONCORD. The ship only measured 50 feet at the waterline and 17½ feet abeam. In other words, the CONCORD was not much larger than our own SARAH ABBOT, but we sailed with nine aboard and the CONCORD had at least 25. We came to learn; Gosnold's crew hoped for material profit.

The CONCORD's crew nursed their weary ship across the ocean in 49 days, probably making their landfall at what is now called Cape Neddick in southern Maine. Thereafter the CONCORD sailed south where Gosnold surveyed Cape Cod and named it for the bountiful fishing. The adventurers then rounded the Cape, transited Nantucket Sound, and stopped two nights along the north shore of Martha's Vineyard, which Gosnold named for his daughter. Finally, the ship sailed down Vineyard Sound and rounded Sows and Pigs reef. On May 24 the CONCORD "came to anchor in eight fathoms, a quarter of a mile from the shore" off an "island Captain Gosnold called Elizabeth's Isle." Today this spot is the islands of Cuttyhunk and Nashawena that were joined as one before the sea broke through at Canapitsit Channel.

The Europeans met local Wampanoags, probably of the Sakonnet band that summered in the islands, on their third day anchored near the West End Pond at Cuttyhunk. According to Gabriel Archer's chronicle of the expedition:

"There came unto us an Indian and two women, the one we supposed to be his wife, the other his daughter, both clean and straight bodied, with countenance sweet and pleasant. To these the Indian gave heedful attendance for they showed much familiarity with our men, although they would not admit of any immodest touch."

In subsequent days some of the English explored the north shore of Buzzards Bay along the coast of what is now Westport, South Dartmouth, and New Bedford. Back at Cuttyhunk, Archer had numerous friendly encounters with Wampanoags and oversaw the building of a fort house on the shores of West End Pond.

Twenty members of the crew prepared to remain at Cuttyhunk for the winter, but they discovered that they had only provisions for six weeks, not six months. Disappointed, Gosnold made plans to return to England with a load of sassafras and cedar logs to sell to shipbuilders and recoup the investors' expenditures. On June 18, the CONCORD sailed to England, leaving the bay he called "Gosnold's Hope," just that—a place invested with unfulfilled desires.

The expedition could hardly be called a failure. Archer's and Brereton's accounts of the trip became books that fueled the English with romantic notions of North America and energized waves of explorers. Many literary scholars believe that Brereton's account of Cuttyhunk was the raw material from which Shakespeare wove his descriptions of Prospero's island in *The Tempest*. Meanwhile, Gosnold mounted a second, successful colonizing expedition to America. This time his colony grew on the shores of another estuary, the Chesapeake. He called it Jamestown after England's new king, and Gosnold died there in 1607 before turning the profit that lay at the heart of his obsession with America.

Some dozen or so years later my ancestor Captain John Smith, after years of exploring the Chesapeake, passed this way to trade for furs with the Indians, map the New England coast, and keep the log that became his *Generall Historie of Virginia, New-England and the Summer Isles* (1624).

During the afternoon of our first day at Cuttyhunk, we saw an unusual Fourth of July celebration: a parade of island golfcarts. These vehicles had become the most popular form of transportation around the hilly isle. On Independence Day, the islanders dressed themselves as American heroes like Betsy Ross and Ben Franklin, decorated about 50 golf carts in red-white-and-blue streamers, and paraded around the island to the sounds of a portable tape player blasting the Boston Pops rendition of *The Battle Hymn of the Republic*. After dark everybody gathered on the beach for amateur fireworks displays and a bonfire the size of a large teepee. Caught up in the nostalgia of Independence Day, we sat around the bonfire with a collection of long-time islanders who helped us piece together Cuttyhunk's history. As the fire snapped and the southwest wind sowed through the beach grass, we pressed close to the flames and listened as residents unfolded the secrets of their island. I listened closely like a detective searching for clues in some unsolved mystery that included giant toads and white whales.

As the story goes, it was not long after the founding of the English colonies at Plymouth in 1620 and Massachusetts Bay (Boston) in 1630, that European real estate speculators and developers rediscovered Cuttyhunk. Thomas Mayew, a Watertown merchant in the Massachusetts Bay Colony, had dreams of living on his own island fiefdom and persuaded the British gentry who held title to New England to grant him a deed for the colonization of Martha's Vineyard and the Elizabeth Islands in 1641. In 1654 Mayew convinced Seayik Sachem of Monument to give up his claims on the islands for "full satisfaction" and "one pound powder" and some "shot." Three years later, Mayew solidified his claims by getting another Indian sachem, Quaquaquinagat, to yield his ancestral claim on the islands for "two coats in full satisfaction for the same." Some deal.

This purchase began a period of almost two hundred years in which speculators divided, subdivided, and traded Cuttyhunk for profit. Caretaker residents survived by subsistence farming and working as ship pilots, life savers, and wreck salvagers. They attended to the growing number of vessels passing through Vineyard Sound en route between New York, Boston, and England.

Except in the minds of the real estate profiteers and seafarers, Cuttyhunk languished, virtually ignored until 1864. Then the yacht THERESA sailed into Cuttyhunk Harbor and seven New York sportsmen came ashore to imagine how Cuttyhunk might make the site for a spectacular bass fishing club where sportsmen could angle for stripers from fishing platforms built on the island's boulders. Immediately, the tycoons set about buying up the deeds for most of the island. Shortly thereafter, the Cuttyhunk Fishing Association had 50 prominent members, a club house that still overlooks Vineyard Sound, and rules that positively excluded women. Among the members and guests the club counted two American Presidents, Cleveland and Taft, rail tycoon Jay Gould, the president of Standard Oil, and many of the other prominent capitalists of the day. But the club dwindled into oblivion during the early-twentieth century as old age overtook the membership. In subsequent years the island survived catering to families of summer "rusticators." During Prohibition the rum-running trade infiltrated the island as "night fishing" became a popular pastime for bass boats hailing from Cuttyhunk.

Today, at the outset of the twenty-first century, SARAH ABBOT's crew found Cuttyhunk life continuing to evolve. The fiberglass boat revolution that began in the 1960s had put the cost of buying and maintaining a cruising boat within the range of middle-class incomes. Now, it seemed that everyone who lived along the New England coast owned a boat . . .

and sooner or later many of those boats ended up on cruises to Cuttyhunk. With cruising yachts packing the harbor every night of the summer, and visitors sleeping aboard their boats, the last of the old boarding houses closed its doors.

During the last decade of the twentieth century, gentrification has set in, and the cost of a modest cottage had escalated to over a quarter of a million dollars. In addition to the island general store and the bakery, Cuttyhunk now sported a new gift shop, a gourmet pizza palace, gourmet coffee emporium, and bed & breakfast inn. And with houses rising from almost every patch of land in the east end village—and the west end a protected wilderness for the rabbits and deer—islanders expected a construction moratorium any year now. Forty souls braved the winter on this rock, 300 flocked to the island during the summer season.

Just what was the big attraction?

This was the question I was asking myself later back in my berth aboard the schooner. The boat was dark except for the searching beams of flashlights as the crew took care of all the little rituals attendant to going to bed for the night, when a boy's voice suddenly echoed from the forward head.

"Hey, Captain, what's this?"

Imagining some incipient emergency, I struggled from my sleeping bag and made my way forward through the vessel's main saloon and the tiers of bunks in the midships fishhold.

When I reached the forward head, I found the boy bent over near the toilet. His eyes and a flashlight beam fixed on a four-foot length of a two-by-six plank directly behind the sink.

"What's going on here? What are all these names? Dan 'Blood' Kurtz, 'Slime' Glassup, 'Plague' Nilson? More than a hundred of them."

"It's a little hard to explain," I began. "We call this 'the Plank'."

"As in pirate ships and *walking* the plank?"

Several flashlights clicked on and pointed toward me from berths both fore and aft of the head's cabin dividing the boys' berths in the fishhold from the girls' quarters in the forecastle.

Clearly, I had an audience, so I paused . . . before choosing my words carefully.

"Not exactly," I began. "Kids sign the Plank using the nicknames they get from each other aboard the schooner. It's all part of joining *The Dead Pirates Society*."

"The what?!!" asked a chorus of voices.

So I explained: About ten years ago one of the crews aboard SARAH ABBOT decided that they needed something like the teenagers had in the movie *The Dead Poets Society* to bind them together, a secret society to celebrate their gusto. Of course, The Dead Pirates Society had an initiation. You couldn't just join because you felt like it; you had to prove you had the right stuff. The crew had to sleep on deck together, bathe in the ocean instead of taking showers, and successfully overcome an unexpected challenge to the group like a treasure hunt or something else the weather or the Bay or the adults aboard threw the crew's way. No one really walked the plank. Dead Pirates just signed their names on it *after* completing the process of initiation. So far there were almost a 180 signatures.

"When do we start?" asked a girl from Los Angeles.

"Stir it up!" I winked. It was an enigmatic call to arms from a Bob Marley reggae tune. And also the motto of The Dead Pirates Society, buccaneer slang for carpe diem—seize the day.

Without a word, our Los Angeles girl slipped out of her sleeping bag and dragged it topside to the schooner's foredeck. The rest followed.

During our second day at Cuttyhunk, while following the island's ribbon of road as it curled around the hills and swept into the moors of the west end, several of our crew met Donna Hunter, a lifelong Cuttyhunker. We found her outside her cottage among a scattering of small gray-shingled houses looking out to the south over Vineyard Sound, the cliffs of Gay Head on the Vineyard, and the Atlantic that rolled in all the way from Europe. Donna sat in an old beach chair carving wooden animals from a board, wearing old black jeans with bleach splotches, a worn-down pink and blue striped shirt, and a red ball cap with Cuttyhunk written in magic marker on the bill. She had an audience of crates and a golden retriever companion who panted as we walked up, and she did not stop to acknowledge us until we got close enough to introduce ourselves.

At last she looked up and offered us seats, and during the next half hour she talked about her connections with this island. Donna told us that she had been off and on the island for 49 of her 51 years, but for the past 25 she had stayed all year round. Really, she wondered, why would any one want to leave? She loved watching the changes that the seasons and the weather brought to Cuttyhunk. She loved the blue sky and stiff southeasterly winds of spring, the fog as it burned off the sea beneath the cliffs on a summer morning. Why would she ever want to leave Cuttyhunk during the golden September days when you could hike all the way to Gosnold's monument at the west end and never see anything but the birds and the rabbits and the deer? And how could she get off the island in the winter when the blizzards came with snow driving at you like a gale of little white nails and the seas outside the harbor cresting fifteen feet?

No, Donna was staying right here on "the Hunk"; she would not change a thing about her life. Now a widow, she spent her days carving birds and fish and helping to raise some of her family's children. To her, life had reduced itself to just about this—sitting here in her chair, carving, and staring off to sea. The only things that broke her reverie were an occasional trip down to the harbor "to see what the wind has blown in," a walk to the little store in the back of a neighbor's house for supplies, or a pause at the bakery to share coffee and scuttlebutt with other islanders.

After our encounter with Donna, one of our crew mused about the calming effect Cuttyhunk had on its residents. And even visitors like us. He said that this island seemed to be a sanctuary, a place where an old seadog such as Donna Hunter could almost stop time.

I liked that term "seadog." It had a way of rolling off the tongue like a sigh that ends as a yawn, and it reminded me of Yankee napping on the cabin top in the shade of the main boom on a hot summer afternoon. A seadog, I thought, would be a very contented being indeed. And stopping time? What middle-aged person like me did not wish for such a thing when stepping ashore on an island, or starting on even a modest, local passage under sail?

III PENIKESE TO THE WESTPORT RIVER

Today, I really felt like an explorer. After decades of sailing around Buzzards Bay, I had gathered up the courage to brave the tricky entrance into the Westport River and see a part of the Bay I only knew from studying the charts.

The morning had come on with hazy sun and a moderate sou'westerly breeze, and we weighed anchor at 0930 to depart Cuttyhunk. I wanted to get an early start so we would reach the mouth of the Westport River and cross the surf-strewn shallow bar at the mouth on the last hour of the rising tide. Leaving Cuttyhunk a mile astern, we were passing a small knob of an island, about a mile square, when I felt a tingling beginning in my arms. Almost treeless with a few weathered cedar-shingled buildings, the island had the look of a shepherd's isle off the coast of Scotland.

Sometimes referred to locally as the "evil island," Penikese had already gained a certain symbolic significance for the crew of SARAH ABBOT. Since our first night aboard the schooner, we had been reading to each other for entertainment from Jan Adkin's novel *A Storm Without Rain*. The novel was a story about a contemporary fifteen-year-old who went through a time warp on Penikese Island and found himself transported into Buzzards Bay's life as it was just after the turn of the twentieth century. Now, for the second time in 24 hours I began wondering if this sail aboard the SARAH ABBOT was taking this crew and me though a time warp of our own. A search for things hidden in the past, things so shadowy that I could not yet see them clearly enough to speak their names.

So once again thoughts of the past began prowling through my mind, and I tried to fit them into my emerging picture of the Bay. I knew that when Bartholomew Gosnold had sailed this route and first saw Penikese in 1602, it was a verdant forest which chronicler Archer called Hill's Hap. Eventually, Gosnold explored Penikese, stole a canoe from four Indians who fled upon the arrival of the Europeans, and logged the island for its first-growth cedars. Like Cuttyhunk, Penikese passed through the hands of numerous speculators during the next two hundred years while their tenants systematically denuded the island forest, raised sheep, and engaged in the lucrative piloting and wrecking trades.

Like Cuttyhunk, Penikese came to the attention of wealthy New Yorkers; in 1867 a tobacco merchant named John Anderson bought the island as a retreat, claiming that "the ever-changing aspect of the sea filled [his] life with rapture." Apparently, Anderson saw himself as a philanthropist and gave the island and a $50,000 trust to Harvard University's great naturalist Louis Agassiz. In 1873 Agassiz opened the Anderson School of Natural History on the island with 28 men and 16 women students. This was the forerunner of the famous Marine Biological Lab in Woods Hole. Unfortunately, Agassiz died the year the school opened. The island institute withered, and by 1905 Penikese became the property of the Commonwealth of Massachusetts.

Against the protest of Cuttyhunkers, the state built a small hospital on the island, hired Dr. Frank Parker to run it, and turned Penikese into a leper colony to isolate persons afflicted with what the public then viewed as a terrible plague. It was from this period that Penikese took the name of the "evil island." Even today, when we asked Cuttyhunkers about Penikese, they invariable mentioned the lepers. On seeing the island now, my mind pictured ghostly souls with missing body parts swaddled in hospital robes and bandages wandering aimlessly along the island's shores or among the sheep on the baren hills.

After the leprosy scare subsided, the Commonwealth closed the hospital, turned out the doctor without a pension, and dynamited the buildings. Until 1973 Massachusetts kept Penikese as a sanctuary for terns, gulls, and cormorants. Since then the island has been the site of a work/study boarding school for delinquent boys. For more than the last twenty years boatbuilding and a homesteader's way of life on Penikese had been an alternative to the Juvenile House of Correction for hundreds of troubled teenagers.

Sailing past Penikese, we saw a half-dozen young men standing on the porch of the main house watching our schooner's progress.

"It's almost like I can feel their eyes watching me . . . like I feel the sting of their envy," said one of our crew.

"Any way you cut it, those guys are stuck like lizzards on a rock, just doing their time," added another. "How would that make you feel?"

"Lonesome. Just like in *A Storm Without Rain*," said a third.

I knew what she meant, and almost unconsciously I asked the deck watch to retrim the schooner's sheets to sail us away with all possible speed.

Like Gosnold, we spied a series of hills and promontories to the north that called us to explore. We had the wind on our quarter, rising as it usually does on the Bay in late morning to blow 15 to 22 knots out of the southwest by afternoon. In an hour and a half we crossed the open mouth of the Bay where the Atlantic swells roll in uninterrupted all the way from Africa. Closing with the north shore, we passed between a container ship and a seagoing tug with an oil barge in tow—both heading northeast to pass through the Cape Cod Canal—probably en route between New York and Boston. Since the opening of the canal at the head of the Bay about eighty years ago, the shipping lane through Buzzards Bay to the canal had become the favored route for ships sailing coastwise in New England. These days as many as 20 large ships a day transited these shipping lanes and the canal.

Even though the route through the Bay was safer by far than the old route around the outer coast of Cape Cod (the Graveyard of the Atlantic), the Bay could still be a ship trap when storms approach from the south. Probably few mariners sailed the Bay without a rise in blood pressure and a sharp eye for changes in the weather. We saw recent evidence of the Bay's perils as we closed with the north shore and passed close to the twisted wreck of a 400-foot cement barge rusting on Old Cock Ledge where it had come to rest after breaking loose from a tugboat in heavy weather.

Further inshore, we passed between several other ledges before spying the 50-foot-high mound of rock called the Nubble at the west end of the long crescent of Horseneck Beach. The Nubble marked the almost imperceptible cut through the beach into the expansive Westport River. During my years on the Bay I had heard that 250 years ago mariners called this river the "Devil's Pocket." Pirates hid their ships here out of sight until they spied an unsuspecting merchantman sailing into the Bay.

The pirate stories captured my fancy, but Westport River was still risky business for a deep draft vessel like SARAH ABBOT. I could feel my breath quicken as we approached a line of buoys leading toward the cut in the beach. The wind had begun to rise, and ahead a southwest swell built to peaks in the shallow water over the shoal that spans the mouth of the river. A half mile off the Nubble, I called the crew to their sailhandling stations, and with two students standing by each of the schooner's three sails, Jackie pointed SARAH ABBOT into the wind while the rest of us lowered and furled the sails as the boat pitched in the seas like a hobby horse. Then we lingered in deep water just south of the bar until we saw a lower-than-usual set of swells approaching.

As the second of the low swells in the wave train approached, I took a deep breath and turned the schooner toward the shore. Adding power to the Volvo diesel, I increased SARAH ABBOT's speed until she rode the crest of this swell. For several seconds the vessel rushed forward like a surfer. Rocks loomed to starboard. The white sand of the shoal glowed beneath the water to port. The beach ahead seemed almost close enough to touch, and for a second I thought that I had made a terrible decision. We were going to strike the bottom, get spun sideways to the waves, and be lost. Then—in the time it takes to snap your fingers—we crossed the bar showing eight feet on the depth sounder. Once in the deeper water of the river, I powered back. The wave rolled ahead of us and broke on the far shore of the inlet.

The last push of the flood tide carried us behind the barrier beach and along a winding channel between sand flats. Ahead, the river opened into 3,000 acres of saltmarsh protected by dunes, gentle hills, farms, and stands of mature maples and oaks. Visiting this area for the first time, I now knew why Gabriel Archer had gushed:

"This main is the goodliest continent that ever we saw, promising more by far than we any way did expect: for it is replenished with fair fields, and in them fragrant flowers, also meadows, and hedged in with stately groves, being furnished with pleasant brooks, and beautified with two main rivers that (as we judged) may haply become good harbors and conduct us to hopes men so greedily do thirst after."

Archer's description still held true for Westport as we found it even though 150 years ago these "stately groves" provided the lumber for shipyards on the river banks that built and operated an active fleet of whalers. Now there were no signs of the whalers. Except for a colony of summer homes on the periphery of state-owned Horseneck Beach, a small fleet of offshore lobster boats, and the ancient houses clustered at the landing called Westport Point; Westport was clearly an agricultural community where horse and dairy farms stood side-by-side with hydroponic lettuce growers on both branches of the river shores.

After navigating two miles up river, we cautiously edged SARAH ABBOT alongside the floating dock at Moby Dick's restaurant as a fierce current buffeted the schooner's bows. Now, the crew's real work began as we prepared to mix our study of marine biology with community service. A few decades ago the Westport River supported a vital shellfish industry, particularly rich in bay scallops. But in recent years pollution from farm runoff, failing septic systems, and boats had depleted the oxygen in the river and the scallops have died.

In response to the deteriorating environment in the river, a group of concerned citizens led by the unlikely partnership between a retired industrialist named Bob Edgcomb and a young environmentalist named Wayne Turner formed the Water Works Group. They conceived the Bay Scallop Restoration Project in hopes of revitalizing the dying estuary by bringing oxygen and scallops back to the river. Beginning with a commitment to reduce river pollution—and with only 400 living scallops just a few years ago—volunteers began raising and planting seed scallops with such success that the shellfish warden reopened the river to commercial scalloping, and in the fall of 1994 watermen harvested 500 bushels, the first commercial harvest in the river in almost ten years.

In the years to follow, Edgcomb and Turner have been working to further increase the number of scallops for harvest, but to do this they needed a troupe of volunteers. Well, here we were. And we intended to stay in the river until we had helped to rig and deploy hundreds of fine-mesh screen bags filled with coils of monofilament line to attract free-swimming juvenile scallops. At this very moment rafts containing brood scallops were anchored over the shellfish beds in the river, and these mature scallops had begun to spawn. A whole river of new life.

IV WESTPORT

On our second day in Westport, the morning came hot and hazy, reminding me of the summer I spent 25 years ago when I fished for crabs with Captain Bart Murphy on Chesapeake Bay. Today was so hot and humid that Margaret teased the crew into squirting each other with a hose on the dock while Jackie and I took over the galley chores and made French toast for breakfast.

Later, lathered in sunscreen, Margaret and the students went down river in a pair of the Scallop Project's work skiffs with 900 spat bags to anchor over the scallop beds. Jackie and I kept busy buying water, fuel, and fresh vegetables for the schooner, but finally we had a chance to kick back and read in the shade of the canvas awning I had rigged over the cockpit. Inspired by the area, Jackie discarded her Tolstoy in favor of a book called *Secrets of Old Dartmouth*. I found time to delve into the students' logs that they were keeping as resources for essays to be written after their cruise ended and they returned to classes at Phillips. For some reason reading these journals quelled my jumpiness a bit.

After exploring Horseneck Beach last night, one girl had written a few words that now began to echo in my head and chest:

"The beach is vast and no one is here. Having all this place to myself makes me feel tiny. There is water and sand all over; my eyes cannot see further. There is no sun, just the moon starting to glow through some clouds. I kind of want to cry but don't have a reason to . . ."

Although hard for me to admit, the truth was that sometimes in recent days the Bay had made me feel melancholy. It was a feeling best described by the word *saudade* that I had learned from Buzzards Bay's large

31

population of Portuguese-speaking immigrants who had come here as whalers and fishermen from Europe, the Azores, and Cape Verde Islands. *Saudade* was a feeling that a person could never quite put into words . . . like the feeling of missing someone or something you did not even know that you had lost. According to legend, *saudade* was a common malady among mariners and explorers like Vasco da Gama and Juan Ponce de León who wasted his life in search of the fountain of youth. But so was sun poisoning and indigestion. Liabilities of the trade.

Whatever the source of my uneasiness, thoughts of loss were stirring in mind as I took in the landscape of Westport. Looking out on the vistas of green shores and meandering river, I thought about how much had been lost or changed in this place, often violently, since the middle of the seventeenth century when the Wampanoags ruled Westport, and the people from the Sakonnet band used Westport for hunting and fishing.

The first big cultural changes to this river basin came with the arrival of European settlers in the 1650s. They named the community from the Westport River to the Acushnet River "Dartmouth" after their former home on England's southwest coast. Many of these first families were Quakers escaping the religious tyranny of the Puritan majority in the Plymouth and Massachusetts Bay colonies where Quakers were hanged as dissenters by the 1650s.

Like the Puritans, the Quakers were religious nonconformists who rejected the Episcopalian Church of England. But while mainstream English citizens lumped the Puritans and the Quakers together as religious fanatics, the two groups were quite different and clashed in New England. Specifically, the Quakers believed in a community based on spiritual reflection, democratic freedom of speech, and collaborative problem solving. They eschewed the evils of violence and war. The Puritans believed in a much more authoritarian community dominated by their ministers, and to the Puritans, violence and war were useful means to resolving conflicts.

Both groups were aggressive capitalists, and from the outset they collided in the English colonies to the north of here in Plymouth and Boston, until the Quakers moved south to look for peace in Dartmouth. For the most part, the Quakers had to buy the Dartmouth land from the original Pilgrims who now saw a chance to turn a profit on the real estate they had all but stolen from the Wampanoags. Miles Standish, the head of the Pilgrim militia, had paid the Indians five or ten dollars for his share of Dartmouth in 1652; he sold the land to a Quaker settler named John Russell nine years later for $210.

What followed was a brutal epoch in American history. Not long after the Quakers began farming in Dartmouth, Massasoit, the great sachem over all of the Wampanoag communities, died. This was the man who had befriended the Pilgrims, nursed them through their first difficult winters at Plymouth, and established a treaty of peace with them that fostered collaboration for forty years. On the death of Massasoit, his sons Wamsutta and Metacom (Philip) looked around them and realized that the English were blatantly usurping the Wampanoag lands. When Wamsutta protested, the English demanded that he come to Plymouth to explain his state of mind. Tragically, Wamsutta died on his way home from the fateful meeting at Plymouth. This left his younger brother Philip as the great sachem of the Wampanoags, believing that the English had poisoned his brother. Philip wanted his ancestral land back for his people, and he wanted revenge. Speaking before a group of concerned English in Rhode Island who hoped to head off an Indian war, Philip stood tall and defiant among forty warriors and counselors and declared:

"The English who came first to this country were but an handful of people forlorn, poor and distressed. My father was then sachem. He relieved their distresses in the most kind and hospitable manner. He gave them land to plant and build upon . . . they flourished and increased. By various means they got possession of a great part of his territory. But he still remained their friend till he died. My older brother became sachem. . . . He was seized and confined and thrown into illness and died. Soon after I became sachem they disarmed my people . . . their land was taken. But a small part of the dominion of my ancestors remains. *I am determined not to live until I have no country.*"

Soon after this declaration, war broke out ten miles from the banks of the Westport River when a farm boy, in what is now Swansea, Massachusetts, shot and killed a Wampanoag raiding English cattle on June 24, 1675. The Wampanoags responded by killing nine citizens on their way home from church. Shortly thereafter, war exploded in earnest. As historian John Fisk, imagined the scene, Indians "swooped down upon Dartmouth, burning thirty houses and committing fearful atrocities. Some of their victims were flayed alive, or impaled on sharp stakes, or roasted over slow fires. Similar horrors were wrought at Middleborough and Taunton; and now the misery spread. . . ."

But the carnage did not last long: fourteen months later Philip died at the hands of an Indian loyal to the English, and the bloodiest war in New England history came to an end. By the mid-eighteenth century, the area around the Westport River and the two rivers to the east had over 10,000 acres in pasture. Shipbuilding and inshore whaling flourished. The Wampanoags never recovered.

Thinking back on all of Westport's violent place in American history and my shipmate's nocturne on Horseneck Beach touched an emotion in me that I didn't want to examine too carefully right now. So I found cheerier inspiration in Bob Edgcomb, the seventy-five-year-old steel company president who had embarked so late in life on this new career as a scallop project czar.

One of the crew's journals captured Edgcomb perfectly for me "with this big smile on his face, wearing the same clothes he was wearing when we met him yesterday—the typical black 'Bay Scallop Restoration Project' ball cap, a thin-skeletoned pair of glasses, dirty and worn blue jeans, and his boots."

We had first met Edgcomb as SARAH ABBOT's crew gathered for lunch under a shade tree at the Scallop Project's cottage headquarters, and he started talking to us about Westport in the earlier years, particularly during Prohibition back in the Twenties.

Edgcomb's face lit up like a boy's as he recalled for us "the bad old days" when this river was a center for smuggling alcohol unloaded from ships offshore and transported into the river in high-speed rum-running boats. Al Capone himself visited Westport once to check on the operation. Local people had a unique way of signaling to the rum runners with their eight-over-eight windows. When the bootleggers saw blinds over the windows, they knew that nobody wanted any bottles; but when they saw blinds over two or three rows of the window panes, they knew that the particular house wanted two or three bottles of whiskey or rum. Back then the Coast Guard didn't know where the channel was, and the bootleggers with local knowledge could continue their booze smuggling every night while the Coast Guard chasing them constantly ran aground.

I liked the way Bob Edgcomb's eyes twinkled with pride as he explained to us how he got involved in the Scallop Project. Conceptually, he said, Wayne Turner first thought of building this enterprise. The idea intrigued Edgcomb, but he realized the project needed a development man to find the money and community volunteers to keep Turner going with his field work on the river. Edgcomb decided he could be that person. Why grow old restoring antique homes when there was real community-building work to be done, he surmised. So it was that Edgcomb began his new career working with schools and environmental organizations, inviting them to Westport to volunteer like us and learn more about the bay scallop—and save it from extinction in the Westport River.

If Edgcomb was the very image of a mature and productive life, his partner Wayne Turner seemed a symbol of passionate youth. The first thing we had all noticed about Turner was his size. As one student noted, "His legs are like tree trunks, and his arms the branches. He isn't just big; he is built!"

And he seemed like a natural leader. Turner wore his Bay Scallop Restoration Project ball cap as much as a badge of pride as a means of shading his sandy blond hair and high forehead. He smiled in an engaging way when he rallied our troops to makeup and deploy "just one more set" of spat bags. Meanwhile, his mud-streaked cargo shorts and shirt with the sleeves rolled up to his elbows sent a clear signal that he was a fellow worker—not a boss.

In spite of this rugged look, Turner proved to be a gentle giant. The best example of this was the day when he brought a boy named Mark along in his skiff with some of our crew to check the spat bags. Mark was a mentally-challenged teenager who loved the river and idolized Turner. But patience was crucial in dealing with Mark because he liked to ask the same questions over and over again. Riding back to the SARAH ABBOT in one of the Scallop Project's skiffs, Mark kept asking what boat our crew was staying on over and over again, even after the crew had told him many times.

After the crew got to the schooner, Mark persisted with this same question, and just as Mark's question got to be a little tedious interrupting the flow of conversation as we all ate lunch in the cockpit, his idol intervened to get Mark's attention. In the wink of an eye, Turner made up a point system to award Mark points for being good, saying that Mark had to earn three billion points.

When Mark asked, "How many points do I have, Waaynee?" Turner said, "One."

Everyone laughed, including Mark. For the rest of the time they were on the schooner with us, Mark kept asking Wayne if he was earning points. If Mark got carried away, Wayne would tell him to settle down and rustle the boy's hair with a big gentle hand . . . until Mark and everyone else was smiling.

Over lunch we heard how Turner conceived of the Scallop Project.

"The actual cleaning up of the Westport River is my bigger agenda," he said.

But Wayne Turner believed that the minute you mentioned environment or pollution, people immediately turned away. On the other hand, if you mentioned economics, people listened. It was Turner's idea to pitch bay scallop restoration as an economic plus to the people of Westport.

Because of the economic benefit of reviving the bay scallop industry for the watermen on the river, the people could see a clear chain of cause/effect from residents cleaning up septic systems and cow farms. And they have pitched in with money and volunteer time.

After hearing Turner's story, one of SARAH ABBOT's crew wrote in his journal:

"This situation reminds me of home. The river I live on is dirtied by the cows on its banks just as the Westport River is. Just like Westport, people at home are turned off by the words pollution and environment, and the thought of cleaning up their farms and septic systems. But if I started a Catfish Restoration Project and people began to come to the river for fishing, then, perhaps, my community would begin to clean their septic systems and cow farms as the people in Westport have."

Reading this entry, I wondered how I should respond to this shipmate's rhapsody, his youthful fire.

In the margin of his log I wrote, "Go for it—like Edgcomb and Turner—stir it up!"

For some reason I fell asleep picturing Bob Edgcomb's smiling face and Wayne Turner's hand rustling Mark's hair. A team, three generations, lacing their lives together with shoals of scallops, an old Indian fishing ground, and a pirates' lair.

V QUICKS HOLE

Our third morning in Westport burst over Buzzards Bay with wind and the clatter of halyards rapping against the schooner's wooden masts. The words "stir it up" were still echoing in my brain when I woke. Right or wrong, I read these words as some kind of signal to get our show on the road.

As soon as we had cleaned SARAH ABBOT, stowed our gear, and rigged the vessel for heavy-weather sailing, we set sail on a rising tide from Westport. Well, actually we motored against the strong river current and a southwest wind, timing our crossing of Dog Fish Bar at the mouth of the river with a moment when the flood current was still fattening the waves on the bar. Nevertheless, we cleared the bar with barely a foot of water under SARAH ABBOT's keel. Westport's pirates, privateers, and whalers in their larger, engineless ships could not have left under such conditions. They must have depended on northwest winds and ultra high tides. Such conditions limited river traffic and commerce—a reason Westport remained a quiet backwater to this day.

Upon clearing the day marker on Half Mile Rock, we set all three working sails on the schooner as we kept an eye on a thunderstorm hovering over New Bedford ten miles away. The wind came out of the sou'west at 18 knots with gusts. But with the tide still flooding from the same direction as the wind, the potentially wicked seas lay relatively flat. Now, each member of the crew stood a half-hour trick at the helm, as SARAH ABBOT hissed across Buzzards Bay at 7.5 knots. The sailing was so good that we decided to press on through Quicks Hole Passage between Nashawena and Pasque Islands and ride the fair current up Vineyard Sound along the southern side of the Elizabeth Islands all the way to Martha's Vineyard for provisions. But passing the deserted beaches of Nashawena and the cliffs and hills of Pasque, the crew vowed to return to these quiet islands.

After provisioning and spending an afternoon and night on the town in the Vineyard's Oak Bluffs, we made good on our pledge to return and anchored off the beach at Quicks Hole—a deserted cove whose dunes and white beach on Nashawena Island had the look of a remote Bahamas isle. At sunset the crew rowed ashore in our 12-foot skiff and tried to collect their thoughts and impressions of this chain of wilderness islands nearly the size of Bermuda.

Later, with everyone asleep, the anchor light set, and the schooner rolling to a gentle swell, everything I knew about this place surfaced in my consciousness as an antidote to—or was it a by-product of—my nagging restlessness. Once again I seemed to be combing my memory of Bay history for something I had lost, picking up pieces of what I knew about this place and trying to put them down in some semblance of order.

Like Cuttyhunk, the rolling meadows, forests, harbor, and beaches of Nashawena—which was part of Cuttyhunk until the early 1600s—have been prized real estate for New England's wealthy families almost since the Europeans arrived on the shores of Buzzards Bay. In 1693 Nashawena, like Cuttyhunk, passed into the hands of one Peleg Slocum, a prosperous merchant farmer and Quaker preacher from Dartmouth. One of Slocum's descendants noted that while his ancestor was an honest Quaker preacher in the eyes of the community, Brother Peleg was also "a merchant on the wrong side of the law"—a smuggler. Given such proclivities, as well as Dartmouth and the Elizabeth Islands' prominence in smuggling right down through the rum-running and marijuana eras, one wonders if the good preacher really wanted this remote island for grazing sheep. Local observers have noted that for a man who called himself a preacher and a merchant farmer, Peleg Slocum spent a notable amount of time traveling to and from the islands in his famous "shallop" boat.

For over 150 years Nashawena remained under the control of the Slocum family. At first so-called "praying Indians," Christianized Wampanoags tended the island, then came white tenant farmers, and finally a few Slocums themselves. Eventually the island fell into the hands of Waldo E. Forbes. Since Forbes' purchase of Nashawena, the island has remained as a part of the Forbes family trust for their descendants.

As the crew of SARAH ABBOT could see when we sailed close to Nashawena and anchored off the beach at Quicks Hole, the island remains unspoiled, and the farm still operates. Under an easement to the Trustees of Reservations to assure its future as undeveloped grazing land, the farm raised shaggy, big-horned Highland cattle that wander the island like prehistoric beasts. During the last decade, eastern coyote packs had invaded and thrived in the Elizabeth Islands, all but exterminating the once-vast herds of sheep. Unless piping plovers are nesting and the area must be closed to protect the endangered birds, the Forbes Trust welcomes the public who come by boat to picnic on the long crescent beach facing Quicks Hole Passage; the rest of the island is private.

Private ownership of the Elizabeths sometimes made me uneasy. I knew that the Forbes family trust had done an exceptionally responsible job protecting the natural environment of the islands, but something about the trust's absolute authority over the islands smacked of feudalism. Yet what were the alternatives for preserving these islands in a natural state? I wished that the Forbes family and their heirs might have an awakening some day soon and give back these islands to the people of the United States as part of the National Seashore.

VI PASQUE

This morning broke gray and misty without a hint of wind. I would have remained curled in my sleeping bag like the rest of the crew, had it not been that a passing flounder dragger returning through Quicks Hole Passage to New Bedford trailed such a rough wake that it sent *Eldridge's Tide and Pilot Guide* tumbling off the navigation shelf and into my face. Checking to make sure SARAH ABBOT was still riding securely to her anchor, I caught a shadowy glimpse of Pasque Island 300 yards across the current-choked passage from our anchorage at Nashawena. In the mist Pasque rose above Vineyard Sound and Buzzards Bay like an Indian mound or a giant grave.

Stripped of almost all of its trees, Pasque's thousand acres of land was never a place that seemed to welcome the world at large. Over the centuries Pasque has gained a reputation as a ghostly island where wind and sea have overwhelmed human efforts to domesticate the land. More than a hint to Pasque's wild character lay in the Wampanoag name for the island: Peshahtaneset, "The Blue Place Where the Sea Breaks Through." This name could refer to both the east and west ends of the island where the boiling currents of Robinsons Hole and Quicks Hole divided Pasque from the woodlands of its sister isles.

About Pasque, I knew little else—and had not really cared to know more in all the years I had been coming here. But now this morning the island made me uneasy, and I turned to the schooner's library to find out why. Historians claim that Pasque began much like the other Elizabeth Islands: for millennia Pasque had been a summer fishing camp for Wampanoag bands. After the Elizabeth Islands came under English control in the mid 1600s, Christianized Indian families arrived on Pasque, presumably to tend the sheep. But the Indians lost patience with being forced into the role of the white man's serfs. Following 40 years of manipulation by the colonists, the Wampanoags began to reassert themselves. On the mainland, the Indian discontent that eventually led to King Philip's War smoldered as braves met to dance the war dances, stockpile guns, and raid settlers' livestock. On Pasque Indian vexation gave rise to a form of free enterprise that became as central to local history as real estate speculation: piracy. The first act of New England brigandry was not committed by Long John Silver or Blackbeard: it was done by Indians, at Pasque Island on September 18, 1667.

As the story goes, the day was a Monday at 2 or 3 a.m. when the ship of Vineyard Captain William Weeks blew ashore on Pasque next to Quicks Hole. The Wampanoags living here refused to give Weeks or his crew anything from the vessel except their clothes, while keeping for themselves the 15-ton vessel and its full load of freight—barrels of corn, meal, and salt pork. Throughout the rest of that year, British colonists became outraged with the Indian initiative at taking something that did not belong to them. As if these islands and this Bay had always belonged to the English.

Eventually, some of these same white men turned to piracy. About 1680 piracy began to flourish around Buzzards Bay and the Elizabeth Islands. One of the first pirate accounts was about a Captain Thomas Pound who sailed a pirate ship until he met a British Coast Guard vessel under a Captain Pease sailing along the Elizabeth Islands. A violent naval battle ensued, and many of Thomas Pound's crew were lost to Captain Pease's men on the MARY. Both captains were wounded, but eventually the Coast Guard vessel triumphed in a raging southeasterly wind off Cuttyhunk. Captain Thomas Pound was taken to Boston along with his crew and found guilty of piracy. But in an odd reversal of circumstances, Pound received a reprieve and found himself sent to England where all charges were dropped, and the pirate was given command of a ship. Years later, Thomas Pound died honored and respected. He was, however, never the man he had been before his pirate days: during his fight against the MARY, he sustained several gunshot wounds and had "several bones taken out." A broken man.

Another famous local pirate was Captain William Kidd. He was born in 1654 in Scotland and had a glamorous career which has turned into myth around Buzzards Bay. For three years before he sailed into these waters, Kidd raided ships throughout the East Indies with the ADVENTURE GALLEY, a 287-ton ship with 34 guns and a crew of 155. One of his prizes, the QUIDAH MERCHANT, is said to have carried 30,000 pounds in valuables. Since Kidd's last stop before being arrested in Boston was at Tarpaulin Cove in the Elizabeth Islands, many local people believe that Kidd hid some of his plunder in the Elizabeths.

One piece of evidence is the testimony of one of the sailors captured with Kidd in Boston. Gabriel Loffe of Long Island, New York, claimed that Kidd left "a pack of goods on shore at Tarpaulin Cove." Curiously, Caleb Ray, the same man who acted as jailer to Kidd and his pirates in Boston, owned a farm near Tarpaulin Cove in the Elizabeths. Found responsible for permitting two pirates to escape his jail, Caleb Ray lost his job as Kidd's caretaker and retired to his land in the islands before finding a chance to assist Kidd in a jailbreak. Local myth assumes that Ray returned to the Island to enjoy the plunder Kidd left here perhaps as a bribe, while authorities whisked the pirate off to England in 1701 for hanging.

Captain Kidd and buried treasure. Right here. I could picture the scene in black and white like an old pirate movie starring Errol Flynn. At the hour of sunset Kidd's ship rode to her anchor 150 yards offshore, her black hull and furled tan-bark sails already silhouetted against the shadowy island hills. The tide was half and rising, and ten men hiked in double file along a thin gray beach. The ship's longboat lay at their backs pulled high on the sand above the rotten eel grass that marked the high tide line. As the men approached a point of land formed from a cluster of boulders, I could see that a trim man in knee boots led the crew forward, waving a cutlass in his hand. Some of the men carried shovels and picks; some shouldered firearms; the last two lugged a chest.

Someone said, "Stir it up!"

Another buccaneer added, "Dead pirates tell no tales!" And everybody laughed. Including me.

Then I thought, "The captain of the SARAH ABBOT had better get a grip on himself. He's becoming unstuck in time."

And what of Pasque after those turbulent years when pirates roamed the Elizabeth Islands? The island changed hands among New England gentry and fell under the domain of the Tucker family from Dartmouth for almost 200 years. One story from the 170 years when Pasque was known as Tucker's Island relates to the American Revolution. During the 1770s a Quaker and British sympathizer named John Slocum lived on Pasque. He fraternized with the crews of British warships that stopped in the Elizabeths during their patrols to harass American privateers in their home ports around Buzzards Bay and Cape Cod. During one frolic, the Quaker learned that the British planned to attack and burn Falmouth the next day. Secretly, Slocum sent word of the impending attack to minutemen in Falmouth who rallied troops and repelled the British.

About a century later striped bass fishing brought a temporary change to Pasque's reclusive character. In 1866 a group of disgruntled members of Cuttyhunk's elite fish club bought Pasque from the Tucker family and set up the Pasque Island Fishing Club with the enlightened idea of permitting women to enjoy this exclusive summer resort. The club—with its clubhouse and servants' quarters at Robinsons Hole—flourished as an outpost for its 24 wealthy members and their families until 1917 when an aging membership, poor bass fishing, and World War I kept the club closed.

A few years later, like many of its sister isles, Pasque became property of a Forbes family trust. Today, members of the family periodically stayed in the buildings that were the remains of the old club at Robinsons Hole. No part of the island opens itself to the public. Pasque is the brooding mystery among the Elizabeth Islands. And in its presence I could not truly sleep.

VII ROBINSONS HOLE

On SARAH ABBOT's second night anchored off the coast of Pasque, the rumble of thunder and the patter of rain on deck kept me tossing and turning in my berth. Then I heard the Chelsea ship's clock in the saloon strike three bells. It chimed one bell for every half hour, eight bells for every four hour watch. Three bells was 5:30 a.m. While the crew slept, I set a second anchor for security, boiled water for tea, and flipped on the radar that I had learned to tune in such a way that it would detect and track thunder squalls. When the tea was ready, and the radar on line, I pressed my face to the rubber mask over the radar screen and watched two squalls heading across the Bay in our direction. The sensible thing to do was to crawl back into my berth and let the squalls pass before rousing the crew, and before consulting with Jackie and Margaret about their agendas for ship keeping and science today. I would not be bored or even anxious about the weather: I had a stack of logs I promised the crew that I would read.

The first log that I picked up took me back to yesterday when the clouds never cleared. But the gray weather had not dampened the spirits of the rest of the crew as it had mine: the general feeling had been that gray skies were a blessing since everyone was suffering from sunburn in spite of megadoses of SPF 15 sunscreens. Margaret said she thought we had a perfect day to see what kind of fish lived in the shallows of these tide-ripped holes, so we motored SARAH ABBOT to Robinsons Hole at the east end of Pasque and secured permission from a Forbes caretaker to conduct our research on the low-tide beach. Here the crew hauled the 100-foot beach seine all morning, capturing, counting, and releasing over a dozen different species of fish ranging from minnows to small mackerel and flounder.

I was discovering that spending time on this Bay had a way of taking travelers into themselves to reconsider where they had been and where they were headed. Sitting on the beach last night, a student watched a flock of seagulls circling and wrote this in her log:

"Each bird knows he is not alone, nor does he need to worry about offending anyone in order to give himself some space or to do as he pleases. These birds just simply live the way they want. Suddenly I want to be a sea bird."

How I knew this fantasy. In my fitful sleep last night, I had dreamed of flying down the Bay like a young, black duck on an autumn day when the Elizabeth Islands were a mottled quilt of reds, yellow, and orange leaves. I was searching for something—maybe a fish for the catching— when I caught sight of a convoy of Wampanoag canoes heading out from the islands, moving west in a line toward a distant shore. And for some reason I followed.

VIII   PADANARAM HARBOR

Our second day anchored in the shadow of Pasque turned out to be a flurry of manic science activity as the students worked on their cruise projects and covered SARAH ABBOT with everything from plankton nets and microscopes to buckets of live crabs and sample jars of dead fish. The crew was so busy that Jackie and I took over the galley chores and grilled dozens of cheese sandwiches for lunch. Margaret kept the energy level high as she scuttled around the deck saying things like "Eh, would you look at that!" and "Good scientists always want more data; don't you think you ought to run that experiment again?" After nightfall, when the students curled up shoulder-to-shoulder in the forecastle to read aloud *A Storm Without Rain*, I heard Margaret tell our crew that she was proud of them: they had the bulk of their cruise projects completed. The teenagers heaved a collective sigh.

Then before the reading even began, I heard our shipmate from West Virginia laugh,

"Y'all smell like my hands after cleaning a mess of trout."

"It's true," said his Greek pal.

"Gross!" moaned the rest of the crew.

Any pretense of reading *Storm* ended there. The crew turned their minds to what they called "the real world." After three days of roughing it in the islands, the teenagers' highest priorities had become a) showers, b) Laundromat, and c) ice cream. It was clearly time to find a civilized port of call: schooner life had begun to get a little claustrophobic. I could use a shower, fresh laundry, and ice cream, too. But clearly I was looking for something more. Something that made my plunges into Bay history seem both crucial and sustaining.

The next morning began with yet more windless and drizzly weather, so I pointed SARAH ABBOT north across Buzzards Bay in search of civilization, and real as well as spiritual sunshine. In nearly calm conditions, the schooner chugged along under the power of her diesel with the crew decked out in bright yellow slickers. A shipmate from Texas steered the schooner almost the whole trip with a determined smile on her face in spite of the rain that pelted her cheeks and smeared her glasses; this was not the same cautious girl who had boarded SARAH ABBOT nine days ago, the girl who asked permission to do *everything*, the girl who avoided taking the helm because she was "afraid to break something." I told her I liked this new self-assurance.

"Stir it up!" she said and flashed me a conspiratorial grin.

Then we pressed on in silence. The teenager steered. I stood watch. We did not need to talk. We had become shipmates.

For a while during the trip we passed in and out of sun showers as the warm front that had settled in two days ago began to break up right over our heads. I had hopes that fair weather would arrive any moment, but a warm drizzle returned by the time we reached the well-known yacht haven at Padanaram Harbor in the town of South Dartmouth on the Bay's north shore. Directed to a mooring by a New Bedford Yacht Club launch, we surveyed the scene. Hundreds of unattended cruising sailboats swinging to their moorings in this narrow harbor, the prestigious Concordia Yacht Yard, the expansive docks and clubhouse at the New Bedford Yacht Club, the village crossroads with their clutch of quaint shops, and the lavish flower gardens decorating baronial homes, all spoke to our crew of old money and leisure time.

On another day, Padanaram might have been the perfect port of call to a gang of mariners eager to stretch their legs and explore. But with the cruise more than three quarters over, and a lot of work behind us, we had begun to run out of energy. Today's persistent drizzle kept us below deck. Eventually, we withdrew to our individual berths with books on local history. Everybody seemed to be looking backwards in time now, not just me.

And I think each of us hoped that reading might carry us through a day when our spirits seemed as soggy as the weather. At one point our Virginia surfer stared out through a rain-smeared window in the saloon and offered a cynical indictment of Padanaram.

"This looks like a place that has never seen trouble," he grumbled.

A number of voices echoed his prejudice.

Later, digging into a book about Padanaram, I began to discover how wrong we had been about this community. More than once this place seemed to stand at the very core of hell on earth.

For the most part, Padanaram shares its Indian and colonial history with Westport and other communities like New Bedford in the township that began as Dartmouth in 1652. The Quakers gave this harbor its name Padanaram because it reminded them of a fertile land in the Bible: according to the book of Genesis, Padanaram is the rich plain adjoining the Tigris and Euphrates rivers where the first Hebrews flourished before settling the land of Canaan. Likewise, the Quakers were fruitful and multiplied after 1660 on the shores of the Padanaram Harbor and the connecting tributary, the Apponagansett River.

Near the center of this community, on what is now Fort Street, still stands the foundation of a stockade house that settler John Russell designed and built as his garrison to protect himself and his neighbors from Indian raids. In July 1675, Russell's intuition about Indian raids proved true in the form of the so-called "Dartmouth Massacre." While braves burned and pillaged 36 of Dartmouth's homes, many of the settlers sought shelter at Russell's garrison and another fortress house nearby. Those who didn't perished in the Indian attack. Ultimately, the violence focused on the garrison. The English fought back with vigor, not only repelling the braves but capturing a number of Wampanoag prisoners. Probably these Indian prisoners were not warriors but rather families who lived directly across the Apponagansett River from Russell's garrison in a place called Indian Town.

Following the blood letting between the settlers and Indians in Dartmouth, the Pilgrim Fathers in Plymouth, including the aged William Bradford, decided that they should round up as many Wampanoags as possible and march them to Plymouth where they might be kept under supervision. To accomplish this task the Pilgrims drafted a noted woodsman from Sakonnet and made him a captain in the militia. His name was Benjamin Church. This tall, broad pioneer prided himself in both his woodlore and his friendship within many Wampanoag communities. From Church's own account of King Philip's War, it seems clear that he hoped to serve both the English and his Indian friends as a peacemaker, but circumstances at the beginning of the war cast Church as a villain. One hundred and twelve Wampanoags (including those from Padanaram who had surrendered to Church believing that the English in Plymouth would protect them) found themselves condemned by the Pilgrims' court, sold as slaves, and shipped offshore, probably to the West Indies. Philip, his braves, and his allies, like the squaw sachem Weetamoe of the Pocasset band, grew wild with rage, and the war spread across New England.

Philip and Weetamoe's forces might have won the war if it had not been for Benjamin Church's respect among the communities of Wampanoags living along the rim of Buzzards Bay. During the summer of 1676, the squaw sachem Awashonks from the Sakonnet band who held sway over many of the groups of Buzzards Bay Wampanoags convinced these people to remain loyal to her friend Benjamin Church and the peace-loving Quakers who had settled the region. Meanwhile, Philip and Weetamoe took their war westward, away from Buzzards Bay and toward the Connecticut River Valley. When Philip returned to the Bay area in August of 1776 to take refuge in the wilderness of his homelands on the Powkanoket Peninsula at Mt. Hope, Rhode Island, Awashonks' braves helped Church to track down Philip.

A disaffected warrior shot his former leader through the heart in an ambush. Another Indian severed the great sachem's head and delivered it to Plymouth where it stood upon a spike in public view for decades.

My rainy-day reading revealed that Padanaram suffered more trauma and losses when the American Revolution broke out a hundred years after King Philip's War. A century of peace had brought prosperity to Buzzards Bay. Third- and fourth-generation settlers had grown resentful and defiant of England sticking its nose into local life by the time the British began impressing American seamen, billeting redcoats in private homes, and taxing tea. Dartmouth minutemen rushed to the aid of their comrades when the showdown came with General Gage's troops at Lexington and Concord. But Padanaram men were bred to the water, sailors more than soldiers, and so it was natural that they took to the sea—as privateers to harass British shipping around Buzzards Bay. Lieutenant John Paul Jones on the sloop PROVIDENCE was a leading figure among the Revolutionary fleet. Jones, an immigrant from Scotland, frequented Dartmouth's harbors and recruited local sailors for privateering.

With the British losing in excess of 450 ships to privateers in 1777, and Jones and his colleagues-in-arms drawing attention to Buzzards Bay, the British Admiralty sent a fleet of about 20 warships to Buzzards Bay on September 5, 1778, with two Dartmouth Tories as pilots. General Gray landed 4,000 troops at Clark's Cove, between Padanaram and New Bedford harbors, and burned 70 ships as well as the shops, warehouses, and homes along the Acushnet River. A few ships anchored at Padanaram and launched troops to selectively burn the vessels and homes of the Tory pilots' personal enemies.

Reading a shipmate's log took me back to 1778 and what it might have been like to be a colonial woman during the British attack. She imagined the defense of Padanaram like this:

"I could hear the marching of the rows of British soldiers in contrast with the 77 untrained minutemen blindly stumbling through the battle of Lexington. I could feel the cold winter wind blasting through the soldiers' bodies as they struggled to keep warm in the seven long New England winters during the war.

"I could smell wood burning as the redcoats torched houses of suspected patriots in Padanaram in 1778. I heard the splashing of water from windows of burning houses as women doused the fires and drenched the British soldiers. Then the mutterings of disgusted British soldiers as they stomped away.

"I am the lady of the house. I'm worried about my brothers who are fighting in the war. I fear that the British soldiers may come to my very door soon. A loud shot rings out and is matched by the piercing screams of a stableboy. The sudden scent of burning wood fills my nostrils. I rush into action.

"First, I fill all my buckets with water from the pump in the backyard and then wait upstairs for the British to come. I see a small group of about five come up over the hill from the burning ships. They have a torch and light my house. I throw buckets of water on the fire and on them. I drench everything. Finally, the sopping-wet soldiers sludge away with strings of oaths upon their lips."

Was my young shipmate's scenario simply a fanciful fiction? I don't think so. On some primal level, she had revisited the eighteenth century: documents show that a woman named Akin acted with exactly such heroism to preserve her house that stands to this day on Elm Street.

Just as eerie as my shipmate's clairvoyant visit to Padanaram's colonial conflicts, are the details of a much more recent melodrama in the town. During the last hundred years perhaps no drama—not the demise of the whaling industry, the devastating hurricane of '38, nor two world wars—has woven itself more deeply into Padanaram lore than the stories associated with Round Hills, the Green estate. The 300-acre manor overlooking Buzzards Bay and Padanaram Harbor from the extreme end of Nonquit Neck was once the home of one of America's most eccentric millionaires. With no less powerful illustrations of the greed and miserliness of Yankee capitalism than rose from the pages of *Moby Dick*, the saga of the Green fortune exposes the festering underbelly of New England enterprise.

Today, Round Hills is a public beach and park for residents of Dartmouth. The sixty-room granite, neo-classical mansion has been turned into condominiums. Except for the transformed mansion, little is left to remind visitors that this point of land was once the family seat of one of the greatest personal fortunes in America. It had belonged to Hetty Green, the so-called "Witch of Wall Street." When she died in 1916, Hetty Green was the most famous miser in the United States. As the *Boston Transcript* reported, "she lived as a poor woman lives, and moved from one place to another in order to dodge those pestering her with appeals for aid."

Green's fortune was the final result of two hundred years of Yankee entrepreneurism. Descended from the Howland family who arrived on the MAYFLOWER, Hetty Green's family moved to Round Hills in the seventeenth century. Starting with one black cow, the family amassed capital through farming, trading with Indians, slavery, and real estate deals. After the Revolution, the fortune grew as ancestors created a merchant fleet to traffic in commodities like rum and Russian iron. The large and profitable Howland whaling fleet of the mid-nineteenth century capitalized the shrewd business deals of Hetty's father, Black Hawk Robinson, a ruthless miser. Obsessed by stinginess, Hetty Green lived much of her adult life in a series of cold-water New York flats. Meanwhile she consolidated and expanded the family wealth through forgery, perjury, and penury before she died and left a fortune estimated between $100 and $200 million to her two children, a reclusive daughter and a flamboyant son who lost a leg due to his mother's neglect.

The land at Round Hills and the fortune belonged to Hetty Green, but her son, E. H. R. "Ned" Green, who shared none of his mother's mania for thrift, transformed the ancestral farm into a pleasure dome. Three years after the death of his mother, Ned Green committed $1,500,000 to erecting his Round Hills estate. Neither Ned's Howland relatives nor the rest of Padanaram had ever seen anything like the 6'4", 300-pound, one-legged man who enjoyed being called Colonel, an honorary rank granted him by a Texas governor. As Arthur Lewis wrote in his biography of the Greens, *The Day They Shook the Plum Tree*, Ned Green "blithely tossed away $3,000,000 a year on yachts, coins, stamps, diamond-studded chastity belts, female teenage 'wards', pornography, orchid culture, and Texas politics."

Before he died in 1936, Ned Green had managed to turn Round Hills into a bizarre and gilded amusement park. Old-guard Massachusetts families like the Cabots, Lowells, Lodges, and Winthrops with summer retreats in South Dartmouth were appalled by what they saw going on at Round Hills. Everyone knew that Ned had filled his mansion with a harem of teenage girls whom he "adopted" and encouraged to call him "Uncle Ned." While the girls were buzzing around Padanaram in Ned's roadsters, or pursuing private interludes with their adopting "uncle" allegedly to work on his coin and stamp collections, Green's wife Mabel drank like a fish and openly cultivated romantic relations with some of the 100 servants who robbed her blind.

Things were no less strange on the waterfront where Ned's 215-foot yacht UNITED STATES, considered the largest and most lavish vessel of her type, sunk mysteriously—a total loss—at her mooring in Padanaram. But Ned hardly noticed: he had other maritime toys including an Italian gondola and the whaling bark CHARLES W. MORGAN which he kept at his dock as a shrine to the glory days of Howland whaling. Ashore, Ned rankled his neighbors by setting up a water tower with a public address system near the beach broadcasting radio music and attracting crowds of perhaps 25,000 from New Bedford to party on warm summer nights. At another moment, Ned became interested in experimenting with means to fight airport fog and make air travel safer. Before he died, Ned had an airfield and an MIT lab on his property doing significant work with cloud physics. But as with everything else, the Colonel lost interest.

In his obituary, *The New Bedford Standard Times* remembered Ned Green as a "friendly, extraordinarily interesting neighbor whose sharing of his hobbies was as notable as his hobbies themselves." Those who knew the Colonel well saw him as an acutely sad man. Following his death, several states and the Federal Government spent years dismantling the Green fortune for unpaid taxes; only after his sister Sylvia died did any contributions of significance go to charity.

rafts of Canada geese paddled among a dozen cruising sailboats at anchor. Snowy egrets and an oyster catcher waded in the shallows. With the approach of a cruiser's dinghy, a coyote rushed her pups off a rocky beach and into the brush on Bull Island. Around their boats, people swam in languid circles as if choreographing their exercise to the chorus of the songbirds.

Even after 25 years of visiting Hadley, the scene eased my heart rate down to about 50 beats a minute, and I could see that this place was affecting my new shipmates the same way. Following this first afternoon aboard the schooner, a boy from Japan made this log entry:

"I feel like I am entering an entire new world, or maybe heaven. Beyond my expectation, the boat was cool yet beautiful. The sailing was great. It was faster than I thought, and I realized that the ocean is incredibly huge in its wind and its waves . . . Everything I did today is something I have never experienced in my whole life."

On this cruise our Japanese shipmate joined a diverse group of students who had come to us from England and Nicaragua as well as America. They brought a new scientist with them. John Rogers rotated aboard while Margaret took over the *Oceans* teaching duties back at the Andover campus. This was John's fourth year with *Oceans*, and over those years he had developed into a first-rate seaman and field biologist. Trained as a physicist and biochemist, John applied for a job with *Oceans* after participating in one of the Sea Education Association's summer institutes for teachers. The idea of hands-on teaching and learning in a marine environment appealed to his natural curiosity, affection for teaching, and love of the outdoors.

Not surprisingly, John is a wilderness hiker, mountain climber, backcountry skier, and explorer when he can break away from his winter teaching job at Phillips Academy where he also serves as the head of the school's Science Division. In spite of his 33 years of age and accomplishments which include a masters degree from Harvard, John is still often mistaken for one of his students. Now, here at anchor at Hadleys, I looked at John's

What a loss. The story of the Green fortune made me shudder, and I wondered if an obsession with money had been handed down through the centuries and generations of the Bay's oldest families. Melville had satirized the greedy, miserly characters of the Quaker ship owners in *Moby Dick*. And so much of the local history that had been churning through my mind during our cruise featured stories of wheeling, dealing, and just plain cheating and thievery. Had dreams of fortune cast a curse on Buzzards Bay? And what if it did? How did such a curse affect me or my crew of incipient Dead Pirates?

After our rainy day of reading aboard the schooner, we saw the sun break over Padanaram Harbor, in late afternoon. Double rainbows glowed over the mansions along the Nonquit shore and above the saltmarsh and woods of the Apponagansett River. The change in weather teased us on deck, and soon a trio of the girls headed ashore in a yacht club launch to see if they could find "any friendly natives." When they returned to the schooner for dinner, they seemed electrified and reported that they had a "spectacular visit" with a man who is sustaining the 300-year-old tradition of boatbuilding in Padanaram. John "Skip" Garfield, the president of Marshall Marine, had shown our shipmates around the shop on Shipyard Lane where he and his crews build classic Cape Cod catboats.

The boatbuilder had explained that until World War I and the advent of gasoline-driven skiffs, pea-shaped, wooden catboats—broad and shallow with one mast rising from the stem and one great gaff-rigged sail— were the vessels of preference for the Bay's lobstermen, clammers, and scallopers. For almost one hundred years catboats dominated the inshore fisheries of the Bay. Today, the design survives largely because of Marshall Marine. Garfield builds 14-, 18- and 22-foot Marshall cats out of fiberglass for sailors who like connecting with tradition as they explore the backwaters of the Bay in a boat whose seaworthiness and carrying capacity has been tested by generations of watermen.

A shipmate's log entry about her visit to Marshall Marine opened the heart of a Bay legacy:

"Affable and welcoming when we wandered into Marsh
boatshop, Mr. Garfield introduced himself by asking us to call
casual attitude matched perfectly his appearance and his wor
man in his forties with longish salt-and-pepper hair, John wore
polo shirt with khaki shorts. As he led us around the boatbuildi
ticed that he looked perfectly at home. While definitely not a
was a far cry from the orderly office setting you associate with
Three men in T-shirts were moving around, laughing and jo
other while working to fit wood trim into a catboat's cockpit.

As SARAH ABBOT's girls toured the boat shop, Skip Garfiel
how his crew lays up the fiberglass hulls and decks in separ
glues and bolts the pieces together. He also led them to a su
2,000 separate parts and a small foundry where he casts the
and rudder fittings. He said that the company has produce
to date—approximately 40 vessels a year. Marshall Marin
market for catboats. And as Garfield talked about the catbo
as a fast and able workboat capable of penetrating the sh
around Buzzards Bay and Cape Cod, the builder's face bea

His attachment to tradition showed through even
sation veered away from catboat history. Asked whether
expand his business, Garfield answered with a definitive
over-expansion was often the downfall of boatbuilding c
having too much fun with his present lifestyle becaus
time to enrich his life outside of his profession. Keeping
gave him the time to help a friend sail a boat from Spa
and join his wife in community service endeavors.

Discovering my crew's enthusiasm for Skip Garfie
my faith in the Bay's entrepreneurs and their enterpri
traditional Buzzards Bay man, a good old boy in a tr
Bay business. He sounded like a man at peace with h
past. I envied him.

---

lot of his time testing to make sure that the
and that both recreational and commercial
rules and only working on open healthy bed

"So why do you carry a gun?" asked a

Sherman cleared his throat and told us
protection because I sometimes have to dea
the 40 miles of coastline I patrol."

He said that he once got a report of man
ing offshore. When he went to the scene,
contained marijuana, left after a boat wreck
investigation by Sherman and others, the
brought to justice.

Listening to this story, our crew started
night, but Sherman put our fantasies to res
ing experiences were once-in-a-lifetime eve
gun yet.

But then he added, "When your numbe
you don't miss."

Sherman flashed a smile of self-assura
smile somewhere before, I think in an old
the gun slinger Billy the Kid.

So here was another local titan, I thoug
Sherman, the visibility improved to about
abruptly, Sherman patted his firearm, claimi
said that he had just enough visibility to sneak
peradoes whom he suspected to be poaching cl
on closed beds in Clarks Cove.

Suddenly being a schooner captain
teenagers around Buzzards Bay seemed like
and a sham—a faint shadow of traditional B
man was doing seemed like life itself. He had
in time, stepped squarely into the shoes of

Bay the present seem
it's vice versa—like
shoulder. Does that m

"Heavy," sighed

"Deep."

"Strange idea,"
was it the kind of ron
bound from a voyage
and age? In Buzzards ith a record-setting 98
what exactly were the e temperatures were in
feeling in me? In this fowing at 25 knots since
lover, we ate lunch and
en the greenhorns got a
ough afternoon in Buz-
g, the schooner dashed
r twelve miles away at
inst SARAH ABBOT at half-
the water and drove for-
f spray arched over the
lves against the rise an

n to bare his young ch
d and drenched his sl
H ABBOT for the advent
rbor at the northeas
from the marine sc
in New England,"
ge to weather agains
ntrance between B
oaks filtered out
water lake. Bou
huge stone ma
ble, and the ha

tangle of blond curls, bright eyes, and fresh complexion and pictured Huckleberry Finn.

At dusk, I invited Jackie to linger with me on deck after setting the anchor light for our night in Hadley. A full moon bathed Naushon's hills and Stone House, the mansion on the crest of a hill in a mercurial light that painted a scene reminiscent of Emily Bronte's *Wuthering Heights*. I could almost picture the ghosts of Heathcliff and Catherine Earnshaw gliding over the highland moors that spread out around Stone House. The call of a loon echoed from somewhere in the shadows as I began telling Jackie just about everything I had ever learned about this place as if I were making a confession about something I had neglected or lost a long time ago.

From time immemorial Wampanoags called this island Cataymucke and spelled the name in numerous ways. At the end of the seventeenth century, colonists dubbed it Winthrop's Island after its owner, a grandson of the first governor of Massachusetts, John Winthrop. But while humans have tagged this island with different names over the course of history, virtually everyone who has seen Naushon has judged it romantic.

Approximately six miles long and a mile and a quarter wide, Naushon is the largest of the Elizabeth Islands. With its satellite islands, Nonamesset, Uncatena, and the Weepeckets, Naushon trails off the shoulder of Cape Cod—just a quarter of a mile from the village of Woods Hole—like a shoulder blade dividing the waters of Vineyard Sound and Buzzards Bay. No island in New England is a more dramatic example of a terminal moraine: Naushon's rolling hills, kettle holes, boulders, and scalloped coast line were nothing less than the debris and aftermath when the great New England glacier pushed down from Canada 15,000 years ago in the last ice age. In contrast to the bold and weathered profiles of the other Elizabeth Islands, Naushon had a gentler, textured topography. The island was rife with forests, freshwater ponds, sheltered coves, and several, spectacular sandy beaches.

A travel article published in the Barnstable Gazette in 1825 gushed:

"Taking the whole island collectively, there could be no better situation for one who wished to turn his back upon the world, and to devote his time to study, contemplation and uninterrupted ease. The poet would find subject for the muse, the student ample room for the pursuit of learning, and the lover of romance a fine range of dreamy reverie . . . One might draw his mantle around him here, and fit himself for earth or heaven, there is a witching about the whole, which entices one to linger around it, and to indulge in melancholy feelings when he deserts it."

Another writer from the early-nineteenth century filled in the picture of Naushon's "witching" environment:

"Naushon is well wooded . . . About three fifths of the trees are beech: the remainder of the wood is white and black oak, hickory and a little pine. About one half of the island is in wood and swamp; and in the swamps grows white cedar . . . Stones lie on the upland, and along the beaches as in the opposite beaches of Chilmark; but the shores are not iron bound like those of Marblehead. . . . Tataug, swappog eels are the most common fish near shore, and alewives in the season in the greatest abundance. The quahog and lesser clam are found within the harbour, also lobster in abundance . . . Ducks are in abundance in the fall and winter."

These descriptions still hold today, and it is easy to see why the prose of Amelia Forbes Emerson in her book *Early History of Naushon Island* waxed with enthusiasm as she speculated about the various translations one might give to Wampanoag words associated with this island:

"Nashanow. It appears that nooshun, with unimportant variations, is used in the superlative degree, 'the best,' 'all in all,' etc . . .

"Katomuch (also spelled Cataymuck and Katamawick) is familiar to the reader and traveler as well as the historian by the name Naushon. The question will be asked why the natives call it Katomuck, as it appears in the testimony. We can only answer that cautumme is their name for the natural year; hence they gave it to planting ground and the planting season. Was this not therefore the aboriginal, Planting Island?

"Katomuck. A great fishing place. Derivation, Kehtamaug, 'chief fishing place'."

In Amelia Forbes Emerson's mind, Naushon must have been the chief fishing place for Wampanoags migrating to the islands to feast, gather food for the winter, and beat the summer heat. She might have been right; a number of Indian shell piles have been found in the vicinity of Hadley, and the waters off Naushon were still dotted with sport fishermen, commercial draggers, and lobstermen on every fair summer day.

"Wow!" said my wife when I had finished my history lesson.

"Yeah, wow!" I echoed. I was getting pretty carried away by the past. But, now, looking at Naushon's shadowy landscape from the moonlit deck of SARAH ABBOT, it seemed as insubstantial as a dream. I suddenly felt the urge to hug my wife to my chest.

XI NAUSHON

Our stay at Naushon proved full of surprises. The second morning of the cruise broke with a wild thunder squall. In Hadley Harbor we heard and felt the wind gusting to over 50 knots. Boats sawed back and forth on their anchor lines like drunken water bugs. Fortunately, only one of the 20 vessels in the harbor dragged anchor, and she managed to use her engine to keep clear of the other boats and to stay off the rocks at the lee side of the anchorage.

After the sun came out again, we found ourselves invited ashore to explore the east end of Naushon in the vicinity of Hadley with Cindy Wish, a summer resident of the island, and her ten-year-old son Eric.

Dressed in shorts and T-shirts, Eric and his mother Cindy were full of welcoming smiles. As we trouped along what seemed to be a bridle path, the Wishes talked about Naushon history, and I gathered that the Wampanoags gave up their claims to the island in the 1650s. Early white owners set up a tenant farming operation raising sheep, cattle, and goats, but remained absentee landlords. Inevitably, Naushon's natural virtues attracted interlopers and squatters, and during the 1720s the owners found themselves caught up in a struggle that persists to this day—the more-or-less constant battle to protect the island's privacy. Concerning this struggle, one of the island's owners explained how he had taken the law into his own hands, expelled the squatters, "turned off their creatures and burned down their cottage."

British ships and troops proved to be just as big a threat to the island's privacy as squatters. During the Revolutionary War the English repeatedly invaded Naushon and "abused the inhabitants, stove the boats and by force [took] away part of their property." The Continental Army responded by building a fort of earth overlooking Tarpaulin Cove and arming it with four small canons and 100 hundred men. But the British raids persisted, and the redcoats burned the barracks and carried off the cannons. Years later Samuel Robinson who grew up the son of a tenant farmer on Naushon during the Revolution recorded his memories of how both British and Americans plundered the island:

"It was during that war, the British came down the Bay, with eighteen sail of transports and other vessels and anchored near the Weepeckets; they then landed about 500 men, and demanded all the stock there was on the Island--remonstrance and resistance were useless, they marched to the Eastern part of the island; and separating, they commenced driving the stock to the Westward as far as Robinsons Hole, where they took it in their boats, and carried it on board—as near as I can remember they took off at this time 1,400 sheep, 35 head of cattle, and 25 horses. This was stripping the island with a vengeance, but this was not all. Some time after a privateer sloop with two tenders [John Paul Jones in the PROVIDENCE?] came and anchored in Hadley. I then resided with my father at Nonamesset. There were remaining of the former stock about 60 cows, 70 or 80 sheep, and one yoke of oxen. The captain of the privateer sent his boat on shore, and the officer after looking around awhile at the stock spied some calves which we had at Nonamesset—he gave us orders to dress him four, and send them onboard in the morning—this we did and carried them on the boat as he directed, which he paid us for. My father went with me onboard the privateer, and after paying us for the calves, he said to my father, 'I shall take what sheep you have got on the Island. I see that they are all yarded, and now my friend, as the wool is no use to me, you may go onshore and commence shearing them,' for it was in the spring of the year, 'and I shall attend to getting them on board and further,' says he, 'if you are faithful in sending all the sheep on board, I will leave the cows and oxen with you.' I very well remember how my father worked to save the wool, and I carted them down to the boats the next day with a soldier marching each side of me."

The sacking of the island was just a fireside tale by the time John Murray Forbes bought the island in 1842. Descended from a family of Massachusetts merchant-princes, Forbes saw the island as a piece of New England history and an exquisite natural retreat he had to own. Ever preservation minded, Forbes devoted considerable personal wealth to re-foresting Naushon and to limiting human use of the island. On his death in 1898, he left Naushon and its smallers satellites in trust for the exclusive use of his direct descendants. The keystone for the Forbes domination of the Elizabeth Islands was in place.

In recent years, the single remaining farm has faltered as eastern coyote have devastated the sheep flocks. These same coyote have reduced the deer herd from 400 a decade ago to about 80 today. Now, there are signs that distemper has begun to thin the coyote packs, and the deer might begin to thrive again. Meanwhile, deer ticks infested with Lyme disease plague Naushon's thick brush. A few years back, Eric Wish almost died from a bite by an infected tick.

Every summer the Forbes family and their celebrated friends—including presidents, senators and foreign royalty—still arrived aboard the island ferry CORMORANT, retreated to the dozen or so houses clustered around Hadley Harbor, and disappeared into Naushon's forests. Visitors were only permitted ashore at Bull Island in Hadley, Tarpaulin Cove, Kettle Cove, Crescent Beach and the Weepecket Islands. A friendly, but firm island constable patrolled Naushon to protect it from the curious and the careless. In the midst of the development that had swept over nearby Cape Cod and Martha's Vineyard, Naushon remained an exclusive oasis open only to those visiting on private boats.

As we walked the upland trails of the island with Cindy and Eric Wish, we noticed that everything looked overgrown with plants. Eric explained to our crew that the Forbes did not want to change anything on the island: it contains an actual virgin coastal forest, one of few untouched areas in the United States.

Meanwhile, Cindy Wish spoke of some of the prestigious individuals such as Grover Cleveland, Dwight Eisenhower, Jack Kennedy, and Bill

Clinton, who had visited the island. Suddenly, I could picture John F. Kennedy walking by fields of bleating sheep and swimming in the cool waters of an island pond. And I could tell that some of SARAH ABBOT's crew were angry that all this was accessible only to the rich and famous. But as our conversation with the Wishes unfolded, we soon realized that any commercial developer would gladly destroy Naushon's forest to build vacation homes and shopping malls. Cindy Wish underlined Naushon's rarity by telling us how, during the 1960s, Naushon barely escaped a plan that would have built a bridge from Woods Hole to Naushon and on to Martha's Vineyard. Then everything that I loved here might have disappeared, I thought.

I felt privileged for the chance to be here as a tolerated, but uninvited guest of the Forbes family. Once when President Clinton was vacationing on Martha's Vineyard he took a yachting junket to Hadley. Clinton arrived amid a flotilla of Secret Service, Coast Guard, and State police boats with Massachusetts Senator John Kerry who has family ties to Naushon. By chance, SARAH ABBOT was heading for Hadley at the same time. But arriving at the entrance channel just after the president's boat, the schooner found herself in a traffic jam of pleasure boats being turned away from the harbor by the president's security patrol. After a short quiz by some Secret Service agents who came alongside, SARAH ABBOT gained permission to enter the harbor as long as the crew anchored well away from the president and went about its business of education. How exhilarating to be accepted into this inner sanctum, but how unfair to all the people on the other boats. Didn't they have a right to be in Hadley, too?

Sure, this event surrounding the president's visit to Hadley had been engineered by his security people, not the trustees of Naushon, but now—for me—the memory brought to the surface again my conflicted feelings about the exclusivity that results from the Forbes ownership of the Elizabeth Islands. The Forbes trust had been an excellent caretaker of the natural treasures of Naushon, Pasque, Nashawena, and the smaller islands. For this America owes them an enormous debt of gratitude.

But now I wondered where else in this country did a single family own so much prime coastal wilderness and chose to let the public share so little. How would the members of the Forbes family feel if they were in the shoes of casual visitors by boat to Naushon or the other Forbes-owned islands? Would they feel grateful because the trust "welcomed" the public to a few acres in the islands, or would they feel they had been thrown some crumbs? Would they feel a swell of pride in America's democracy, or would they feel something like indigestion?

Following our visit with the Wishes at Hadley, we weighed anchor, hoisted sail, and made our way through Woods Hole Passage and along the southeast side of the island to visit Tarpaulin Cove. Even though it was a fair Sunday in July, we found fewer than a dozen boats at anchor here. A great white crescent beach made an arc around the deep, broad cove. Green rolling hills, a swamp maple forest, a lighthouse on the point and one lone barn of a house—that used to be the tavern for the sailors and pirates—completed the scene.

When the crew rowed ashore to pull the beach seine and collect data for their cruise projects, we met Gary Hodges, Naushon's assistant manager and security force. We saw him coming down the beach on his horse. From a distance, we could see his mirrored sunglasses reflecting the light. He wore a cowboy hat and binoculars around his neck. The man must have been my age, 50, but he looked inexplicably younger, like a poster boy for the Texas Rangers.

After dismounting, Hodges invited us to the edge of the beach where the white sand meets green dune grass. By way of introduction, he told us that he had been a field biologist and forest ranger in Oregon, Washington, and Colorado before coming to this island in 1985.

Our crew had some questions for Hodges. As he answered, the beach seemed hushed—despite 20 to 30 people swimming nearby—as if everybody and everything was listening.

He explained to us the basic geological facts of Naushon's formation from glacial sediment, then moved on to the history of the island. One anecdote he told about Tarpaulin Cove seized my imagination. According to Hodges, conflict returned to Naushon during the War of 1812. Events reached their peak when the little American sloop TWO FRIENDS with a volunteer crew of Cape and island men set out to raid the British privateer RETALIATION at Tarpaulin Cove.

An American sailor remembered the event this way:

"The sloop TWO FRIENDS of Nantucket, a coaster commanded by a Falmouth man, Captain Weston Jenkins, was in Falmouth . . . It was the evening of October 28, 1814. There was moon up but it was raining. The wind was southeast when we started, but by the time we came to Job's Neck it had died away. We were in sight of the privateer; our captain had divided us into two companies,—one stayed down in the cabin, the other was on deck.

"There was a board all around the gunwale to screen us and we all lay down. No one was to be seen but two men walking about the deck. The privateer fired and we laid to; presently we saw her barge putting out for us. When it came close to they hailed us and said, 'What sloop is this?' Captain Jenkins answered, 'The WILLIAM of Falmouth.' 'Who is in command of this sloop?' By that time he was right alongside. Captain Jenkins said, 'I am,' and stamped his foot,—and they saw men enough then! We all jumped up at the signal and the men below came right on deck. The man in the barge lifted his gun to fire, but it only flashed in the pan.

"One of our men was kind of excited and he jumped right into the barge and took that man and threw him neck and heels right o' to our deck. He couldn't ha' done it if he hadn't been so excited."

The Americans demanded the British surrender, put twelve men on the RETALIATION, and sailed their prize back to Falmouth, leaving the island in peace at last.

As Gary Hodges related this tale and others, we got the feeling that he had more of an agenda than just giving a history lecture to our floating high school class. We sensed that he somehow felt connected to those earlier American defenders of the island, and that by passing on these stories he was somehow reaching out to pull us into a tribe.

Finally, before he remounted and rode off, Gary Hodges talked about why he preferred to patrol the island on his horse instead of in a jeep. He said he felt that traveling by horse was more in keeping with the motto of the island, "leave things as you find them."

I saw my shipmates nod when he said this. The man and the motto made sense. And no matter how much I questioned Naushon's exclusivity, I could not find fault with the island's philosophy or the people who work here. My mind filed Gary Hodges with Donna Hunter, Bob Edgcomb, Wayne Turner, Skip Garfield and John Sherman, under "lucky buggers." They seemed to know something I didn't. Or connect with this place in a way I hadn't.

After meeting Hodges, the crew spent a few hours towing the seine and preserving species for observation and dissection. Exhausted, they turned into their berths almost immediately after dinner and a short session of reading *A Storm Without Rain*.

Before falling asleep, I read a shipmate's log about last night when he undertook a marathon study of changes in water chemistry at Hadley. His reflections made me think of the kind of things the young Charles Darwin wrote in *The Voyage of the Beagle*:

"I had to do my cruise project, 24 hours water research, which is to study the change of water's character during 24 hours by testing every 4 hours. I did a total of 6 tests, starting with 3:45 in the afternoon. Mark, Roy, and I slept on the deck to see the stars and to test at midnight. I've looked up at the sky until the 11:45 test. There were nothing but shiny stars on a dark, black sky and a shooting star every 10 minutes. I realized how small I am; I wouldn't even be a piece of plankton compared to this boundless space. I thought about how different the night is in Osaka where you can never see the sky like this."

Reading this log entry reminded me how much I admired these kids.

True, being out here in the islands on the schooner was an adventure, but these young scientists were probably working as hard or harder than they did back in their own high schools. I didn't know if I would have spent my precious summers in such intense academic pursuits when I was a teenager. Jackie told me that when I had epiphanies like this about the crew I should tell them. Tomorrow I would.

XII WOODS HOLE

Tonight the crew turned in early. As the stiff northwest wind set SARAH ABBOT's halyards clattering against the masts, I curled under my sleeping bag in a flannel shirt and jeans; this was the first time in almost two days that I had been able to return to my log keeping. We had sailed this morning from Martha's Vineyard after a day and a night in Oak Bluffs where we had ridden out a spell of dirty weather. With the wind howling through the anchorage at 35 knots, and a hard rain flailing the decks, the crew had spent a lot of time below working on their cruise projects while I continued pouring over local history. Virtually every square inch of horizontal surface inside SARAH ABBOT got buried beneath microscopes, dissection trays, sample jars, notebooks, texts, and students.

The scientist's berth overflowed with springs, cylinders, and rubber tubing as John Rogers rebuilt devices known as Nansen bottles that we used for taking water samples from different depths in the Bay's water column. Meanwhile, WMVY, the Vineyard's radio station, kept us humming with a steady diet of blues and funk. Dinner at a local pizzeria, a night at the movies, and several runs to the Laundromat to dry wet gear helped to keep up our spirits.

This morning had come with intermittent drizzle, but lighter winds. Good enough weather to set sail on the early tide and fair current for Woods Hole. But we were not more than a mile out of the harbor when the first squall jumped us. The new crew responded like veterans, and we doused all the sails in less than a minute. By the time the wind was gusting over 30 knots, we had the engine thrumming and SARAH ABBOT steaming to weather at five knots. Everyone except our Nicaraguan shipmate and me went below decks to ride out the weather in their berths. Several of the crew looked a little green, and two of them lost their breakfasts as the wind whipped Vineyard Sound into haystacks of foam.

With visibility down to a sixteenth of a mile, SARAH ABBOT tracked toward Woods Hole. I kept watch for the constant parade of ferryboat traffic on the radar while our student helmsman steered a steady course. Just as we reached the stiff current boils at the choke point in the shipping lanes to Woods Hole Passage, the squall passed and the sun broke through the ragged cumulus. Totally tuned to the same frequency, the helmsman and I slapped each other a high five. I had not felt so good in weeks.

Woods Hole, the only deepwater port on the south side of Cape Cod, rose out of the sun-streaked mist with the look of a Roaring Twenties seaport transformed into a college town. The massive hulls of the Nantucket and Vineyard ferries lying at the Massachusetts Steamship Authority dock had the bulky look of passenger liners in black and white movies. At the next wharf to the west lay two 125-foot schooners, the Sea Education Association's school ships WESTWARD and CORWITH CRAMER, with the yards of their square sails canted into the wind. Beyond the schooners lay what looked like a trio of tramp steamers, actually two research ships for Woods Hole Oceanographic Institute and one for the National Oceanographic and Atmospheric Administration. Rising behind the shipping were the cupolas and three-story red brick or stone buildings of the Woods Hole Oceanographic Institute and the Marine Biological Laboratory.

We found a strong mooring in Great Harbor among a collection of house boats that look like small cabins afloat. As soon as we had SARAH ABBOT squared away, and our most recent complement of wet gear hung on the booms to dry in the sun, John Rogers took his students ashore for a close encounter with North America's mecca for marine scientists.

Even though I had been passing through Woods Hole for decades, I felt that this visit as well as my reading from local histories stretched my understanding of the community. To begin with, I discovered that in spite of its busy ferry terminal and marine science institutions, Woods Hole was not a distinct municipality as I had always imagined. This settlement was just one of a half dozen villages that made up the town of Falmouth.

Woods Hole existed not because of some legal act of incorporation but because of its geology. In fact, the Hole had been a jumping off place for something like the last 12,000 years. When the glacier began to recede at the end of the last ice age, it left a terminal moraine forming the ridge of hills that are now the southeastern shore of Buzzards Bay and the Elizabeth Islands. The Atlantic's sea level lay 200 to 300 feet lower than it does today, and North America's eastern seacoast stood at George's Bank at the edge of the continental shelf, a three-day walk from Woods Hole. Mowing Hill in Woods Hole stood as a promontory overlooking the vast plains of tundra that are now Vineyard Sound and Buzzards Bay. At such vistas paleoindian hunters could camp and scout for herds of caribou and mastodons before sweeping down onto the plains in pursuit of their quarry.

As the glaciers melted and the sea rose, Nantucket and the Vineyard became islands about 7,000 or 8,000 years ago. Archeologists know that in those days the so-called "archaic Indians" began seasonal migrations to this area to fish, and—as in later centuries—Woods Hole made a convenient point of departure for Indians headed to their summer camps on Nantucket and the Vineyard. When the ocean overwhelmed the highlands south of Woods Hole forming the Elizabeth Islands some 3,000 to 5,000 years ago, Woods Hole became the place where Indians staged their summer migrations to the islands. Remains of the archaic Indians' presence in Woods Hole existed in the form of mysterious stone piles left alongside Woods Hole Road near the Quissett campus of the Woods Hole Oceanographic Institution. Archeologists speculated that these stone piles marked sacred sites, formed boundaries, or composed astronomical calendars. In recent history, Woods Hole was a jumping off place for the Wampanoags as they traveled by canoe from their major settlements near the north shore of Buzzards Bay to satellite villages like Mashpee near Woods Hole, and Gay Head on the Vineyard.

Jumping off places are, almost by definition, remote. Woods Hole's location on the tip of Cape Cod's shoulder saved it from the English for a while after the arrival of the Pilgrims. Even though the English had driven many Indians off their traditional lands during the first 50 years following their arrival, Woods Hole remained Wampanoag country until 1679. In that year a clever nonconformist named Jonathan Hatch persuaded a local Indian, Job Notantico, to sell Woods Hole to a confederacy of 14 Englishmen—a mix of real estate entrepreneurs and Quakers fleeing the religious tyranny of the Puritans in places like Sandwich, Plymouth, and Boston. In the deed the authors refer to the property as a neck of land "commonly called Woods Hole Neck," so one can only speculate as to the origins of the name. Presumably, it comes from a translation of the Wampanoag word describing a woodland bordering a tide-ripped channel, the "Hole," between the neck and the Elizabeth Islands.

From his youth Jonathan Hatch had a reputation for initiative and self-reliance. Apprenticed at age 14 in Salem, Hatch ran away at 16. Captured in Boston, he was whipped and "committed as a slave" to the same man. Escaping again, Hatch took refuge with his mother at Yarmouth on the Cape. Thereafter, the young Hatch retreated to the woods, befriended the Wampanoags, learned their language, married, and supported his family trading with the Indians. More than once he ran afoul of the law for supplying guns and alcohol to Wampanoags. In the 1660s Hatch built a tavern at Sucanesset (Falmouth Center) beyond the prying eyes of Puritan judgment. Here he served the needs of travelers going to and coming from the islands.

If Hatch or any of his partners had high hopes for reaping the profits of a real estate boom on their subdivisions at Woods Hole Neck, none of them lived to collect the pot of gold. When the Revolutionary War broke out 120 years after the original purchase, there were only ten houses at Woods Hole. But in keeping with the character of a jumping off place, the waterfront had already featured rival ferry services and competing taverns for 50 years.

While American colonists showed little more than a passing interest in Woods Hole, the British fleet saw it as a prize for plundering. The so-called Battle of Falmouth began on April 1, 1779, when the British fleet, anchored at Tarpaulin Cove on Naushon Island, sent a raiding party to Woods Hole with a Tory guide to show the way to Manassah Swift's farm. The story of that night survived in an account by a descendant of one of Woods Hole's original proprietors. It seemed that the Tory guide baited the British soldiers by telling them that Swift's wife made exceptionally good cheese.

"All at once their mouths began to water for the good woman's cheese, and cheese they would have. So while the main body were robbing the stalls a party drew off and proceeded to the house. The woman was alone with her children. She met the party at her door and inquired if they had a commander. A man stepped forward saying he had the honor of commanding the company, to whom she replied that her house was defended by no man and she presumed him to be so much of a gentleman as to have no desire to molest a woman and her children. He asked her if she had any cheese. She replied yes, but no more than for her own use. He said that he would buy her cheese, to which she answered that she had none to sell, and besides, they shouldn't have a crumb. With the sneaking guide to lead, they proceeded to the cheese room and two of the soldiers ran, each of them his bayonet into a nice fat cheese. This dastardly act raised the woman's wrath. She stationed herself at the door and, as they retreated, she grasped the cheeses and slipped them from the points of the bayonets into the ample folds of her blue checkered apron [and] commenced with her tongue such a well-directed fire as completely to subdue them. She called them a valiant set indeed—fitted for just two things, to rob the roosts and to make hen-pecked husbands. They could not stand this broadside but rushing to the door were glad to make good their retreat and join their companions with the poor old dead cows on the beach. The worthy dame, however, stood at her door shouting their disgrace as long as they were in hearing.

"Patriots fired on the thieving soldiers, and they beat a retreat, their boats loaded with the carcasses of some of the stolen cattle. Vowing revenge, the British returned two days later intending to burn Woods Hole and Falmouth. But thanks to the warning sent to Woods Hole from John

Slocum, the tavern keeper in the Elizabeth Islands, four companies of patriots met the redcoats as they came ashore at Surf Drive Beach and repelled them."

Sweet, sweet liberty. Such were my thoughts while the crew lingered by the seal tank and exhibits of indigenous fish at the small National Marine Fisheries Aquarium at the west end of the village. Later, the crew wandered toward the center of Woods Hole. They followed Main Street along the shore of Great Harbor on its way to the Steamship Authority ferry docks at the other end of town. Here, in the center of the village, the community took on the look of a college town complete with tall academic buildings belonging to biological research facilities, outdoor restaurants, cafes, dim bars, boutiques, and a bookstore.

But what caught the crew's eyes more than the landscape were the people. Tourists shared the narrow street and sidewalks with tweedy researchers riding bikes, skateboarders, and clutches of laughing teenagers in cutoff jeans. Gaggles of graduate students toted backpacks and briefcases in and out of laboratories and took breaks to lounge with cold bottles of fruit juice or deli sandwiches on the lawn of a small seaside park. Taken collectively, the local citizenry lent Woods Hole something of the funky energy usually associated with Harvard Square. With one distinct difference: in the byways of Woods Hole, women appeared to outnumber men by about two to one.

Social observers have long noted the strong influence of women over the centuries at Woods Hole. With most of the village men involved in seafaring, women were the people who remained ashore not only to manage their children, but also to oversee family finances and businesses.

At no time were women more of a presence in Woods Hole than during the whaling era between the 1820s and 1860s. Women wove the fabric of the community as it expanded to 34 houses and 200 souls. In the whaling ports of Nantucket and New Bedford, the community women, called the *gray* ladies because of their conservative fashions, became dominant civic figures. So it was in Woods Hole too, as whaling transformed the sleepy village into a boom town. Many of the local men shipped out in search of their fortunes for three- and four-year voyages to the Pacific whaling grounds. Some got rich, but quite a few never came home. Meanwhile, women stepped forward to staff the shops, inns, and whale oil manufactories. With the constant leavings of the men, the women learned hard lessons about the precariousness of love, and adapted. Many of the pillars of the community followed the example of one Woods Hole Hallett family member: she had lost four husbands by the age of 21 and married nine times.

Woods Hole's deep harbor made it a natural whaling port, and one of the whaling industry's great entrepreneurs, a Falmouth man named Elijah Swift, sought to put the harbor to good use. He built a commercial wharf and shipyard called the Bar Neck Wharf Company, constructing ships here as well as building a full-fledged oil refinery. The heart of the refinery, the stone Candle House, still stands on Water Street. Another enduring legacy of Woods Hole whaling is the story of the whaling bark AWASHONKS.

Named for the famous squaw sachem of the Sakonnets, the 352-ton AWASHONKS took shape in Elijah Swift's Woods Hole yard in 1830. She left after Christmas (like the PEQUOD in *Moby Dick*) in 1833 on a voyage after sperm whales in the Pacific. Twenty months later the whaler anchored at Namarik Atoll just north of the equator with the hope of taking on fresh fruit. Typical of such events, the islanders rowed to the whaler in their canoes and came aboard with the intent to barter. But in the case of the AWASHONKS, the islanders came aboard in hordes. Before the crew had time to react, the islanders grabbed the 14 cutting spades stored on the quarter deck and used for butchering whales. The "AWASHONKS Massacre" ensued as the islanders nearly severed the captain's head and slew the first and second mates as well as many of the crew.

The hero of the day was a nineteen-year-old Falmouth boy, Silas Jones, serving in the apprentice position of third mate. The fury on deck drove Jones and a band of sailors below decks in the forward part of the ship. While the islanders murdered, whooped, and plundered on deck, Jones led three or four sailors aft to the main saloon where they opened the armory. Then, armed with pistols and muskets, Jones and his men surprised the islanders from the poop deck.

For an hour the sailors who had fled into the ship's rigging watched as Jones repelled the islanders' attacks with musket volleys and the decks grew dim beneath a cloud of gun smoke. When the smoke cleared, the decks were awash in blood, and the surviving islanders dashed ashore in their canoes or swam for shelter. After attending to the dead and wounded, Jones, the only surviving officer, captained the AWASHONKS on a 50-day voyage to Hawaii where he delivered the ship into the hands of the American consul. Years later, Jones sailed as captain on the last whaler to ship from Woods Hole. The AWASHONKS continued whaling until 1871 when she was crushed in the ice near Point Barrow, Alaska, along with much of the remaining Yankee whaling fleet. I discovered her figure head surviving as a display in the New Bedford Whaling Museum: barely a person stopped to take note, her story— one of the great tales of Yankee seafaring—all but lost on citizens of post-industrial America.

After this squally day the shipmates were feeling hot, sticky, and foul smelling as they stretched their legs ashore. Jackie seemed to have a firm sense of their mood when she wondered aloud if we should give the galley watch a holiday and stay ashore for hot showers and a restaurant feast. The crew actually cheered. Following a dinghy trip to collect fresh clothes and shower supplies—and an hour spent at the Woods Hole Yacht Club oohing and aahing over the forgotten joys of warm, fresh-water showers—the crew marched back into Woods Hole village with clean T-shirts, dry jeans, and shower-slicked hair.

For our cooks' holiday we chose Woods Hole's traditional gathering place of salts, scientists, and Dead Pirates—Captain Kidd's bar and restaurant. A clapboard and gray-shingled wharf house facing Main Street and stretching out over Eel Pond on stilts, Kidd's looked like just the place where you would expect to find buccaneers. Entering through the dimly-lit tap room with its long bar, round tables, barrel stools, and smoke-stained mural of Captain Kidd burying his treasure at Tarpaulin Cove, we saw shadowy figures huddled together. Some wore the sea boots or the oilskin bib overalls of fishermen, and a ceiling hung with life preservers left by mariners from around the globe testified to Kidd's international popularity.

Light breaking from a sunny enclosed porch overlooking the pond beckoned to off-duty scientists. Here we gathered at a huge round table to munch mounds of homemade French fries, gobble thick Kidd Burgers, and eavesdrop on the conversations of researchers sitting at neighboring tables. When Dr. Robert Ballard, who had led the teams that discovered the TITANIC, joined a group at a nearby table, you could tell by the long silence that settled over SARAH ABBOT's young crew that they felt in the presence of a god. I felt the same. What a day! If I was on some kind of search, Woods Hole must have been a final refuge. Or, possibly, a threshold. A jumping off place.

XIII   HIDEAWAY COVE

Our second morning in Woods Hole arrived hot and still. At 6:30 a.m. Great Harbor looked like a mirror kissed now and then by the ripples of striped bass feeding on pogies. Insects of a half dozen varieties buzzed through the schooner and roused the crew. Feeling sweaty and gritty, scientist John Rogers cajoled everybody into leaping over the side for what he called "the Breakfast Club swim."

After breakfast we all went ashore where John gave the crew a behind-the-scenes look at Woods Hole's marine science complex. He told us that virtually none of the academic buildings we were seeing existed a century ago. Spencer Baird, Assistant Secretary of the Smithsonian Institute and a naturalist, fell in love with the wealth of marine organisms he found at Woods Hole and convinced Congress to fund a new agency based there to oversee America's marine resources in 1871. Known today as the National Marine Fisheries Service, it raised its labs on the shores of Great Harbor, and Woods Hole still remains today the base for the agency's sea-going research vessels and the site of the great little aquarium—complete with a petting zoo of sea creatures.

Baird's reputation and the Fisheries' early work in Woods Hole quickly attracted other marine scientists to the area. In 1888 Harvard scientists raised $15,000 to start the Marine Biological Laboratory. Since those days more than 30 Nobel laureates pursued research at the Marine Biological Laboratory, the library grew to be the most complete repository for marine science data in the world, and the Marine Biological Laboratory evolved into a year-round operation through its association with graduate programs at Boston University. Watson and Crick did some of the research leading to unraveling the mysteries of DNA.

Meanwhile, during the 1920s the Marine Biological Laboratory's director and secretary raised $3 million from the Rockefeller family to fund a new project, the Woods Hole Oceanographic Institution, to support offshore marine research. The money financed the building of the world's largest steel-hulled ketch, the ATLANTIS, one of the few vessels in the world designed specifically to carry a crew to sea for oceanographic research. With the "A Boat" leaving and returning regularly from Woods Hole, the Woods Hole Oceanographic Institution flourished, and government money came flooding in to support research that could help American submarines use the presence of underwater temperature gradients to avoid detection. Since World War II the federal government, through the Office of Naval Research and the National Science Foundation, has been a primary supporter of the Woods Hole Oceanographic Institution and its state-of-the-art research ships KNORR and ATLANTIS II. It did not take much of an imaginative leap for our crew to see how today's teams might utilize the same equipment used to find the wreck of the TITANIC to salvage a sunken Russian nuclear submarine or bomber.

The least known of Woods Hole's scientific institutions was the United States Geological Survey, a contingent of over 100 cartographers, topographers, mineralogists, and geophysicists. These scientists work out of rented space at the Quissett Campus and oversee the exploring, assessing, and mapping of America's offshore mineral resources in areas like the Baltimore Canyon which had been sited for offshore oil fields.

As our tour ended, John told us that the newcomer to Woods Hole's collection of marine-oriented think tanks was the Sea Education Association. Begun in 1975, SEA had become America's most respected program for introducing marine science to undergraduate college students. With its two large steel schooners and a campus on a former estate facing Woods Hole Road, SEA offered semester-long courses for collegians, and some summer institutes for teachers and high school students, that teach oceanography, nautical science, and maritime studies. Students spent half their time studying ashore and half their time on an extended cruise off-shore aboard the schooners WESTWARD and CORWITH CRAMER. In many ways SEA was the inspiration for Andover's *Oceans* program aboard SARAH ABBOT, although SEA focused on deep-sea research while *Oceans* looked carefully at coastal Massachusetts.

The climax of our exploration came when we found ourselves invited into Dr. Michael Moore's lab in the Woods Hole Oceanographic Institute's Red-field Laboratory overlooking Eel Pond. Michael Moore was a veterinarian with a doctorate in marine biology as well. Using an enzyme called cytochrome P450, he and his assistants were trying to identify and quantify man-made toxins in eels, flounders, and whales as a barometer for measuring the effects of pollutants on a variety of ocean species.

Entering the lab, we saw a spectrometer sitting on the sturdy, plastic counter in the cramped lab surrounded by a monstrous centrifuge, computers, buffers, and solutions of every color. So far everything seemed more or less the way we had pictured a science lab on the cutting edge of marine biology. But then tall, lanky Michael Moore appeared with his nest of wild blond hair, a black T-shirt, faded khaki shorts, and Teva sandals. A look of surprise crossed the faces of SARAH ABBOT's crew: this man was not the nerdy little professor in a white lab coat that they had pictured as the maestro of a world-class science lab. Moore looked way too laid back and casual to hold those heavy-weight doctorates and attend to the details of subtle biochemistry.

But as Moore's fair-skinned arms carved the air while he explained his project—and he elaborated on his findings about liver damage from toxins in flounder from polluted Boston Harbor—the crew fell under the spell of his posh British accent. In short order, this scientist had us looking through microscopes at slides of diseased liver tissue. The lesson had begun, and nobody was questioning any longer their new teacher's dress code. In fact, some of us were wondering how we could volunteer to join Moore on his field trips to study whales as far afield as the Antarctic.

Personally, I was fitting Moore firmly in the sea boots of the whalers who had sailed from this port more than 100 years ago.

The air temperature felt like an oven. As soon as we all got back aboard, I jumped into a bathing suit and took a long dip in Great Harbor. Everyone else followed. Afterwards we drank two gallons of lemonade and consumed dozens of apples before turning our attention to the peanut butter and jelly sandwiches supplied by the students on galley watch. A southerly breeze began stirring the waters out on Vineyard Sound, bringing with it the taste of salt, the scent of fish and golden haze.

Over lunch someone asked me where we were heading next. I explained that our next port of call would be the city of New Bedford; unfortunately, we were stuck here for two more hours before the tide turned fair for us to navigate Woods Hole Passage back to Buzzards Bay. Except for the chatter of a crane loading gear on a research ship at the dock, silence descended over SARAH ABBOT until someone groaned.

No one moved. The crew sat in the cockpit dazed, eyes fixed on remote patches of water. Unconsciously, one girl scratched flakes of dry skin from her sunburned shoulders. Another girl chewed on the end of her pen as she pretended to review data for her cruise project. A boy clipped his nails while his left knee bounced up and down to the rhythm of a rock and roll tape playing in his head.

"What's going on here? What's up with you guys?" asked John Rogers who came back on deck after pouring over his teaching notes below in the saloon. "Has the sun made you brain dead?"

One of our shipmates from England looked up from doodling in her log.

"I feel like I need to move. I've had bloody enough of this harbor. I want to go windjamming," she announced with her English accent.

"Me too," sighed a comrade.

"I want to sail and end up in some place that is completely fresh and wild," added another. "No civilization, pleeease!"

At first, I wanted to lash out at this student and tell him that this wasn't the *Love Boat* and I was no Captain Stubing. We had an educational agenda here. But then I saw Jackie give me a look like "Be cool, Ahab." Then I counted to about 35 silently until the lightning in my brain went down a few volts so I could think again.

As the static cleared, I realized that I was not alone with this jangled sensation. The crew knew how I felt. Just like me they wanted relief from this feeling of being lost or trapped or whatever it was.

Our shipmate's use of the word "windjamming" really was the clue to point us out of this stalemate. Windjamming is journalists' jargon describing the jaunty look of a late-nineteenth-century ship—usually a square rigger but sometimes a schooner—plunging through the seas under a heavy press of canvas. True deepwater sailors in the days of commercial sail rarely used the term. But modern sailors in the late-twentieth century sometimes say windjamming when they speak of making a passage without any help at all from an engine. To go windjamming is to submerge yourself in the romance of wooden ships and iron crews nosing among strange and wild places under a spread of sail.

Now, after days of dirty weather and commercial harbors, this mild summer day and the fair wind made us yearn to go windjamming aboard SARAH ABBOT as the local fishermen say, "out where the buses don't run." Until you've been stuck hanging on a mooring and heard the call of the sea, you can't imagine that waiting for a tide to turn can be such torture. But in my experience, seafarers are not patient by nature; it is only the rhythms of their environment that make them so.

"I think we need an adventure," said Jackie.

As usual she was absolutely right. With a crew and captain in this itchy state of mind, a long, slow motorsail to New Bedford in these light winds could prove to be a tedious passage laced with the scent of exhaust from the diesel engine. And New Bedford's urban harbor—rife with the hooting horns and growling engines that came with the arrival and departure of one of America's largest fishing fleet—would never meet our needs for solitude.

Once Buzzards Bay had been very different from modern New Bedford or even Woods Hole. Once this Bay must have been what F. Scott

Fitzgerald had called "a fresh green breast of the New World [where] for a transitory enchanted moment man must have held his breath in the presence of this continent." But the vision of such a place still seemed shadowy and out of reach to me and the crew as well. We needed to seek out some pristine corner of the Bay, discover a place to call our own. A place beyond time, a neverland, a hideaway.

So the adventure began.

Bartholomew Gosnold's exploration of Buzzards Bay in 1602 records an extensive collection of small coves and islets suitable for sheltering a vessel full of explorers. While some of those places like Hadley Harbor and Cuttyhunk became the destinations of choice for the yachting crowd, and other anchorages like Padanaram, Woods Hole, and New Bedford spawned substantial communities, pristine anchorages remain scattered around Buzzards Bay. To find them what you needed was a sense of safe weather, an eye for out-of-the-way nooks depicted on Bay charts, and the care to explore such places with a dinghy and sounding lead to get a clear picture of the depth, bottom contours, and sediment which were sketched incompletely or inaccurately on government charts. To discover such a place was to feel like Gosnold and John Smith. To anchor at such a place was to stand in the sea boots of Captain Kidd. The location of such a hideaway and the route to the place always remained a secret kept by a crew. Dead Pirates told no tales.

Like Kidd's pirates on the ADVENTURE GALLEY and Gosnold's crew on the bark CONCORD, we began our voyage of discovery with no help from an engine or electronic navigation instruments. When the tide turned fair in Woods Hole Passage, the crew of SARAH ABBOT assembled at their sail-handling stations and hoisted sail. First, the mainsail went up, then the foresail. Next we dropped the mooring, hoisted the jib, and fell off the wind on starboard tack. With all sheets trimmed, halyards coiled, and dinghies trailing in a line astern, we tacked beyond Great Harbor and ran north through the Hole with a fair wind and tide. Gaining Buzzards Bay, we began a stately tack to windward at four knots.

This was one of those passages you sail in your dreams. The southwest wind teases the hair on the back of your neck, the water makes a soft hiss rushing along the lee rail, the sea crisps in gentle swells, and the sun hangs in the west like a red balloon. Aboard, the crew trades off tricks at the helm, peels oranges for each other, and mounts chorus after chorus of Bob Marley's "Jammin." Chicken stew simmers on the galley stove. As an old captain told me decades ago when I worked on his skipjack catching Chesapeake oysters under sail, "Ain't no other way to do this thing; just steer by the wind and follow the water."

So we did. Centuries seemed to have peeled away like hours when at last we dropped the jib and ghosted into a deserted island cove half the size of a soccer field. Drawing within 40 yards of the shore we could see the white sandy bottom glowing. Then we doused the foresail, veered into the wind to stop the schooner, and let go the anchor. The wind on the mainsail drove us backward to set our hook in the sand. SARAH ABBOT rode in about ten feet of water while the crew dropped and furled the main as if they had been born to it. Then the galley watch passed out steaming bowls of chicken stew to all hands.

Ashore, herring gulls circled by the hundreds above high, grassy dunes— a sure sign of a rookery. Dozens of cormorants stood guard, drying their bat-shaped wings on the exposed rocks of a nearby reef. With the flocks of weeping gulls and osprey fishing in the shallows like *wabacucks*, the Wampanoag's white-headed eagles, we had a vision of how Buzzards Bay looked to the Native Americans and the early European explorers. The distant hills glowed an unnatural green and the dunes, grass, and rocks faded to pastel hues as the sun blazed red over the mouth of the Bay. As the sun set, the water first turned gold, then silver, and finally purple.

The student crew watched all this from the beach where we had left them for two hours of solo time. Spread out among the sand and boulders each of them found a private place, a hideaway to witness this cove and record their impressions and thoughts in their logs. One girl wrote:

"The sun is slowly dipping towards the ocean. As I look across the hard and craggy beach, long shadows are painted across each surface, each edge. A seagull is perched on almost every rock, and the numbers of seagulls mystifies me. I stare at them, mesmerized by their smooth and winding motions. . . . I lower my head as if to bow in church, and stare at the rocks. Something shifts in my stomach. That secure feeling is lost momentarily."

Somebody else in this crew had begun to share my reveries—both their peace and uneasiness. Now what?

The next thing I knew, it was late at night aboard after everyone had climbed into bed. The oil lamp over the saloon table guttered with a wick needing to be trimmed. Prompted by a crew of students who were all beginning to act a little twitchy, I was telling the story of the ghost aboard SARAH ABBOT. Having lived with the story of a ghost for almost 15 years, I often neglected to mention the story to new crews. The ghost had become as commonplace to me as, say, the odd short plank on the starboard waterline used to repair the damage after a runaway mooring barge struck the schooner 18 years ago. But inevitably something strange happened aboard or a shipmate heard a rumor about the ghost from a previous crew, and I found myself relating the tale again.

His name was Bert O'Neil, and he was the first owner of the schooner which served as his private yacht from 1966 to 1979. Bert had made a success of running an auto dealership near Lunenburg, Nova Scotia, but cars were not the love of his life. This schooner which he named SKYLARK was. Twice he had won the Governor's Cup schooner races with her. But as much as Bert enjoyed racing his schooner, he also loved cruising in her or just sitting aboard at her mooring with a fire going in her coal stove on a foggy day. The schooner was his thinking spot, his secret place. But suffering ill health, Bert sold his schooner in 1979 and died shortly thereafter.

I knew none of this when I bought the schooner in 1984 with the purpose of putting her to work for Phillips Academy *Oceans* program. SKY-LARK and Bert O'Neil were merely names in the sheaf of papers I needed to document the schooner under American registry and change her name to

SARAH ABBOT in honor of a woman who believed in hands-on learning. Madame Sarah Abbot had begun Abbot Academy, the girls school that merged with Phillips in the early 1970s.

An unexpected encounter with the spirit of Bert O'Neil occurred about a year after I bought the schooner. Following SARAH ABBOT's first summer sailing for the *Oceans* program, I took the schooner to Martha's Vineyard to compete in a revival of the International Schooner Races, one of America's most dazzling sporting spectacles during the first three decades of the 1900s. In their heyday, the races drew enormous crowds and media coverage to watch elimination trials and final duels between the fastest schooners in the American and Canadian fishing fleets. The BLUENOSE, immortalized on the Canadian dime, was the swiftest of the swift during the 1920s when Grand Banks fishing schooners were viewed as the most graceful, elegant machines to be designed by humankind. In that era yachtsmen had draftsmen imitate the great fishing schooners' looks a thousand times over.

But with the Depression and the arrival of reliable internal combustion engines to drive fishing boats, big, labor-intensive schooners vanished from the working waterfront just as fast as steam locomotives disappeared from the railways two decades later. The last International Schooner Races between Canada and the U.S. were sailed in 1938. Smaller auxiliary power schooners continued to fish the inshore waters into the 1960s, particularly in Canada's Maritime Provinces, but no one built new fishing schooners. In the States building schooners out of wood became all but a lost art after the 1950s. In Nova Scotia where no one ever seems in a hurry to trade old ways for the new, a few designers and builders continued to squeeze a living from building schooners—more or less on the lines of the great Grand Bankers—for nostalgia racing and cruising. One such builder was David Stevens and one of his boats was SKYLARK/SARAH ABBOT which he launched in 1966 and sold to Bert O'Neil.

During the second half of the twentieth century, wooden boat connoisseurs and schooner lovers formed schooner associations in the U.S. and Nova Scotia to support and preserve the historic design, and in 1985 the two groups decided to revive the old races for a weekend of racing at the Vineyard. At least seven vessels sailed from Nova Scotia for the races. The Americans had a dozen, and one of those was SARAH ABBOT who had now forsaken her Canadian heritage to sail under the Stars and Stripes.

Of course, the crews of the Novi schooners who arrived at the Vineyard to race were more than a little curious to see SKYLARK/SARAH ABBOT: not only had she once been a star of the Canadian schooner races, but she had also been so seriously damaged during a grounding shortly after Bert O'Neil sold her that she had required a major refit.

Shortly after my crew and I had dropped anchor in the harbor at Vineyard Haven, dinghies full of Canadian crews began rowing alongside to introduce themselves. During one such visit, I discovered one of the Canadian women seated in the schooner's main saloon crying. Not quite sure what had caused this outbreak or what to do, I sought out one of her shipmates on deck and asked his counsel.

"She's me old mate Bert O'Neil's daughter," said he. "It's a hard thing her being back aboard a vessel that's so stamped with the spirit of her father. You can't blame the lass; Bert's still here all right. I can feel him, too."

It was after this that my crew and I heard the story of Bert O'Neil's love affair with my schooner.

"That explains the footsteps I keep hearing on deck," said my eight-year-old son Noah who shipped aboard as cabin boy.

"Yeah, right," I thought. I had never heard footsteps unless they were my own, and I don't believe in ghosts.

Nevertheless, when the races began I sailed the schooner as if she was a borrowed, prized possession. I was so cautious that I refused to fly the boat's fisherman staysail even in a moderate breeze, and consequently we lagged behind Canadian boats that Bert O'Neil had routinely beaten. At the awards ceremony where the Canadian boats garnered more than their share of the trophies, I even found myself referring to my schooner as SKYLARK, not SARAH ABBOT. Was I spooked?

Time passed, and the schooner returned to her work for *Oceans*.

From time to time a student asked a naive question about who was disturbing our sleep by walking the deck in the middle of the night. Occasionally, a crew member sleeping in the forecastle, the forward cabin now reserved for females, claimed to awaken in the dark to feel a benign, shadowy presence standing between the tiers of berths. I joked: maybe the students had heard or seen the ghost of Bert O'Neil keeping watch over his schooner. But I hardly took these reports seriously.

Then one quiet night while SARAH ABBOT swung to a mooring in the protection of Sakonnet Harbor in Little Compton, Rhode Island, I felt what seemed like a sharp tapping on my shoulder waking me from sleep. Rising on my elbow and looking around, I saw no one and nothing amiss in the main saloon and galley beyond my quarter berth. But then I heard the footsteps. Starting over my berth, the steps proceeded with a firm, measured gate to the bow, paused, then returned. Immediately, I guessed that the student crew was playing some kind of joke on me so I dragged myself out of my sleeping bag and climbed on deck to see not a soul. But just two yards off the starboard beam I saw a 40-foot lobster boat which had slipped its mooring gliding toward a collision with SARAH ABBOT. Swiftly, I grabbed the boathook and parried the lobster boat away. Then I roused the scientist, and together we got a line on the lobster boat and lashed it to a vacant mooring. Given the speed and direction of the lobster boat, it would have hit with enough force and sharp edges to fracture planks on the starboard side of the schooner, putting her out of commission for at least a month *or* sinking her on the spot with all hands asleep below.

"That was some luck," I confessed to the scientist after all the excitement had passed.

"You owe Bert, big time," she said seriously.

"Really?" I asked.

She gave me a looked that said, "You bet your bosun stripes, bucko."

Then she added, "Surely, you've noticed that this boat has a guardian angel."

"Right!" I jibed sarcastically and headed for my sleeping bag. But sleep eluded me.

Over tea the next morning I challenged the scientist to make her case for a guardian angel, hoping to see the holes in her data and dismiss Bert O'Neil as so much romantic wishful thinking.

To my surprise the scientist cited a dozen moments when the schooner had sidestepped disaster against all odds. One recent instance had been particularly disturbing. SARAH ABBOT had been motoring out of the west end of the Cape Cod Canal dead into the wind and a four-foot chop when the vessel began to develop engine trouble as a tug and oil barge overtook us from astern. Caught between a strong westbound tide rushing us along from astern and the wind and seas in our face, SARAH ABBOT began to wallow in the swells as the engine lost power, perked to life, and began to fade again. Then the schooner lost steerage. Meanwhile the tug and barge drew within 100 yards and came on strong at eight knots. Shoals and rocks on both sides of the channel kept us fixed in the tug's path with no chance to run and nowhere to hide. Suddenly, a strong intuition told me to hoist the foresail even though the channel ahead lay dead to windward. Then, with the tug and barge barely 40 yards astern, the engine caught again and revved heartily for about 30 seconds before expiring . . . just long enough for us to regain steerage and drive the schooner adjacent to the only point within a mile where we could make a left turn and navigate under sail into a pocket of deep water safely beyond the channel, tug, and rough seas. If any of the factors in the equation had changed even slightly, we would have had a hard, potentially-catastrophic grounding on the edge of the canal or a collision with the tug and tow. But we had escaped.

"Bert," explained the scientist as we relived the close shave.

"OK," I sighed. "I'll take that kind of luck any day!"

So I gave in to the myth and began folding Bert into my thinking about SARAH ABBOT. If it made people feel better to believe they sailed aboard a schooner whose good fortune came from the watchful eye of her dead captain, so be it.

Years passed, and the schooner's good luck continued unabated as she defied the odds, surviving two direct hits from hurricanes on Marion

Harbor and two fluke fires in the engine room. She also gained a reputation for having a nose for finding whales off Cape Cod when even the whale watching fleet came up empty handed. Perhaps, best of all, SARAH ABBOT, with a student crew, won second place—to a Nova Scotian boat, unfortunately—in another replay of the International Schooner Races at Gloucester. And somewhere during those six or seven years a crew aboard the schooner dreamed up the Dead Pirates Society, giving Bert O'Neil supreme status in our pantheon of "Immortals." Every cruise someone has heard the footsteps on the deck or felt the presence in the forecastle. And Bert's legend grew.

But when John Rogers stepped aboard as a scientist some years ago, his mind went into spasms one night when a crew member asked me to tell the story of SARAH ABBOT's ghost. John actually laughed out loud.

"That's preposterous," he guffawed when I had finished the story.

"Open your mind to the possibility," challenged a student caught up in the romance. "Maybe Bert O'Neil's ghost is bound to this schooner for eternity."

"In your dreams," chuckled John.

The next several days passed without incident until one night when we swung to a mooring in Oak Bluffs at Martha's Vineyard. Some time after 3:00 a.m., I woke to a shake and a whisper. John stood beside my berth.

"Get up. Someone's on deck."

With that remark, he charged topside to accost the intruder.

Dragging myself free of my berth to back up John, I heard the brush of his bare feet circle the boat from bow to stern before I reached the cockpit. When I got there, I saw a wry grin taking shape around John's lips.

"OK," he laughed. "You got me. That was a pretty good joke."

"What do you mean?" I asked.

"There's nobody on deck except us," he explained.

We both walked around the deck and scrutinized every boat in the anchorage and every ripple on the water. Nothing stirred, not even the harbor ducks and gulls.

"I heard footsteps so loud that they woke me up. Then I listened while the steps walked around the boat. I wasn't dreaming," John assured himself. "Tell the truth, you were on deck. This is a joke, right?"

I shook my head "no" and laughed at John's confusion; I had truly been asleep.

"Where was Yankee when you got up?" I asked John.

"Asleep on the saloon floor. I tripped over her and woke her when I came to get you," he added.

"Then I guess it wasn't her you heard, and if one of the kids had gone on deck, she would have gotten up to follow," I surmised. We both agreed. Yankee had been proving herself as an alert watchdog ever since her puppy days when she deterred thieves from coming aboard during a six-month cruise of the Bahamas Islands.

"Who did I hear?" challenged John. "Bert?"

I shrugged: "Your guess is as good as mine."

So the legend persisted, and SARAH ABBOT continued her run of good fortune. Fact or fiction, the ghost of Bert O'Neil was balm to my restless soul on this particular night out where the buses don't run. And now something changed for me. Somehow windjamming to Hideaway Cove was a turning point. This was not the end of my search: I knew I was looking for something more than I had found in windjamming with the crew, the pristine beauty of Hideaway Cove or ghost stories about Bert O'Neil. But I also guessed that coming here had set me on the right course. If I could only sail it.

XIV NEW BEDFORD BOUND

A light fog loomed over our cove at sunrise, cutting the visibility to a half mile, and tinting the day with orange light when I rowed Yankee ashore for her walk on the beach. My first thought was to rouse the crew to share this moment when all the world had shrunken to the size of this small cove, a wooden schooner, shoals of menhaden winding through the clear water, and the distant calls of gulls. But the sighs of the sleepers persuaded me to brew my tea quietly and retreat to the deck for an hour alone with SARAH ABBOT, the cove, and my chamomile. Generally driven to get work done—like reading the crew's logs, writing in my own, or studying charts—at spare moments like this, I yielded to a different impulse and found myself dissolving in a meditation on our next port of call, Buzzards Bay's commercial center, the city of New Bedford.

For as long as I could remember the first images that came to mind when I thought of New Bedford rose from Herman Melville's *Moby Dick*. This city of over 100,000 souls, where I had shopped and dined regularly for 25 years, never broke the surface of my consciousness with pictures of its huge fleet of steel fishing trawlers, Coast Guard station, massive fabric mills, marine chandleries, Portuguese neighborhoods, expressways, and auto traffic. These contemporary images that I knew so well only came to mind *after* I had sorted through the mythical vision I have of the port from reading *Moby Dick* with the same lip-murmuring rapture as my grandfather read his Bible.

For me the name New Bedford always conjures images of a dark December night in the early 1840s, when a young school teacher from New York by the name of Ishmael wanders into town in search of the adventure of his life—a voyage on a whaling ship. The night moans with the sound of the north wind and stings with spitting snow. Ishmael finds "such dreary streets! blocks of blackness, not houses, on either hand, and here and there a candle, like a candle moving about in a tomb." I see the shadowy figures of the African-American church where Ishmael stops, and I hear the creaking of a sign "faintly representing a tall straight jet of misty spray" with the words underneath "The Spouter-Inn—Peter Coffin." Inside, the walls display a "heathenish array of monstrous clubs and spears, some thickly set with glittering teeth resembling ivory saws; others tufted with knots of human hair, and one sickle-shaped, with a vast handle sweeping round like a segment made in the new-mown grass by a long armed mower."

Then there is a noise starting up outside and the landlord's "hurrah" for the crew of the GRAMPUS home from a three-year voyage to the whaling grounds off Fiji. Finally, there is a dark sleeping room where Ishmael lies tossing under the covers on a corncob mattress when his shipmate and friend-to-be appears: a tall, lithe South Sea islander with a bald head, a candle in one hand . . . and a shrunken head in the other. Queequeg the harpooner, his face tattooed with dark squares.

This is my New Bedford. And even after more than two decades of living virtually in its shadow, its whaling industry cast a spell over me. By the 1830s this harbor—long just a wilderness fringe to the town of Dartmouth—had become the whaling capital of North America. With Nantucket Shoals, the Chatham Bars, Stellwagen Bank, and Cape Cod Bay attracting dolphin, pilot whales, minkes, humpbacks, right whales, sei whales, and fin whales, as well as the occasional orcas and blue whales to feed, the Massachusetts coast has a long tradition of whaling.

Artifacts found in shell middens around Cape Cod and Buzzards Bay show that the Wampanoags fished the waters for marine mammals. Even before colonizing the land, Europeans hunted whales off New England. As early as 1614, my ancestor Captain John Smith abandoned his voyage of discovery to hunt whales along this coast. From the early days of the Europeans' arrival, colonists squabbled with their government about who had rights to the profits associated with drift whales that came ashore. Why all the fuss over stinking, dead whales? European whalers could not keep up with the growing demand for lubricants and lamp oil refined from whale blubber. In the seventeenth century you could make a fortune selling oil boiled out of a dead whale's hide.

America's commercial whaling began in 1644 when the village of Southampton, Long Island, created wards along the beach with caretakers in charge of cutting up and rendering drift whales that washed ashore. Shortly thereafter, men began sailing and rowing to sea in longboats with which they could sneak up to a whale and drive a harpoon through its heart while it lunged along the surface refilling its lungs before another dive. Soon the whaling industry spread to Nantucket, the outer edge of Cape Cod and Martha's Vineyard.

While the majority of the men in the fisheries were of European decent and Quakers in faith, a number of Wampanoag Indians were brought into the hunt because of their traditional knowledge of local waters and whale behavior. In addition, the Wampanoags' talent for throwing spears made them first-rate harpooners. Such a man was the fictional Tashtego, a harpooner in *Moby Dick*. Another was the real Amos Smalley, the man credited with killing the white sperm whale believed the very incarnation of the Wampanoag's giant Maushop, and the inspiration for Melville's angry leviathan. Both Tashtego and Smalley were Aquinnahs—"Gay Head Indians" or "Gay Headers"—Wampanoags from the southwest corner of Martha's Vineyard.

At first, whales were plentiful just off the beaches, and whalers put to sea in flotillas of longboats. But as whales grew scarce, the hunters began building larger vessels for cruises of a few weeks or a month in search of whales. Initially, these boats were small, shallow draft vessels, mostly sloops, built to negotiate the shoal water around Nantucket and the Outer Cape. During these early days of American whaling, the cartoonish-looking right whale—with its mammoth smiling face, stubby pectoral flippers and delicate tail—became the principal quarry of the hunters. The whale's thick coat of blubber made it buoyant enough to float after killing unlike the more muscular humpbacks and fin whales that also frequented Massachusetts coastal waters. Because the right whale floated, its carcass could be fixed with a marker flag and temporarily abandoned while the hunters moved on to kill more whales in the herd. After the hunt, the whalers lashed the dead whales together and towed them to a beach for rendering.

Relentless hunting quickly thinned the herds of Massachusetts' right whales so that whalers found themselves sailing on longer and longer voyages, pursuing the right whale northeast to feeding grounds off Newfoundland and Labrador and south to its calving grounds off Savannah, Georgia, and northern Florida. For these trips that might last months, the whalers needed larger, seaworthy vessels like two-masted brigantines weighing between 20 and 40 tons. These vessels the whalers began equipping with tackle, cutting tools and boilers—the "try works"—in order to strip the carcasses of blubber and boil it into oil that could be drained into barrels and stored below while the hunt continued. It was on these offshore trips that Yankee whalers first fell in with the herds of sperm whales that range along the edge of the continental shelf feeding on the giant squid that gather there. Captain Christopher Hussey was the first Nantucketer to kill a sperm whale in 1712.

The event changed the industry. Here was a new fishery. Just as the right whale and other baleen whales were growing scarce, this toothed monster, the sperm whale, appeared in large, unhunted herds—easy picking for mariners with stout vessels to brave rough passages offshore. An additional incentive to hunt the sperm whale was its huge cache of fine spermaceti oil, the purist natural lubricant and best burning oil in the world. The spermaceti filled the melon of the whale's head, the so-called "Heidelberg tun." By killing a sperm whale, a whaler could virtually double the profit he made by taking a right whale of equal size. Needless to say, such profitability appealed to the shrewd business minds of the Quakers who dominated the New England's whale fishery.

So the Yankee hunt for sperm whales began, led for the most part by Nantucket's whalers. The longer, offshore trips in dangerous sea conditions called for ships that were larger and more powerful than the small

New England brigantines. The new ships, built largely on the north shore coves of Buzzards Bay, were generally three masters and bark rigged, more than 100 feet in length with 300- to 400-ton displacement. They carried course after course of square sails and drew 12 feet (or more) when loaded. These ships were self-contained factories for the slaughter and rendering of whales into oil. A whaling ship's hold might store a thousand barrels of oil. In other words, the modern whaling ship was an adaptation of the trans-Atlantic merchant ships. The new vessels proved a great step forward in terms of efficiency, but they had one problem. They rode so deep in the water that they ran aground in the shoals around Nantucket's harbor. Yankee whalers needed a deep water port.

Enter the Acushnet River.

In my reading aboard SARAH ABBOT, I had discovered that as early as 1750 settlers kept a try house on the western shore of the Acushnet River. While great whales have been rare in Buzzards Bay proper, pilot whales and minkes sometimes appear today and were probably plentiful enough to support a modest shore-based fishery in the eighteenth century. Furthermore, a steep underwater bank known as the "27 fathom line" that lies about 18 miles south of Martha's Vineyard and Cuttyhunk remains to this day a favorite feeding grounds for great whales like fins and humpbacks. Russell and fellow whalers may have harpooned large whales here during settled summer weather and sailed with them 45 miles on an easy downwind passage back to the Acushnet River.

Whatever the circumstances, the Acushnet River already had a tradition of whaling when Bedford Village began to emerge as a settlement in the 1760s, and whalers, some from Nantucket, migrated here. With its deep water, protected harbor, shores thick with oak and fir well-suited to shipbuilding, and land links to the population centers of New England, Bedford Village had many advantages over Nantucket as a center of commerce. The town boomed. Between 1770 and 1775 the town of Dartmouth (mostly on the shores of the Acushnet) records the annual fitting out of 80 vessels of 6,500 tons for the whaling industry with 7,200 barrels of sperm oil and 1,400 barrels of whale oil taken each year.

But in February of 1775 the British Parliament passed a law restricting the New England's trade with foreign nations. The bill sent the whaling industry and the import-export dependent American economy as a whole into depression and proved the final incentive for the colonies' revolt.

Thoughts of the American Revolution had just begun appearing like shadows in my mind when all three of my female teenage shipmates appeared on deck to clean their teeth wearing their pajamas and carrying their toothbrushes and cups of water. The morning rituals had begun. I heard Jackie stir from her quarter berth and slap a Stan Rogers folk tape in the cassette player, fill the tea kettle, and fire the stove. Within seconds the sound of Rogers' voice and his fiddlers came romping from the boat speakers with the lilt of a Highland fling. The song was *Fogarty's Cove*, a Nova Scotian fisherman's homecoming chantey. It's a real foot stomper, and hardly had the first verse begun when the crew erupted. I heard clapping from the boys in the fish hold as Jackie and John broke into a clog dance in the saloon. On deck the girls dropped their brushes and cups, hooked arms with each other, and began a fling on the foredeck.

When Rogers and his musicians hit the chorus, the crew sang,
"She will walk the sandy shores so clean
Watch the combers rolling
'Til I come to wild Rose Chance again,
Down in Fogarty's Cove."

The effort left us breathless, but roused. Before we gathered for breakfast, the crew assembled at their sailhandling stations to hoist sail and weigh anchor. Then with a breeze beginning to stir at about six knots, SARAH ABBOT reached north into the fog toward New Bedford. While the crew dressed and ate, Jackie and John stood the helm. I plotted our course and kept an eye turned to the radar scope. The coming and going of fishing trawlers and a half dozen rock ledges planted like booby traps around the entrance to the Acushnet River urge a mariner to keep a sharp watch on his position in these waters.

As the sun glowed through the fog from overhead but horizontal visibility dropped to a quarter mile, SARAH ABBOT ghosted toward New Bedford with no landmarks to steer by. On the scope I could see the Mosher's Ledge buoy as well as the clearly-defined peninsula of Sconticut Neck jutting far out into the Bay to the east. It occurred to me that except for the anachronism of radar, the year might have been 1775. At that time, in this place, an American vessel made history.

With the outbreak of conflict between the colonies and their mother country, England began seizing American whalers on the high seas, impounding the ships, and impressing the American crews to sail aboard ships of the line or English whalers. While such actions virtually closed down the Yankee whale fishery, it left hundreds of vessels and thousands of rough, able seamen out of work. Broke and angry, mariners from the Acushnet River were primed to strike back. Twenty-four days after the battles at Lexington and Concord Bridge, three days after the Continental Congress elected George Washington Commander-in-Chief of the colonial forces, a rider galloped into Fairhaven Village on the eastern shore of the Acushnet River opposite Bedford. On his arrival two military companies were drilling in a field, and they heard the horseman's news that the English 20-gun warship FALCON had captured two local sloops in Vineyard Sound. These sloops were now manned and armed by the British and sailing in Buzzards Bay as decoys that might overtake American vessels. The date was May 13, 1775.

Primed to retaliate, 25 Acushnet River men, their drummer, and two commanders, Captains Nathaniel Pope and Daniel Egery, put to sea aboard the 40-ton sloop SUCCESS to take on the English. The winds being light, the SUCCESS drifted with the tide out of the harbor and along the west coast of Sconticut Neck during the night. It was a long night, thick with fog. While the two captains and the drummer boy kept the watch on deck, the 25 minutemen lay silent, secreted in the hold. Shortly after sunrise the deck watch aboard the SUCCESS spied one of the sloops that the British had commandeered riding to an anchor in the fog. Although the wind was calm, the tide carried the SUCCESS closer, prompting the watch on the anchored sloop to warn the approaching vessel to bear off to avoid a collision.

"Aye, aye!" came the response from Captain Pope at the helm of the SUCCESS. But he held to his collision course while stamping on the deck to warn the men below to prepare for action.

"Sheer off, you'll be into us," called the watch again.

"Aye, aye," responded the Yankee captain again, then he lay the SUCCESS alongside.

At this moment the drummer on the Yankee vessel rolled his drums and the minutemen sprang from the hold. They overwhelmed the British watch before they could cut free of their anchor cable with an ax and surprised eleven armed officers and men sleeping below. The wind came up, and shortly thereafter, Captain Pope, one minuteman, and the drummer sailed their prize and prisoners to anchor off Fairhaven.

Meanwhile the SUCCESS, under Captain Egery, stood out to sea and soon found the second decoy sloop at anchor in a cove to the west and making sail. A chase ensued. When the Yankee vessel approached within rifle range, Egery ordered a sharpshooter to take a bead on the officer in British livery who shouted orders and ducked in and out of cover of the companionway. The shot felled the officer, more shooting followed, and the English struck their colors. Before the evening Quaker meeting, the SUCCESS and her second prize swung to their anchors in the Acushnet. The British lieutenant who had been shot survived with the help of a local surgeon. The doctor removed a buckshot which had pierced the skin of the officer's forehead, slid along the surface of the skull, and lodged flat, thin and sharp at the back of his head. The officer shook off the wound philosophically, saying that his family had often been called a hard-headed lot.

For a short time this aggressive show of Yankee patriotism embarrassed and dismayed the largely Quaker population of Bedford and Dartmouth because no war had yet been declared. Many voices argued that the prisoners should be returned with apologies to the captain of the British FALCON, but patriotic sentiments prevailed and the prisoners were hauled off to jail in Taunton. A few weeks later, on June 17, sympathy for the captain and the crew of the FALCON waned to nothing when the very same ship sailed into Boston Harbor and joined the naval bombardment at the Battle of Bunker Hill.

Visions of the SUCCESS and her triumphs faded from my mind as SARAH ABBOT approached the shipping channel into New Bedford. Now the fog began lifting and the breeze swelled. Soon the turreted lighthouse rising from shoals on Butler Flats fell astern, and a parade of 90-foot steel fishing trawlers and scallopers streamed toward us. With names like SÃO FILIPE, the fishing boats signaled the dominance that Portuguese immigrants from the Azores have achieved today in the cod, haddock, flounder, and scallop fisheries whose home base is New Bedford/Fairhaven. With a fair weather report these vessels were heading out for one- or two-week trips to the fishing ground on Georges Banks 80 miles east of Cape Cod, once the domain of fishing schooners like SARAH ABBOT. The fishermen waved at us with sad smiles as our schooner passed more than a score of these outbound workboats in close quarters. I would like to think that the men's sad smiles grew from nostalgia for the days when SARAH ABBOT's course had been sailed by deep-laden schooners crashing home from the banks. But it is just as likely that the healthy-looking females who waved back from our schooner inspired more wistfulness or *saudade* than thoughts of the good old days.

Passing through the gate of the hurricane dike built to protect New Bedford Harbor from future devastation in the vein of the killer hurricanes of 1938 and 1954, we left the scents of salt, sassafras, and bird rookeries behind and breathed diesel exhaust from the trawlers. Instead of the hiss of a smokey sou'west wind and the cry of gulls, we heard the clatter of machinery as trawlers unloaded plastic tubs of fish or filled their holds with ice for a coming trip. Once inside the harbor north of the dike, we saw a swarm of fishing boats darting, swerving, and backing around wharves, shipyards, and fish processing plants. As we headed into the wind and struck sail, we saw a large Coast Guard cutter tied to the government pier and heard her testing sirens, bells, and whistles. The old stone buildings of long-dead whaling merchants on Johnny Cake Hill and the mansions of sea captains poised against the horizon along County Street seemed to shimmer like a mirage as the summer heat blanketed the port. Hardly paradise. Yet the crew assembled on deck to look at America's largest Atlantic fishing port as if they were eight-year-olds seeing Disney World for the first time.

"This place is rad!" said one shipmate.

"Funky," teased another.

Rad and funky. Those words pretty much summarized the history that I know of this town that was once one of the richest cities in America.

With the outbreak of hostilities between the colonies and England in 1775 and the Declaration of Independence a year later, the Continental Congress realized the need for a navy to parry the British domination of the seas. The bad news was, of course, that Congress barely had the funds to support an army let alone a navy. Congressional appropriation for 13 warships was hardly enough to protect America from the ravages of the British fleet. George Washington and his colleagues needed another alternative. The good news was that with as many as a thousand American whaling vessels and merchant ships idled by the war, and ten thousand mariners "on the beach," the new nation had a navy just waiting for a commission.

SARAH ABBOT's visit to Padanaram on Cruise One had conjured a lot of images for me of those days when more than 600 Massachusetts vessels sailed as privateers, claiming ever-larger number of prizes to reach a peak in 1780 when the Admiralty Court in Boston condemned 881 prize vessels. While no records document how many Buzzards Bay vessels joined the privateer fleet, anecdotal evidence points to the Bay, and particularly the Acushnet River, as a hotbed of privateering. One story about John Paul Jones' privateer activities in the waters off New Bedford always kindles a vision in my mind.

After patrolling the southern New England coast aboard his 12-gun sloop of war, the PROVIDENCE, Jones put into the Acushnet River and took on

crew: It was not just their deep tans or the salt-
their T-shirts and shorts. Seven days ago when
arded SARAH ABBOT in Marion, all of their moves
tative. Now they moved with the confidence of
y walked with rolling gaits, slung backpacks
and laughed with wild anticipation of the
e city. Showers, ice cream, and restaurant
. Along the waterfront and in the streets I
urn and follow the progress of the crew as
Hill. Eventually, smiles crossed the old
at thoughts or memories these young
soned watchers.

ff to town recalled my skipjack days on
oung man full of the love of the sea
forget the strength that I felt in my
er a day of dredging oysters along
ain Bart Murphy aboard the RUBY
lent, and so right with the world.
e from finding myself fixed
th my seafaring ancestors. Not
hteenth-century Chesapeake
haling harpoon I had found
ed years after the iron's last
FORD, I felt like Ishmael,
kind of personal pride in
d what not."

s among the buildings
day, Jackie, John, and
150 years the mis-
retired sailors had
need of spiritual
aw Father Maple

a load of scrap iron at Bedford Village. Such scrap iron was the preferred cannon shot for firing high into an enemy's rigging and carrying away her sails and yards. The scrap also had devastating anti-personnel capabilities.

When a British brig of war appeared off the Acushnet River, Jones took the PROVIDENCE to sea covered with cotton bales to protect his crew and stormed into the fight. Faster and more maneuverable, the American sloop outsailed the larger English ship to gain better firing positions. Meanwhile, the enemy guns hammered back with thunder and lightning. But equipped with the scrap iron and protected by the cotton bales, the sloop's cannon began reducing the brig's rigging to tatters. Eventually, the enemy struck the Union Jack in surrender. But as the PROVIDENCE drew near to take her prize, the English skipper raised the colors again and, comparing the sloop's crude single-masted rig to a ship's tool, demanded to Jones, "Surrender your damned old serving mallet!" With the renewed challenge, the PROVIDENCE worked close to the brig and fired a tremendous broadside that ripped through the English crew and provoked a second and final surrender.

Jones brought his prize back into the harbor where witnesses reported "that the blood of the killed and wounded was running down the sides of the brig when she came to port." The English dead were buried on a small hillock on the shore of Bedford Village. Construction has twice forced the bones to be disinterred, and today they rest in Oak Grove cemetery.

Taunted by such incidents of Yankee audacity, the British staged a major retaliation on September 5, 1778. In the words of one British commander, General Clinton, "I left the fleet and ordered Major-General Gray to proceed to Bedford, a noted rendezvous for privateers, etc., and in which there were a number of captured ships at the time."

I pictured the scene for my crew. After companies of redcoats had scoured both sides of the Acushnet River, they set fire to eight sail of large vessels from 200 to 300 tons, most of them Yankee prizes; six armed vessels, carrying from ten to sixteen guns; and a number of sloops and schooners of inferior size. The total destruction amounted in all to about seventy vessels.

Ashore the British wrought equal devastation: Twenty-six storehouses at Bedford, several at McPherson's wharf, Craw's Mills and Fairhaven were destroyed. These were filled with quantities of rum, tobacco, sugar, molasses, coffee, tea, medicines, gunpowder, cotton, sailcloth, cordage, etc. Two rope walks also burned.

As the village burned, the brig NO DUTY ON TEA, enveloped in flames, floated from McPherson's wharf and grounded on Marsh Island. Other vessels drifted on the islands and shores as far down as Fort Phoenix.

Hearing this story, one boy aboard SARAH ABBOT wondered why the Yanks had not put up a fight. The truth is that they had tried. But most of the men who were not Quaker pacifists had left town to join the army, navy, or privateer fleet, and the Dartmouth villages were virtually undefended. There was a small company of about 80 colonial soldiers stationed at the head of the Acushnet River, but they spent most of the invasion fleeing and trying to reposition themselves in the face of British brigades. Nevertheless, the Yanks were the first to spill blood. As the British troops marched east from Clarks Cove along what is now County Street, armed with muskets hid in the cover of woods near the head Street and fired on the redcoats. Two men died. Now roused fired without provocation on three local men walking up No man's head was "entirely cut to pieces"; his two compa quently. Meanwhile, the British began burning just the western side of the Acushnet River.

But when they came back the next evening on the eastern banks of the river, the British m invasion, minutemen from surrounding t Fairhaven to save what was left of the Acus hungry for a fight, some of the minutemen began murmuring about retreating when barge loads of redc near Fort Phoenix at about 8 p.m. and fired at buildings nea Seeing that the fight might be lost before it began, the youthful Mu, rael Fearing of Wareham placed himself at the rear of the minutemen line of defense, drew his pistol, and declared that he would shoot every

climb to a pulpit shaped like the bows of a ship and preach his fire and brimstone sermon about Jonah, the whale, and a vengeful God.

Now, watching our crew enter the Bethel, I suddenly remembered the conversation that had taken place during the final sail up the Bay with Cruise One. Then a shipmate had referred to Buzzard Bay as an "elbow in time," saying that in this bay the present seems to be bending back to the past—like an arm with its hand reaching back to scratch its shoulder. I had puzzled over the meaning of the metaphor when I had heard it that day. But at this moment something clicked in my head, and I realized that all day long the crew and I had been reaching back and scratching at the Bay's past. On Johnny Cake Hill the ghosts were all around us.

About these streets of New Bedford Melville had written, "Nowhere in all America will you find more patrician looking houses; parks and gardens more opulent than in New Bedford. Whence came they? How planted upon this once scraggy scoria of a country? Go and gaze upon the iron emblematic harpoons round yond lofty mansion, and your question will be answered . . . In New Bedford, fathers, they say, give whales for dowers to their daughters."

Well, at least they did in the days 150 years ago when Ishmael strolled these streets and Johnny Cake Hill stood at the center of town. Whaling had built New Bedford in a hurry following the Revolution with 73 ships and 39 brigs belonging to the port in 1805. The struggles with England that lead to the War of 1812, including the impressment of Yankee whalers and merchant mariners on the high seas, retarded the New Bedford's economy for a few years. But the port escaped any direct attack by the British and their warship the NIMROD which stalked the Bay, and the port began to boom again when hostilities ceased. Ever bolder, New Bedford whalers ranged farther afield to roam from the South Pacific to Hawaii in search of sperm whales and further north to the Sea of Japan and Alaska to hunt the oil-rich bowhead whale. By 1847 whalers numbering to 254 sailed from New

Bedford with a total worth of more than $6 million. The number of ships grew to 319 vessels in 1855.

Captains' and merchants' mansions sprouted like tiger lilies along the hill crests and shady back lanes of New Bedford and Fairhaven. During this rambunctious golden age the port's strong Quaker background made it a center for abolitionist sentiments and a haven for escaped slaves like the great abolitionist leader Frederick Douglass. Hundreds, perhaps thousands, of former slaves passed openly through New Bedford. Many were recruited to sail on whalers instead of struggling on to Canada with the help of the Quakers until the Fugitive Slave Law of 1851 drove operations underground. Daggoo, the black harpooner aboard Melville's ill-fated PEQUOD, may have been such a recruit.

Meanwhile the waterfront teemed with marine industries of every sort, seamen from all over the globe, and vice whose quantity and variety boggled the mind. One of the most infamous bordellos was know as "The Ark" because it was literally a floating whorehouse built from the hulk of a retired whaling ship. Connected in rumor with a murder and other nefarious acts, the Ark scandalized the moral safekeepers of the community to the point that in 1826 a mob attacked and burned the floating brothel. However, in true New Bedford spirit of rising from its ashes, a new Ark soon appeared. This floating house of ill-repute was also burned by a rioting mob in 1829 who then went on to burn other flesh palaces. While city authorities quelled such vigilante justice for the next two decades, a pair of murders in 1851 drew another mob to burn the bordellos on Howland Street, a noted resort for drunken sailors and a place that abounded in dance halls, saloons, gambling dens, and brothels. For many of New Bedford's nineteenth century mariners, the motto might easily have been, "Live fast, die young"—carpe diem. Dead Pirates all.

Visiting the Seamen's Bethel, one boy in our crew discovered a personal connection with young whalers who had been shadowed by hardships and death. He wrote this in his log:

"I stood and walked to the far corner, reading various tablets on the walls—tributes and remembrances of lost sons, husbands, fathers. Some died while on board a whaling vessel. Many died in whale boats. They were pulled overboard into a dark, fathomless sea. Never to be seen again. Or they vanished into the great jaws of a sperm whale. I could not imagine such a fate. But what I noticed most were their ages. Hardly any were above thirty. I've always known that death at an early age is one of the greatest tragedies. At the Seamen's Bethel, it was all I saw."

Such dark thoughts sometimes haunted me, too. If ever a person wanted to feel the pangs of *saudade* and know the torment of inexplicable loss, he or she could find no more poignant inspiration than inside this chapel.

Later when the crew crossed the street from the Bethel to the large Georgian building housing the New Bedford Whaling Museum, we found the museum packed with whalers' longboats, porcelain brought back from three-year voyages to the Far East, and scrimshaw carved on whales' baleen or teeth.

We also found the LAGODA, a recreation of a New Bedford whaler built and rigged to half the size of a seagoing ship. She was towering over the main gallery of the museum like a child's dream of a pirate ship. Here, my shipmates climbed aboard and walked the decks of the LAGODA. I could see far away looks in their eyes and guessed that they were picturing themselves at sea with Ishmael, Queegueg, Tashtego, and Ahab. Later, they lingered at exhibits and watched a documentary film of one of the last whaling cruises made under sail, the whale hunted in the traditional Yankee way from a longboat with harpooner. When the movie ended, our crew left in silence. One of the girls looked around at the closed bars and dusty streets as the crew drifted through New Bedford's streets in search of soft-serve ice cream.

"It's all gone," she said.

"What?"

"The glory," she said.

Amen, I thought.

True, the whaling industry had spiraled into a fast decline following the discovery of petroleum in Pennsylvania in 1859 and the outbreak of the Civil War in 1860. But New Bedford hung onto its wealth—if not the romance of the sea—into the first decades of the twentieth century. The new source of wealth came from textile manufacturing, and the industry grew in New Bedford as whaling had before it—as a consequence of the shrewd opportunism that characterized Yankee/Quaker entrepreneurs. Seeing the Industrial Revolution sweeping through New England, and towns like Fall River and Lowell growing rich almost overnight from mills that spun and wove raw Southern cotton into fabric and garments, a group of New Bedford investors dreamed of a having a piece of the action.

As one historian wrote: "The general sentiments of the citizen were in opposition to the introduction of manufacturing by incorporated companies and preferred those conducted by individual capital and enterprise, and such as were in connection with the whaling and shipping interests. Particularly so were the mechanics, who regarded the organized and disciplined labor inimical to the labor interests."

In other words, the citizens of New Bedford had grown fond of the free and independent lifestyle—the easy money, adventure, and frequent lazy days—that came with seafaring and its associated shore businesses. Manufacturing seemed a dull and slavish business.

But the mills came. By the turn of the twentieth century, New Bedford ranked third in the nation for the number of mechanized cotton spindles in operation, fourth for the number of looms. Wamsutta Mills had six buildings, three stories high and longer than two city blocks. Inside 220,000 spindles spun cotton to thread and 4,500 looms wove fabric. And Wamsutta Mills were hardly the only textile makers in town. Other giants like Potomska, Acushnet, and Hathaway spread their cloth factories through the north and south end of the city where neighborhoods of cheap, frame three-story boarding houses, and apartments dwellings rose up to accommodate tens of thousands of immigrant workers drawn to the jobs.

Eventually, the boom went bust. Like so many other manufacturing enterprises in New England's older industrialized cities, New Bedford's textile companies felt the Depression like a sledgehammer. Mills cut back on shifts and laid off large numbers of workers. Some of the mammoth spinning and weaving buildings that lined the Acushnet River north of Pope's Island went dark forever. You could no longer hear the steady hum of the looms along Acushnet Avenue. Always grimy, the vast acres of tenement houses that had grown up around the mills turned to slums.

When I thought back on the hard times following the decline of the textile industry during the Depression in the 1930s, I was certain that a new dream had already begun to take shape for New Bedford. With the Depression came the technological revolution that brought the advent of reliable motor-driven offshore fishing boats. Such vessels spelled a shift away from the traditional schooners and dory fishing for ground fish using long lines. The new powerboats made it easy to pursue fishing with highly-efficient otter trawl nets towed off the stern. Now, swifter, smaller vessels crewed by many fewer people could make shorter, faster fishing trips to Georges Banks and return with fresh fish.

The development of waterfront ice works and fish processing plants accelerated these changes as did increasing consumer demand for fresh fish. Physically closer to Georges Banks, and blessed with extensive wharves, underutilized waterfront land, and excellent railroad and highway access to the fish markets of New York, New Bedford eclipsed Gloucester and Boston's traditional domination of the New England fishing industry. Customers sought New Bedford's fresh fish with more fervor than they had formerly purchased salt-preserved cod and haddock fillets. New Bedford boomed again. Waves of Scandinavian, Portuguese, and Cape Verdean people with extensive repertoires of fishing skill immigrated to staff the fishing boom at sea and ashore. In fact, so many people of Portuguese ancestry have settled in New Bedford that the city is considered one of the largest settlements of offshore Portuguese people outside of Brazil.

With the immigrants came more fishing boats, and between the end of World War II and 1990 ever larger numbers of fishing trawlers began calling New Bedford home until the harbor rippled with a fleet of commercial vessels more or less equal in number to the whaling fleet during the Golden Age of the 1840s and 1850s.

But just like the whalers before them, New Bedford's fishermen pursued their quarry with abandon. Just as the whales had grown scarce under the pressure of relentless hunting, so have the stocks of cod and haddock. Faced with a total collapse of the New England fishing industry in the 1990s, the National Marine Fisheries Service imposes harsh quotas on local fishermen that limit the number of days each year a vessel can fish. The combination of generally-poor fishing and quotas have driven more than half of New Bedford's fishermen out of business.

Now, as SARAH ABBOT visited the port on the threshold of the new millenium, we still found plenty of activity around the waterfront. But this was high season for cod, haddock, flounder, and scallop fishing, and the dozens of steel fishing trawlers tied to the wharves with nobody aboard were reminders of "busted trips" when the boat could not meet her expense and banks foreclosed on delinquent mortgages. Since 1995, under pressure from Massachusetts legislators, the federal government had been dedicating millions of dollars in relief funds to support boat buy-back programs and retrain fishermen, the "lumpers" who unload the fishing boats, and workers furloughed from fish processing plants.

To get a local perspective on the most recent rise and fall of the port's fishing business, I took the crew to visit Marty Manley, a 40-year veteran of the fishing fleets who has given up captaining offshore draggers for the security of managing the city marina on Pope's Island.

Meeting Manley made quite an impression. For some of our crew, the impression began with the look of Manley's office where a note tacked to the front of his desk read, "Do not even *think* of smoking!" Glass paperweights and family photographs cluttered his desk. Photocopies of off-color, humorous quotations decorated the walls along with a photo of a hundred-foot fishing boat. A window looked out onto a collection of sailboats, motor yachts, and three stainless-steel scallop boats docked at a nearby wharf. The room smelled of coffee and dairy creamer. Sitting behind the desk, Manley wore a men's casual, button-front shirt that stretched tightly over his full chest and stomach. The sun had left a permanent pink shade on his clean-shaven cheeks and nose. Squint lines around the eyes and his gray, thinning hair, placed Manley in his late fifties.

Manley told us how he had been the manager of the commercial docks in New Bedford for more than eight years. Before becoming manager, he had spent most of his life as a fisherman. Like many of the males in New Bedford, he started fishing on his father's boat at age sixteen, sweeping up and opening scallop shells on the main deck. By age forty Manley owned several boats. When he decided to take a land job, he sold all but one boat and gave half his company to his son. Then he mentioned that his son and "our" boat was currently fishing for scallops off the New Jersey coast.

"I try to talk to the boat every day by radio," he said. "Sometimes I really miss it out there. But going to sea is a young man's game. Do it while you can."

"Dead Pirates' talk," I thought. "Stir it up!"

Eventually, our conversation turned to the current crisis in the New England fishing industry.

"I can tell you the problem," blurted Manley. He leaned back in his chair and rested his hands on the back of his head. "The problem is that the government should have just shut down the harbors."

When we said that we didn't understand, Manley began clicking his ballpoint pen to an ever-quickening rhythm as he explained that the sharp decline of scallop and fish populations in New England waters came from overfishing "because the National Marine Fisheries didn't do its job." Manley claimed that he had been warning fisheries biologists of the problem since 1986. But according to him, the Fisheries did virtually nothing to stop "multi-million-dollar fishing companies from sending out oversized boats with crews working 24 hours a day catching everything they could find."

"They just never listened to me," Manley complained. "We had union meetings, and I sent God knows how many letters asking them to shut down the harbors. They didn't want to listen."

Now, according to Manley, the belated steps which the Fisheries Service was taking to solve the problem were not working. Manley worried that the Service's plan that limited the number of days each boat can fish per month was bankrupting family-run fishing boats. He also complained about the policy of the Fisheries to enlarge the mesh-size of scallop and fish nets in order to spare smaller species and younger fish.

"The damned fish nets don't even work; they kill five thousand pounds of fish for each marketable five hundred pounds they bring up. And the scientists don't give their changes time to work," he continued. "They tell us one size for the scallop nets, wait through one season, and enlarge the size again. We need at least two seasons to test the new sizes out. Each one of those fishermen has to buy two new nets each season. Damn, we must be keeping the net companies in business."

Manley threw his hands wide as if he were a religious figure begging for mercy. Then he ripped out a piece of paper from a file on the desk and handed it to us. I read the address of the Fisheries Service at the top of the paper. The letter was in opposition to a proposal which allowed large fishing corporations to buy licenses from independent operators. In it Martin pronounced the large fishing corporations "rapists of the sea" as he repeatedly emphasized the "little guys" who put their "lives on the line" while on the boats. To his way of thinking, the fishermen on the small family-owned boats were soldiers sacrificing their lives for the sake of the "American way." The government and big industry were clearly the villains in the New England Fishery.

Before filing out of Marty Manley's office, one of our crew asked Manley if he thought the fish population in the New England waters would return to its previous levels.

"Sure," he said confidently. "There have always been booms and busts, but the fish always return. The small fisheries somehow survive. All they can do is wait out the lull. This business never really changes drastically. The sea giveth, and the sea taketh away."

More Dead Pirates talk.

XV HEADING OUT

No doubt Marty Manley spoke for hundreds of New Bedford fishermen. He knew the harbor and the fishery, and our crew wanted to trust someone with such confidence in his theories. But we all knew that confidence could not bring animals back. This fish bust was not necessarily like the fluctuations of the past. Americans had polluted and overused the New England coastal waters for too long. Unemployment in New Bedford was already twenty percent and rising.

Today, even when you visit New Bedford from the sea, your overwhelming impression of the city comes from the crumbling hulks of the textile mills, block after block of shabby tenements, and clusters of unemployed men. Graffiti are common. So are the baseball caps and baggy clothes associated with urban street gangs. Hardly unseen in the older cities of the Eastern U.S., these images now seemed nevertheless more than a little disturbing to me. This city was just hard for me to look at when viewed against the natural beauty of Buzzards Bay's landscapes and the romantic history of Wampanoags, colonists, freedom fighters, Quaker abolitionists, and whalers.

With such thoughts in my mind after I reboarded SARAH ABBOT and sat in the shade of the saloon to write in my log, I was beginning to regret my decision to spend the night tied alongside ERNESTINA. Her black hull made the old schooner seem like a funeral ship, an icon of times long gone, a monument to *saudade*. So I literally jumped to my feet with enthusiasm when the rest of the crew clambered aboard and I heard a shipmate exclaim, "Let's blow this pop shop!" Rarely have I heard the call of the sea expressed with such colloquial urgency.

Jackie caught my eye and nodded.

"Let's go. We can make a fish stew for dinner underway."

"We just need about ten minutes to take some water-column samples," added John Rogers. "Where are we going?"

"How about some place where the wind blows free, some place where we can swim?" suggested one of the girls.

"How about one of those quiet New England villages I'm always hearing about?" promoted another.

"You mean one of those places with wooden sailboats bobbing in the harbor, stone wharves, and cedar shingled houses on narrow shady streets?"

"You've got it."

"Well, that's Mattapoisett," I explained. "We can be there a little after sunset."

"Cool!"

So it was that all hands assembled to handle the docking lines with smiles on their faces. ERNESTINA's crew cast us off, and SARAH ABBOT backed out into the harbor. Then we set sail to the easy rhythm of the commands that once echoed all over New Bedford Harbor.

"At the helm, head her up. Clear your sail ties. Free the main sheet aft. Stand by the main halyard. Hoist the main. . . ."

With the mainsail stretched to the masthead, the crew hoisted the foresail and jib as well. The entire operation took less than two minutes. Now the crew coiled the halyards on the foredeck and returned to the cockpit for the next set of commands.

"Fall off to port. Stand by to trim the main sheet. Make the main sheet fast."

So the schooner began to sail. First slowly as she worked away from the wharves and fishing fleet in the hot fluky air eddying down Johnny Cake Hill to the harbor. Then, as we gained the channel, and clear air came at a steady 22 knots over the starboard beam, the schooner heeled sharply to port, flashed her red bottom paint to the city and accelerated toward the cut through the hurricane dike and open water.

From the bridge of one of the trawlers at the wharf, a balding Swede waved and shouted, "SARAH ABBOT, finast kind!"

As the crew waved back, a shipmate asked, "What's that all about, what does 'finast kind' mean?"

"Fisherman talk—Dead Pirates lingo," I explained. "People have probably been saying that for centuries around here. It's kind of like teenagers saying 'cool' or 'be cool.' 'Finast kind' is an affirmation or a wish like 'looking good' or 'bon voyage'."

"Or 'so long' like you might never see the other person again?" asked one of the guys.

"That too," I guessed. Then I added, "A lot of boats and crews left this harbor and never came back."

"Where'd they go?"

"Fiddler's Green," I answered.

The crew gave me blank looks. They had never heard of Fiddler's Green, the sailor's euphemism for a magic kingdom beyond death, so I tried more conventional terms.

"The happy hunting ground, the elysian fields, nirvana, heaven."

"Oh," gasped several of our teenagers casting their eyes to the horizon.

Silence settled over the schooner, and I guessed that this leave taking and the conversation had somehow drawn each of our thoughts to a consideration of our individual mortality. My thoughts turned to some statistics: during a 68-year period between 1830 and 1897, more than 668 schooners and 3,755 men sailed out of the port of Gloucester, Massachusetts, never to be seen again. And while I didn't know the statistics for whaling ships and crews lost at sea, the sinking of the PEQUOD, rammed by a white whale, in *Moby Dick* certainly painted a vivid portrait of the dangers inherent in the whale fishery.

Now, as the sun settled in the west and cast a copper light through the haze, only the rushing of the waves and the creaking of the schooner's lanyard rigging against the deadeyes of the shrouds broke our silence. A steep foaming sea rolled behind SARAH ABBOT as we eased sheets and veered northeast around Sconticut Neck. The vessel sawed left and right, careening before the breaking waves. Not wanting to torment a less experienced person with standing a trick at the helm, I relieved Jackie, sat down straddling the wheel box like a bronco rider on his mount and tried to settle the schooner on her course into the purple haze ahead.

As I steered gloomy thoughts roamed my brain. I pictured the disaster that spelled the virtual end to New Bedford's whaling industry. The year was 1871. Trying to rebound against the triple threats posed by the Civil War's economic decimation, the growing petroleum industry, and the scarcity of whales, most of the remaining whaling fleet, approximately 40 in number, completed their voyage around Africa and north through the Pacific Ocean to arrive at the hunting ground for the oil-rich bowhead whales along the western coast of Alaska. As the Arctic ice receded with the onset of summer, the whalers passed north through the Bering Straits, pursuing the whales right to the edge of the pack ice. It was common practice to tie the ships to the ice flows while the crews hunted the bowheads from whale boats. The hunting was good, but unusual westerly winds struck in mid-August and drove the ice packs rapidly toward the coast. The ice set in so fast that some ships tied to it or anchored in its path had to cut their lines to escape the oncoming crush of slabs piling upon slabs. All that saved the fleet from being driven ashore or crushed was the depth of the massive ice flow. The ice was so thick that it grounded in about 24 feet of water, leaving a narrow band of open water not more than a half mile wide between the ice and the shore where the whalers could anchor. They remained trapped in this precarious position for ten days. Meanwhile the hunting continued with crews cutting up the slaughtered whales on the ice and dragging the blubber to the ships for rendering into oil.

On August 25 a northeast gale blew up as the captains had hoped, and drove the ice four to eight miles offshore giving the fleet an escape route to the open sea. But whaling was good, and in the captain's estimation, they still had several weeks of good hunting before west winds locked the coast in ice for the winter. The whalers paid no attention to the warnings of local Eskimos who encouraged the whalers to leave with all haste or face devastation. Then, on August 29, the wind freshened from the southwest and drove the ice toward shore with such rapidity that several ships were caught in the flow. The rest of the fleet retreated to the narrow band of water running along the shore from Point Belcher at the north to two or three miles south of Wainwright's inlet. The ice field stretched out to sea as far as the ships' lookouts could see, and on September 2, the fleet suffered its first casualty. Heavy ice surrounding the brig COMET pinched the boat until her stern was forced out of the water and her timbers cracked. During the three or four days she sat thus, crews from other ships helped to salvage the ship's gear and cargo before the ice relaxed its grip and the COMET went to the bottom. The next ship to suffer this fate was the bark ROMAN. A day later, ice took the famous old AWASHONKS, and the refugee crews were dispersed among the remaining 31 ships at anchor.

Growing worried, the whaling captains parlayed and decided to send a small boat expedition south through the shallow open water along the beach to see how far the ice extended. When the small expedition of three boats returned, they bore bad news. The ice pack extended about 80 miles to the south: it was utterly impossible to free the fleet. The good news was that seven whalers remained clear of the ice to the south of the flows and all had volunteered to carry the refugees from the icebound fleet. Hearing this information the captains decided to abandon the fleet to save the lives of their crews.

On September 14, crews on the 31 ships anchored near Wainwright's Bay hauled down the Stars and Stripes that had flown over their vessels and hoisted the flags again, flying upside down as the traditional symbol of distress. Thereafter, the crews abandoned their ships and formed a flotilla of about 100 whale boats that rowed and sailed south along the beach in search of the seven rescue ships. These castaways numbered 1,210, including captains' wives and children. After spending the first night of the exodus camped among sand dunes where a weak fire, over-turned boats, and sails sheltered the refugees, they continued south until they spied the rescue ships. But as they reached open water, a vicious southwest gale set in. Only exceptional seamanship kept the whaleboats from swamping before the soaked and exhausted human cargo could reach safety aboard the seven ships anchored in open water. One of those savior ships was the LAGODA. No wonder her image has been memorialized in the New Bedford Whaling Museum.

Ten days after the abandonment of the fleet, the majority of the rescue vessels reached Honolulu to discharge the refugees. Not one person had died, but 34 ships, including 22 from New Bedford, had been lost. The financial devastation equaled $1.5 million worth of ships and cargo, most of which was uninsured. While Yankee whalers returned to the Arctic for a few more years, never again would a whaling fleet of such size and wealth sail from this Buzzards Bay port. The industry, as New England had known it for 150 years, was dead.

As SARAH ABBOT hurtled northeast into the growing darkness, the crew shrouded themselves in hooded foul-weather gear for warmth and stared blankly ahead as the evening haze thickened into a violet fog that seemed to follow us up the Bay. It swirled over West Island to our port, obscured the wink of lights seven miles to the south at Woods Hole and, finally, rolled ahead of us to consume the flashing beacon on Cleveland Ledge. Venus and a few stars appeared overhead, but the night smelled and felt like ink as I steered down the combers by the red glow of the compass light. Finally, the galley watch passed up warm bowls of fish stew to their shipmates on deck, and we ate in silence.

Quiet on a vessel with a crew of teenagers is rare and often the adults had to impose reflection times so each of us could escape from the closeness of living in tight quarters with eight other humans and a dog. But tonight an unnatural silence ruled. Even after dinner when John passed out chocolate chip cookies and Jackie brewed tea, the crew sat in stony silence. And after a day in which New Bedford's ghosts had spun a web around me like this fog, I knew that it was more than just the cool, damp wind against my back that made me shiver.

XVI MATTAPOISETT

Radar found the Nyes Ledge bell buoy for us. As John steered the schooner, I watched on the pale, green scope while the blip that I had identified as the buoy passed abeam the schooner at about 25 yards on our port. With all the crew gathered on watch for the buoy and lobster trap floats that often booby trap the surrounding waters to catch the lobsters on Nyes Ledge, we all heard the buoy clanging away in the rowdy seas. But none of us saw it in the gloom and fog, not even when we veered north and passed it again.

Within 10 minutes of changing course, we felt the seas subside and the air grow warm and scented with hay. No question, our northerly course had taken us from the open Bay to the sheltered waters in the lee of Mattapoisett Neck. The inner harbor and the town wharves on the large cove lay a mile and a half ahead.

"Listen," called one of the crew after the rush of wind and waves had subsided to whispers.

"It's a brass band," guessed one of our teenagers pointing into the fog ahead.

We all cocked our heads, and one by one smiles broke over the crews' dark faces as we recognized the strains of trombones, clarinets and piccolos romping through *Stars and Stripes Forever*. Seconds later SARAH ABBOT broke out of the fog as if she had punched through a veil, and there—no less than a mile ahead of us—lay the lights of Mattapoisett twinkling around the cup-shaped harbor where a field of sailing yachts bobbed at anchor. At the far end of the channel leading between the moorings, a gallery of bright lights shone over a gazebo in the center of a waterfront park. There, on a raised stage beneath the cupola of the gazebo, a band infused the night with John Philip Sousa's patriotism. A crowd with blankets and lawn chairs spread across the park. Even from this distance, you could tell that people were clapping their hands and tapping their feet to the oompah rhythm of the tubas.

"Is this some kind of celebration?" asked one of the crew.

"Just the weekly band concert," I explained.

"Towns still have such things?"

"Not many," John guessed.

"How quaint," judged one girl.

She had that right. Except for the cars parked on the big stone wharves near the gazebo, Mattapoisett had the look of some kind of Yankee Brigadoon emerging from the shadows of the nineteenth century for one festive summer night before disappearing into the past again. The cedar shingled and white clapboard Cape-style houses and the rambling Victorian mansions ringing the harbor stood as trim and proud as they had a century ago when shipbuilders and whaling captains had lived here and made Mattapoisett boom. Granite wharves that jutted into the harbor recalled that history, and the park where the band played bore the name Shipyard Park. Across Water Street from the park, the Mattapoisett Inn, which still welcomed mariners to its screened porches, claimed to be the oldest continuously-operating seaside inn in America. Standing watch over the village, the Tudor clock tower of the school house looked like something drawn on a page from a fairy tale.

A fashionable summer retreat since the days when Supreme Court Justice Oliver Wendell Holmes built his vacation compound here, Mattapoisett remains a town colored by its seafaring past. Many of the residents continue in the trades of their forefathers, working as boatbuilders, merchant mariners, or marine tradesmen. Mattapoisett is a town where large numbers of the citizenry make daily trips to sit on the benches at Shipyard Park or the wharves, watch the comings and goings of vessels, and gam with each other. This is a village where the most respectful way to greet a man is to call him Captain. Here was a town where virtually someone in every family had built or—at least—owned a boat.

Luck was with SARAH ABBOT. No sooner had we rounded up into the wind off Shipyard Park and dropped our sails, when a voice called from the end of a wharf to offer us a nearby vacant mooring. So it was that we got a ringside seat on the rest of the band concert. As the band played the final bars of *When the Saints Come Marchin' In*, the crew rowed ashore to stretch our legs. While our teenage crew pursued ice cream from a vendor on the wharf and lingered on the swings at the town beach, John, Jackie, and I called time out for a round of cold beer on the porch of the inn. Not once, but twice, people who must have seen me lead our crew ashore called me Captain and brought a sudden smile to my weathered cheeks.

Jackie, John, and I woke the next morning to a hot sun beating on deck at 6:30. The warm, moist feel of my pillow against my cheek, and the glaze of sweat I felt around my eyes reminded me of waking up aboard a boat in the tropics.

"I feel all cramped up," whispered Jackie as she dragged out of her berth with a web of thick, dark hair covering most of her face. Her night shirt looked streaked with wrinkles. "I think I need a run and a swim. How about you guys?"

"Something curled up in my mouth and died last night," moaned John as he wandered into the galley and pumped a cup of water from the spigot. "Must have been swell living like this on a whaling ship for about three years."

"Ah, the romance of the sea," I mumbled and fell back against my sticky pillow.

"If it gets any hotter, we won't even be able to jog," groaned Jackie. "Come on, heroes."

When I peeled open my eyelids and wiped the sweat away, my wife stood over me, already changed into a sports bra and jogging shorts. She had her running shoes in hand. John scrambled out of the forward head in his gear. I was doomed to exercise.

So it was that we left our teenage crew sleeping aboard the schooner, and the three of us rowed ashore for a jog around Mattapoisett on what promised to be the hottest day of July. Hardly had we started our jog up Cannon Street, leading inland from the wharves, when the past began to rise all around me. Whether by chance or design, Cannon Street had no cars on it. White clapboard and gray-shingled Cape Cod cottages lined the street in tight flanks. These homes were not contemporary architects' visions of quaint cottages by the sea; these were the real things—homes of captains and shipbuilders—dating back to the 1700s. Steep roofs, uneven eaves, narrow shuttered windows, and corner posts all stood raked at odd angles by time and strong winds. Picket fences and luxuriant rosebushes trimmed the tiny yards. Not yet fully awake, I lumbered down the street, half expecting to see the "gray ladies"—mistresses in the plain, full skirts they wore winter and summer—slipping from the old wooden doors to water the petunias in their window boxes.

Running through the shady neighborhood east of the wharves where the homes of nineteenth-century shipbuilders mixed with turn-of-the century summer mansions, we eventually reached Ned's Point Lighthouse on the northeastern shore of Mattapoisett Harbor. West of the lighthouse stretched the boulder-strewn shores of the inner harbor and hundreds of pleasure boats tethered to their moorings; east lay a mile of sandy Crescent Beach open to Buzzards Bay. Exclusive summer cottages raised on stilts to survive hurricanes dotted the shoreline and reminded me how this town got its name.

Nineteenth-century historians claimed that the translation of the Algonquin name Mattapoisett meant "place of rest." While more recent writers questioned the accuracy of such a translation, noting that Algonquin place names almost always described a geographical feature not an event, the nineteenth-century translation always felt right to me. Nothing about this town ever seems frenzied; jogging down Crescent Beach on a hot July morning, with only the swoops and calls of gulls and terns to break the silence, was more like a vacation than a workout.

But however you translated the village name, the fact remains that the Wampanoags valued this place. Pilgrim settlers learned the name from the Indians shortly after arriving in Plymouth, and by 1640 the name Mattapoyst appeared in the record of the Plymouth court in connection to Captain Miles Standish. Apparently, Standish and a partner had made a claim on Mattapoisett but had never developed the land because Wampanoags refused to give up their traditional rights to the property. This confusion of ownership was the typical state of affairs in the Plymouth Colony as the "Old Comers" who had first settled Plymouth set up their court and laid claim to virtually all the territory that they could explore and define without regard to Indian ownership. Once a settler had a claim to the land endorsed by the Plymouth court, the settler only needed to persuade local Wampanoags to give up their rights in order to own the land free and clear.

But the Wampanoags did not give up their claims in spite of several attempts to relieve the Indians of this place which the court generally referred to as the "lands of Sepecan [today, Marion] and places adjacent." Archeological evidence and lore identifies Mattapoisett as a popular summer camp where inland bands of Wampanoags came to fish, swim, and enjoy the cooling breezes during each summer. Numerous "kitchen middens"—shell heaps from Indian clam bakes—have been found under the sands along Mattapoisett's shores, and a ridge to the northwest of the village has long been called the Indian Burial Ground because of bones and sepulture discovered there.

In 1666 the Wampanoag sachem Metacom (King Philip) granted the right to sell the lands of Sepecan to two subordinate chiefs, Watchapoo and Samson, but they did not sell, unless it was to pass the land to three other Wampanoags—Papamo, Machacam and Achawanamett. These three men petitioned that "being the Right owners of the land heer mensioned doe desire to have them recorded in the Court of Plymouth Collonie that soe we may preserve our lands for our children." Clearly, these Wampanoag owners sought to legitimize their claims on the land in the face of the growing tension that had been developing throughout southeastern Massachusetts following the mysterious death of Metacom's brother Wamsutta in 1662.

Sensing correctly that war between the colonists and Indians loomed, the three Indians restated the boundaries of "land called by the name of Mattapoisett" again before the court in 1673.

When King Philip's War broke in June of 1675, Mattapoisett—and probably this very beach where Jackie, John, and I jogged—served as an exceptional place of rest and the site of a turning point in the conflict. The woodsman, Indian friend, and colonial hero of King Philip's War, Captain Benjamin Church, recorded this turning point at Mattapoisett in his book *An Entertaining History of King Philip's War*. As the crew of SARAH ABBOT had learned during our visit to Padanaram on Cruise One, about a year of bloodshed had passed when Church met with Awashonks, the squaw sachem of the Sakonnet band, to secure a treaty that "pledged her fideli-tie" to the English colonists and offer the services of her warriors on the English side of the conflict. But when Church reported the offer to Ply-mouth's governor William Bradford, the leader grew skeptical about Awashonks' sincerity and demanded that she proceed with her braves to Plymouth to make a show of good faith.

The squaw sachem felt manipulated. But Church persuaded her to make the trip by saying that he and his men would meet her along the north shore of Buzzards Bay on their return trip to make certain that all had gone well in her meeting with Plymouth's leaders. Church had ex-pected to meet Awashonks at Agawam (Wareham), but when the Indians did not arrive, Church and his party continued west to Mattapoisett until they came to a shore where there was a wide view of the bay. Here—prob-ably on our jogging beach between Ned's Point and Angelica Point—Church found Awashonks and her Sakonnet party running races and holding a feast on the "sands and flats."

Following a banquet on bass, eels, flounder and shellfish, the Sakon-nets built a bonfire from "a great pile of Pine Knots and Tops," and the Indians gathered in a ring around the fire. Church recalled the scene:

Awashonks and the oldest of her people kneeling down made the first ring, and all but the stout, lusty men standing up made the next, and all the rabble, a confused crew, surrounded on the outside. Then the Chief

Captain stepped in between the people and the fire, and with a spear in one hand and a hatchet in the other danced round the fire and began to fight with it, making mention of the several nations and the companies of Indians that were enemies of the English; and at every tribe named he would draw out and fight a new fire brand, and at finishing his fight with a fire brand he would bow to him and thank him. When he had named them all and fought them, he struck down his spear and hatchet and came out. Then another stepped in and acted the same with more fury if possible than the first. When about half a dozen of the chiefs had thus done, the Captain of the Guard told Church that they were making soldiers for him, and this was something of a swearing-in ceremony. Now, Awashonks and her chiefs declared that they were all ready to fight for the English.

When the ritual ended, Awashonks gave Captain Church "a very fine firelock." He responded by assuring her that Plymouth's leaders and he had confidence in her allegiance and she could count on the English to protect her people and territory.

Now with his Sakonnet militia, Church moved through the coastal lowlands north of Buzzards Bay rounding up band after band of Indians who remained loyal to Philip during the summer of 1676. Church's job grew easier as the English troops rallied throughout central Massachusetts to drive Philip's warriors and their families south into ambushes by Church and the Sakonnets. Sometimes the captured Indians joined to fight alongside Church and the Sakonnets as they pressed toward victory. Finally, Church cornered Philip in Rhode Island where an Indian loyal to Church and the English slay the once-mighty sachem.

As compensation for defeating Philip, Plymouth Colony ignored the claims of Papamo, Machacam and Achawanamett, and passed an act granting Mattapoisett and the land further to the east along Buzzards Bay to white soldiers who fought with Church. These lands that the Indians had refused to sell for more than 50 years now fell under English control as the spoils of war. The Indians who had lived on these lands, including those who had fought with Church, were commanded by the colony to "take up their abode from the western most side of Sepecan River and sow easterwards to Dartmouth bounds." In other words, much of what we now know as Mattapoisett became an Indian reservation with three lesser sachems acting as overseers.

But even this solution to the "Indian problem" did not last. In 1679 a group of 30 colonists formed the Rochester Proprietary and bought all the "lands of Sepecan" along the north shore of Buzzards Bay, stretching between Dartmouth and the head of the Bay and extending inland to Middleboro. Thereafter, the proprietors of the Rochester territory promulgated a regulation forbidding Indians who had not lived in Rochester for three years from hunting or catching deer within the territory limits. Since many of the Wampanoags were migrants driven to this land after the war, few could claim hunting rights and had to move west to pursue their traditional lifestyle. One tough Indian named Will Connett held out for his claim on the land between the Sippican River east along the shore to the head of the Bay, Agawam (Wareham). Connett carried his claim to the courts, and arbitration won Connett a proprietor's share of the lands of Rochester. But Connett's name quickly vanished from community records. Maybe he died or perhaps, like so many of the Wampanoags, he just sold out for a pittance and headed west to rebuild his life among refugees far from this place of rest. Except in Connett's case, no record exists that the Wampanoags were ever paid for the "lands of Sepecan." The rightful owners of the land—Papamo, Machacam, and Achawanamett—were likely among the many Indians rounded up by Church and deported by the Plymouth leaders as slaves to Bermuda and the West Indies. Mattapoisett and all the surrounding territory—more than 70 square miles—had become Rochester, named for the oyster-rich coastal region of County Kent, England, where the new colonists had once lived.

After Jackie, John, and I had looped back to the wharves in the center of the village, and rinsed away the sweat on our bodies with a water hose on the Long Wharf, we returned to wake the crew for a morning swim. They had a big day ahead: science project work ashore and on the boat, and a meeting with one of the town's historians who we hoped would add to our picture of Buzzards Bay during the nineteenth century—the golden age of whaling and tall ships.

We had hardly finished swimming laps around our schooner and eating a dozen bowls of frosted flakes, when a trim, grandfatherly man in a ball cap hailed SARAH ABBOT from the Long Wharf. Here was our historian, Seth Mendell, a retired teacher from the Avon Old Farm School and a life-long Mattapoisett resident who had made an avocation of piecing together his town's past. Like most of the local citizens, Mendell admitted to loving boats. No sooner had I rowed him out to our schooner and introduced him to the crew, than he requested they give him a detailed tour. As a pair of girls led him below to see the forecastle where they bunked, I saw the seasoned teacher emerging as Mendell tapped his knuckles on one of the schooner's varnished cabin walls and smiled.

"You know a wooden boat like this is a living thing, a floating history lesson," he said. "And don't just think of the boat's life as the history of her classic schooner design. Think of all the oak and Philippine mahogany in her. Imagine that each of the trees that make this boat has its own story to tell. Think about the people who built this schooner in Nova Scotia—the hows and the whys and the wherefores behind turning a pile of lumber into a beautiful living thing. I built a wooden boat once—not this big, 36 feet—but it was one of the greatest achievements of my life!"

From this introduction to Mendell, we all sensed that our time with him was going to be infused with his passion and that what he had on his mind was boats built of wood. According to Mendell, such vessels were as much at the heart of Mattapoisett's history as Indian clam bakes and King Philip's War. During the hour Mendell kept us spellbound with his stories in the cockpit of SARAH ABBOT, we learned the breadth and depth of Mattapoisett's maritime traditions. He told us that the village traced its ship-building roots to the first English settlers who came here from Kent, which was noted for its shipwrights. Many of Mattapoisett's early settlers spent the first years of their American immigration in the villages of Scituate and Marshfield where they also built boats and ships. So when the colonists arrived in Mattapoisett many of them naturally took to building boats on the gently-sloping shores of this harbor where the surrounding forest afforded nearly limitless oak for framing and planking, pine for decks and spars.

Initially, Mattapoisett's builders constructed small sloops and schooners for freight and transportation. Often these vessels took shape as collaborative efforts during the winter when the so-called farmer mechanics could spare the time. Working by "rack of eye," these builders constructed their vessels without any plans or models. They simply squared off the largest log that they could find for a keel, attached the stem and stern, set up midship frames or "ribs" that "looked right" and added a few more frames to suggest the tapering of the hull toward the bow and stern. With this rough skeleton in place, the shipwrights stretched ribbands, thin pieces of fir strapping, around the frames along the length of the skeleton at different heights. The ribbands marked the shape to the hull, and the shipwrights could then add dozens more frames to fit the lines produced by the ribbands. With all the frames in place, builders planked their vessels, and finally added the interiors, decks, and spars.

According to Mendell, the first record of a whaling vessel sailing from Mattapoisett/Rochester was the sloop DEFIANCE which began a near shore hunt for whales in 1771. Other local vessels like the ROCHESTER also sailed for whales during the early days of the fishery, but most of these boats came and went from Nantucket as it was an official port of entry and Mattapoisett was not. Lost on Great Point Rip off Nantucket in 1774, the ROCHESTER was far from the only vessel that never came home during these early years of whaling. Records show that during the days of coastwise whaling from sloops and schooners, about twenty percent of the fleet came to a sorry end every year.

In the face of such losses and dreams of fortunes made on whale oil, Mattapoisett's shipwrights thrived. With the arrival in 1765 of a professional large-ship builder named Gideon Barstow from Hanover near Plymouth, Mattapoisett craftsmen switched from building 50- to 65-foot sloops and schooners and began building square rigged ships over 100 feet in length and 300- to 400-ton displacement. Some ships like the 650-ton

GEORGE LEE were absolute behemoths. By the onset of the nineteenth century, more than a half dozen shipyards ringed the shores of Mattapoisett's inner harbor where large granite wharves had been built specifically for rigging out the tall ships. Records are incomplete, but estimates place the number of vessels built in Mattapoisett during the golden age of shipbuilding (1783-1860) at 300 to 400. During these heydays, the village swelled to a hundred dwellings.

Seth Mendell's father Charles recorded some images from those days:

"The whole waterfront was a scene of intense activity; vessels with their tall rigs towered over the wharves; half-built ships bellying up on the stocks; caulkers perched on the scaffolding, encircling the hulls as their flailing arms hammered in the oakum; shipyards and wharves covered with lumber and whale oil casks; plodding oxen hoisting timber from the schooners, packet sloops, gleaming new vessels fresh from the yards, and older New Bedford whalers which had come around to be hauled up and repaired. Rope walks, blacksmith shops, cooper shops, blockmaker shops, sail lofts, whale boat shops— everything going full blast to complete the ships. And in the evening when the clangor of the hammering ceased in response to the bell which rang at the foot of Gossips Lane, now Mechanics Street, the ship carpenters could be seen each trundling home a wheelbarrow full of chips and blocks of wood to be used as fuel for the evening's fire."

The whaling industry was Mattapoisett's biggest customer, and such ships as the ACUSHNET (aboard which Herman Melville made his 1841 whaling voyage that gave rise to the novel *Moby Dick*) came to live here. Not only did Mattapoisett supply ships for the huge New Bedford and Nantucket fleets, but village mariners owned over 50 ships of their own. Yet whaling ships were hardly the only types of vessels built at Mattapoisett. The town built coasters, merchantmen, steamers, and even Cape Horners like the OSCAR and the MT. VERNON which carried Forty Niners from New England to seek their fortunes in the California gold rush. Among these merchantmen was the ship MARTHA captained by Seth Mendell's great great grandfather who brought back a set of blue Lafayette china for his wife that is still on display in Seth Mendell's home.

But like the related whaling industry, the shipbuilding boom in Mattapoisett began spiraling into decline in about 1860: the discovery of oil in Pennsylvania and the development of iron ships during the Civil War spelled an end to Mattapoisett's prosperity. After the war the shipyards began closing, and the town built her last ship, a whaling bark named WANDERER in 1878. What a swan song for the builders! The WANDERER distinguished herself over almost four decades, whaling well into the twentieth century. Driven ashore and wrecked at Cuttyhunk in a 1924 nor'easter, WANDERER was the last whaling vessel to sail from New Bedford. Her legacy persisted for many years as the Stars and Stripes, that we now saw flying in the breeze ashore over Shipyard Park, waved from the WANDERER's mizzen mast—rescued from the wreck to serve as the park's flagpole.

The sun seared with such heat by the time Seth Mendell had finished his stories that I rigged the cockpit awning to give us a little shade as soon as I had returned from rowing Mendell ashore. Meanwhile, the crew cooled off with long swims before downing gallons of lemonade from the thermos in the galley and eating a mound of what we had begun calling "Dead Pirates soul food" or "The Sacred Pee Bee and Jay." These were peanut butter and jelly sandwiches made in assembly line fashion on the table of the main saloon by the two students on galley watch and passed to hungry mouths on deck wrapped in a paper towel along with an orange or an apple for desert.

When the breeze came up at about 15 knots out of the southwest around noon, our comfort improved. Some of the crew spread out on the foredeck or in the shade of the awning to write in their logs, analyze the data for their cruise projects, peer into microscopes at tiny creatures they had been collecting, or take water temperature/salinity samples. One duo rowed our dinghy in circles around the schooner while towing a plankton net to sample the chartreuse-colored plankton that was blooming all over the inner harbor.

While John moved from one student to the other asking pregnant questions about their cruise projects and teaching them strategies for sharpening their research and analysis skills, Jackie and I retreated to our bunks where an open hatch in the stern lazarette locker set up a wind tunnel effect over our berths and made them a cool shady place to read. Jackie lost herself in an Amy Tan novel. I tried to catch up on my reading of the cruise logs that one student after another delivered to me as the afternoon passed.

Listening to Seth Mendell's evocation of the whaling era in Mattapoisett and New Bedford had inspired one girl to thoughts about women's roles aboard whaling ships. She wrote:

"Seth Mendell told us a story about one wife, just 18 years of age, who knew exactly what to do in an emergency. The ship, which was heading for San Francisco, met a storm rounding Cape Horn. The woman's husband, the captain, caught rheumatic fever and fell unconscious. The first mate had previously failed in leading a mutiny against the captain, and was locked up. That left the second mate in charge. He was a fine whale man, but he didn't know how to navigate. None of the crew, all forty from varied and assorted countries, knew where they were. The young wife's father had been a captain, and he had shown her how to use a sextant. With this knowledge, the 18-year-old girl got her ship safely into the port in San Francisco.

"At the whaling museum I saw a photography exhibit. The wife of the captain of the LANCELOT took pictures of all the stages needed in catching a whale. The first picture was of the crew on the crow's nest looking for the spouts of moisture that indicate the presence of whales. The next showed the crew and the harpooners getting into the chase boats and lowering themselves over the side . . . Seeing all the pictures of the process helped me to imagine what it would really be like to be aboard a whaling ship. We have much more space and luxury than the sailors did back then. Instead of the disgusting smell of boiling whale blubber, we have the mixed aroma of peanut butter and jelly and dog. The main difference, however, is that a woman no longer has to be a wife of a captain to hold a role of importance aboard a boat. On SARAH ABBOT a woman might be a journalist, a scientist, a sailor, a fisher, or even a Dead Pirate."

Sea fever. This girl had it worse than just about any of us. It got under your skin and into your head with such virulence that the very act of sweating could spawn visions of blue water passages and whales lunging and spouting their way through a school of bait. I knew. The only cure was to set sail or to sleep, perchance to dream.

Later, as night fell, the exhausted crew decided to drag their sleeping bags on deck and sleep under the stars. They had heard from John that sleeping on deck as an entire student crew was the first phase of their initiation into the Dead Pirates Society, so one of the crew proposed that they get on with the challenge. None of his shipmates disagreed, and by the way I heard them talking and laughing before I feel asleep, I had the sense that they were enjoying having claimed the deck of this schooner as their own.

XVII STICK FISHING

I awoke the next morning in the dark. The rumble of a heavy diesel engine beat right through my dreams, and I heard a boat approaching so close to SARAH ABBOT that the cavitations of her propeller echoed through the planks next to my ear like a siren. Fearing a collision, I leapt on deck to see six sleeping bags huddled together like a litter of puppies on the foredeck. The silhouette of a long bowsprit swept past the schooner's stern. One of the passing boat's crew stood at the very tip of the bowsprit lashing a long-shafted harpoon to the cage of stainless steel tubing that keeps a man from falling overboard when he's out on this long nose of the boat. From the flying bridge came a few shrill words among the crew: "The bait's runnin'. Whales come right with 'em. Old Mr. Needlenose'll be there, too. Gee, we're gonna have us some trip. Finast kind!"

I knew this game. Stick fishing. There was a persisting belief among the seamen in the old whaling ports like Mattapoisett: a man who can stick a sea monster with a harpoon and master him is a lion among men, a demigod, a Queequeg. From the days of *Moby Dick*, serving at the side of such a harpooner had been the dream of generations of Yankee Ishmaels craving the taste of sea adventures.

Once, more than 15 years ago, before the *Oceans* program had begun, I had felt the incipient restlessness of sea fever coming on. It was what Melville called the "dank, dark November" in the soul that drives a person to sea just as surely as the promise of riches or undiscovered countries. As a young man in the days after my year working on the Chesapeake, I had come to Buzzards Bay and Mattapoisett seeking a new adventure; I had gone stick fishing from this port aboard a boat named the

SHAN-LIN, and I still remembered that day like few others. Standing in SARAH ABBOT's companionway in the fog and the darkness, I pictured my stick fishing adventure as if it were all happening again.

The SHAN-LIN is no PEQUOD, but like many of the square riggers that carried Melville and thousands of other whalers to the offshore whaling grounds, SHAN-LIN traces her roots to Mattapoisett. She is a 44-foot custom sport fisherman, and from the wharf she looked like a set for a beer commercial—long sharp nose, thin blue flanks, flying bridge and skeletal "tuna" tower (the crow's nest) reaching 30 feet overhead. Not so different from hundreds of other boats tied in anglers club slips from Montauk, New York, to Eastport, Maine. Except for one thing: that bowsprit, or pulpit ringed with lifelines, stretches 15 feet off SHAN-LIN's bow making her look to the unschooled eye like a half-erected bridge. But fishermen and mariners know the pulpit is SHAN-LIN's calling card, proof of her membership in an exclusive club: this pulpit makes her a stick boat, one of fewer than 50 serious harpooners still working New England waters.

We have thick fog . . . 20 yards visibility. Still, we steam at 20 knots—over the bars at Nantucket's Great Point, south across 40 miles of shoals and current, toward the wreck of the ANDREA DORIA. The 600-horse diesel blares away like a stuck trombone. My sweater turns to wet plaster in the drizzle driving over the flying bridge.

"Where are we now?" I ask the skipper. He raises his face from the hood over the radar scope.

"Between a rock and a hard place," he says in an even voice. "Jaw's backyard." I can't tell if he is kidding. He rolls his shoulders unconsciously. Preparing himself for what may be to come, I imagine.

After a while, he adds in a solemn voice, "We're headed out south of Nantucket and Martha's Vineyard, the old Indian whaling grounds." He says these words as if this fact somehow sanctifies these waters.

Will we see whales, I wonder.

"They're around," says the skipper, "at least their ghosts are."

Skipper Tom Brownell is my man. The harpooner. In his early forties, he has the broad back of a football lineman. His thick neck and razor-cut, sandy hair suggest a career in the Marines. But Brownell is no brute: a full, unwrinkled face dominates. In another place he might have been a priest or an ice cream vendor.

In fact, ashore Tom Brownell is none of these characters; he is the manager of Mattapoisett's Brownell Boatworks, builder of more than 125 sport fishing boats and leader in the design and construction of yacht-hauling tractor trailers. They say on the waterfront in Mattapoisett that Tom Brownell's eye for business is the "finast kind." So they say, too, about his touch with the harpoon. "He don't miss," another stick fisherman told me. "If you want to see a man who can really use the iron, you best sail with Tommy."

Brownell shrugs off his reputation. "I'm just a weekend fisherman," he tells me. "Some guys do this for a living."

True enough, but by pressing the issue, I discover that Brownell descends from a line of New Bedford whalers and generations of harpoon fishermen. He has spent every summer since age seven fishing with seasoned harpooners out of Mattapoisett. At 14 he stuck his first fish.

"It's definitely in the blood," he confesses. "From the first time I saw an iron buttonhole a swordfish, I knew nothing else could equal the excitement."

That is the game—swordfish, Xiphias gladius. The broadbill. Not Moby Dick, but not cod or bluefish either.

"Magnificent animals," says Brownell. "Bold, fast and mysterious. Nobody really knows much about them. They're not like sharks or marlin. People understand where those fish go—their patterns and feeding habits. But swordfish? Hard to tell how they live, and not even the scientists at Woods Hole can tell me how old a swordfish is even though I've sent in a dozen tissue samples."

As the SHAN-LIN charges on through the fog, I wait for Brownell to fill me with more lore about our quarry. But the harpooner holds back as if he doesn't want to give away the swordfish's secrets, or maybe to show that he is not impressed simply by its size, reputation, or value.

He does not say, for example, that the average Xiphias weighs in at 250 pounds, but fishermen have landed individual fish weighing more than a thousand pounds and stretching over 12 feet. Nor does Brownell note that some Asian cultures assign mystical properties to its flesh or call it the ruler of deep-sea fish because of its agility and its bravery when attacking a boat. The harpooner does not admit that he has seen an angry swordfish ram and nearly sink a 32-foot bass boat.

Instead of building a yarn of heroic proportions around the Xiphias, Brownell just stares ahead into the fog and sighs, "The more you go hunting for these critters, the less you realize you know."

"Aw, gee," ribs Tommy Borges, a wiry fellow in a green ball cap. "We've landed 400 of these suckas together, and now he's gettin' modest on me."

Brownell shrugs off the jibe and suggests Borges might go up in the tower and not come down for about eight hours.

Borges pays no attention and descends to the main deck to help lank John Clark assemble the harpoon and line. These two men, Borges and Clark, are Brownell's mates. Not only do they know every function on the SHAN-LIN, but they also know every facet of the harpooner's work: the three men have been fishing together for almost 30 years.

They are keeping alive a Mattapoisett tradition that traces its origins back to the days when local whalers, tired of globe wandering and threatened by the discovery of petroleum, turned their harpooning skills on the schools of broadbill that show up south of Cape Cod each summer. Even 125 years ago swordfish had the reputation of being a restaurant delicacy, and with the growing crowds of vacationers on Cape Cod and the islands, the harpooners found a ready market. So it has been ever since until the more efficient, less demanding long-line trawls and gill nets displaced the harpooner on most commercial boats.

Today aboard SHAN-LIN the trawlers and net fishermen take the blame for Tom Brownell's pensiveness. Down on the main deck coiling harpoon line Borges explains, "Bad summa. Them long liners been takin' all the fish. Dirty buggas! Wipin' the fish right out."

"This weatha, too," adds Clark. "How you gonna see the fish if he's here. Black fog, black water..."

At the controls the harpooner is rolling his shoulders again. Is everyone nervous, or am I just imagining things? Over the grumble of the engine, I hear Borges turn down Clark's offer of a beer. Borges says he isn't drinking until we have an F.O.B.—fish on board. In a desperate attempt to be useful I go down into the cabin and polish everyone's sunglasses. I hope we will need them on the fishing grounds.

At 1100 hours Brownell cuts the engine back to idle and SHAN-LIN ghosts along at six knots on a new heading—northwest. Slick calm.

"Look at that," the harpooner says to the crew and points to a set of flashing numbers on the control panel. Water temperature 69.7.

"Supa," exclaims Borges trying to generate some enthusiasm.

As SHAN-LIN crosses into 30 fathoms of water the fog lifts. Suddenly we have more than a half mile visibility.

Brownell purses his lips into a near-smile, "Let's go get 'em!"

Clark slaps me on the back and motions to the tuna tower with a jerk of his head, "Get on up; we're fishin'." We pull on our Polaroids and climb.

From the tower the ocean looks faceless and dark gray. Unchanged from here to Portugal. Yet these are the grounds. Four hundred years ago Wampanoags hunted "black fish," pilot whales, from their canoes here. Three hundred years ago colonial whalers began hunting until they had depleted the herds of great whales like the humpbacks and fin whales drawn here to feed. Now, says Brownell, the whales are back; it's a good sign. There is plenty of bait, and if the whales are here to feed, Xiphias will be here, too.

Experience tells Brownell that if the broadbills are basking, it will be at this temperature and depth. Two miles north or south of here you would rarely see a swordfish, and even along this 27 fathom line, the Xiphias have preferred haunts. Places called the fingers, the hole, the dump or—where we are—the corner.

Why these places and nowhere else? Brownell and his crew have stopped trying to figure it out. Perhaps swordfish like these areas because they host large schools of squid, herring, and sand eels—staple foods for Xiphias gladius and whales. But no one can be certain, because the broadbills are found basking on the grounds, not ripping through the bait schools slashing everything in sight with their 4- to 5-foot cutlass beaks. Here, it's the whales you will see breaking the surface with mouths overflowing with squiggling bait, says Brownell.

While Borges lashes the harpoon horizontally across the pulpit and feeds the line aft to a tub of coils and an orange float the size of a beach ball, Clark and I scan the water for a broadbill. We are watching for the tall dorsal fin, the scythe of the upper tail lobe or a fluorescent-purple torpedo shape below the surface. Secretly, I am watching for a small gray cloud that appears suddenly 15 feet above the water, the signature of a great whale.

Suddenly four gulls wheel in a circle off to starboard. Water roils beneath. I glimpse a sickle-shaped fishtail breaking the surface.

"Two o'clock, three boats [lengths]," shouts Clark. Borges is pointing with his right hand and grabbing for the harpoon with his left. Already Brownell has turned SHAN-LIN toward the action.

But just as fast as the ocean seethed up, it goes flat again. The gulls break formation. For seconds, nothing. Then the roiling, the flash of the tail again and, for a second, a long black fin. It races off to port.

"Skilly," shout all three men.

"Let him go," judges Brownell. "He's fishing, too."

A quarter of a mile off, bait fish break the surface pursued by a long webbed dorsal fin.

"What on earth was that?" I say to no one in particular. "It looked prehistoric!"

"That theya was Johnny Clark's sista," responds Borges from the pulpit.

Clark spits down at his mate. "Skilly," he tells me. "That's what we call skillagalee, the white marlin. Fair eatin'."

"Hard as heaven to stick," Brownell adds from down below on the bridge. He says skillies are fast and skittish. Minor fish. We could have taken that one, but that isn't why we came out here, is it?

"Come on, Clarky, put me on a horse," urges the skipper.

Off we go jogging northwest again. I still feel the adrenaline pumping through my arms and legs. Wonder if it's the same for the others. Clark scans the sea and doesn't give off a clue.

I barely have time to settle down before Clark is shouting again, "Ten o'clock, four boats."

"Big fella," I add, trying my best to contribute.

In a second we are almost over the long, dark shape. It seems giant—over 10 feet for certain. Faster than I can see Brownell has taken Borges' place in the pulpit. The harpooner stands poised; the dart just skims the surface of the water.

Ten feet in front of the pulpit the shape surfaces. I brace myself for the thud, then the lurch of the big fish ripping the coils of line overboard.

"Your mother," curses Brownell. He doesn't throw the iron. Instead he drags it across the fish's back. The fish actually seems to like the feel and rubs against the harpoon for several seconds. When it finally twists away from the bow, I see it clearly—a good 400 pounds of blue shark.

"No way," sums up Brownell. "Last time I fooled with a big shark he tried to tear the boat apart. Came right up underneath us and began banging against the hull. Had to cut him loose before he tore up the rudder."

"By George, you guys in the tower are doin' one heck of a job today," snipes Borges from down on the bridge.

At 1300 hours our course still remains northwest. We haven't seen anything but unbroken ocean in two hours. For all that time John Clark has been shifting his weight rhythmically from one leg to the other. I find myself doing the same so that the tower actually vibrates. Borges leaves a clear trail of burned out cigarettes in our wake. Brownell is still rolling his shoulders. Fog has closed down the visibility to about a quarter of a mile. I can't imagine finding a whale out here, let alone a swordfish.

Borges joins Clark and me in the tower; the experienced men talk strategies. They say this is the day they need a spotter plane. Some of the other stick boats use them. The cost, $100 an hour and $200 for every fish the plane finds, really seems like small change when one considers how much searching a plane can do and how a single fish might earn the boat $2,000 to $4,000. But today fog grounds the spotter planes in Nantucket and Plymouth, and on fair days Brownell doesn't much want the planes' help. It doesn't quite seem like fair play. Still, he would use one, they say, if it makes the difference between landing a broadbill or having a busted trip.

Busted trip. The words sting. None of us wants to imagine that is what is coming; we cannot dwell on the idea that we may cover 350 miles of dangerous waters and spend over $500 for fuel just to come home empty. I hope we will take a skilly or shark or tuna or something before we tie up in front of all the critical wharf watchers in Mattapoisett with a busted trip. But who knows.

"Better not think about it," counsels Borges. I block out worry with a daydream about lions on a beach. They play like young cats in the dusk. I love watching them romp in my mind. Perhaps I have lifted the dream from one of Hemingway's fishermen, but borrowed or not, the lions help. They make me feel strong and at ease.

Suddenly Borges is shouting: "Three o'clock, five boats."

Brownell, wearing T-shirt and khakis, sprints to the pulpit, and takes the iron across his body, dart facing left because he's a southpaw.

"Where is he, where?" calls the harpooner.

Borges points 20 yards off the starboard bow.

"He's runnin'," shouts Clark.

Brownell lifts the harpoon over his head and leans his torso far out over the safety rail on the pulpit.

"Jasus, Tommy, Jasus, don't throw it," shouts Borges. "Easy, now, easy; we're comin' around." Now, Borges drives from the steering station in the tower. Clark and I point with extended arms at the shadow that is a fish.

The engine guns for a second. SHAN-LIN turns "down sun" on the fish.

"Here we go. Here we go. Nice fish, nice big fish," announces the harpooner.

The swordfish is a giant grease spot slipping toward the pulpit at three knots. Brownell stretches out over the pulpit and leads the fish with the dart. The right hand guides the shaft; the left palms the heel of the harpoon. Closer. Closer. Strike.

Just as the fish moves to the left of the pulpit, Brownell rises out and up, then thrusts the iron down into the water until he seems balanced on it like an acrobat. The broadbill never surfaces, nor does it sink; it takes all of the harpooner's weight even when he rises a second time on the shaft and drives down. Brownell looks within inches of falling overboard.

"He's nailed!" shouts the harpooner and falls back into the pulpit, pulling the shaft of his weapon away from the dart and line implanted in the fish. Whoops sound in the tower. I hear my own voice warbling involuntarily. Brownell jogs back off the long pulpit and up the foredeck, arms held in victory over his head. Clark climbs down from the tower, and he and Brownell slap hands—high five—like a pair of Pittsburgh Steelers.

"My God," I wonder as my body vibrates with adrenaline, "if harpooning a swordfish feels like this, harpooning a whale must feel like being struck by lightning!"

"Big sucka," says Clark.

"Finast kind," purrs Brownell.

Meanwhile the fish runs off to westward towing 60 fathoms of ⅜-inch nylon line and the orange ball. Out of sight.

"Goin' deep," surmises Borges. "Tryin' to run for home."

The deep dive and the tugging on the unsinkable ball take a toll on the wounded fish. Within 20 minutes the ball sits motionless on the water, and we cruise up alongside. We are all on the deck now. Borges gaffs the ball aboard and Clark begins hauling back the fish by hand, one coil of line at a time. This is a tug of war. Brownell takes over and twice has to let the Xiphias run off with nearly all of the line he has muscled aboard. It is liking watching Spencer Tracy in *The Old Man and the Sea*.

At last the fish begins to circle. Now the coils of line form in Brownell's hand. The muscles rise in a thick hump across his back. The line is so tight that the water jumps from it like champagne bubbles.

The fisherman talks to the fish, "Come on, boy, come on. You wanna kill me! We can't do this forever." His voice is low, almost intimate. In Spain I have heard matadors talk to bulls like this before driving the sword. "This is our fate," they say. "Let us help each other."

The fish cooperates. He circles closer, swimming steadily, without panic. Now the dorsal and the blue scythe of the tail cut the surface. He circles twice more off to port, then rolls on his side. For a second we are face-to-face with his great black eye, like a camera lens. On the third circle, barely moving now, the fish stops. It sinks right down beneath SHAN-LIN's stern.

"That's it," says Brownell. "He's had enough."

Within seconds Brownell has towed the fish up against the port quarter of the boat and John Clark lassos the broadbill's tail. We heave on block and tackle until all but the head of the fish stretches into the sky. It is a magnificent creature, but already the shimmering purple in its flanks has begun to fade to a grayish silver.

"Whatta monsta!" testifies Borges. "Watcha think, Johnny, easy 900 pounds, yeah?"

"A thousand if he's a pound," says Clark.

Brownell bends over the side and slits the great fish's throat. The water turns cherry red.

Minutes later Brownell holds four feet of the fish's sword in hand as he looks over the 11-footer.

"Beautiful fish," he beams, "terrific fighter."

Borges, Clark, and Brownell slap each others' hands—high five—again in victory.

"Great team," chants the harpooner, "great teamwork."

We all lend a hand soaking down the rocket-shaped carcass with buckets of sea water. Borges shovels on hundreds of pounds of cube ice from the ice chests and covers the body with wet canvas to keep it fresh until we can get to one of the buyers we've radioed to meet us on the wharf. Clearly, this is a ritual, and we keep our voices quiet. I try to imagine how Brownell must feel right now. For some reason I am reminded of the lions on the beach.

Suddenly Clark's voice breaks into my reverie.

"Nine o'clock, five boats!"

I stumble to attention. Maybe it's a whale. Beside me Clark sights the target and takes the tower steering wheel in hand. He turn us toward the fins off to the south. For a second he opens the throttle, but just as quickly he backs off. Another blue shark.

Someone curses. We circle the shark slowly—amazed by his size and absolute fearlessness. He rolls on his side and shows us man-eater's jaws.

"Wouldya just lookit," gasps Borges.

At first I think he is speaking about those jaws, but then I see him pointing out to sea. Within sight are a half-dozen stubby dorsals of full-grown blue sharks parting the dark water.

Brownell cuts the engine to idle.

"Who's for a swim?" he jokes.

The sharks move like indolent moths around us. It is as if we are not even here.

Unlike the harpooner I do not see the humor in this. Suddenly, a sense of euphoria and competition wells up inside me. I want to be like Melville's Queequeg; I want to be a harpooner. Before I know it I have opened my mouth and begun to speak: "Come on, let's take a shark with us."

Borges sweeps his hand toward the pulpit: "Be my guest."

The urge to prove myself, the call to battle, and the need to quell drive me to the brink of the pulpit before I look back at the three men on the bridge.

"Go ahead," says Brownell with no real encouragement in his voice. "I'll take you through it step-by-step."

A shark idles across our bows. Through the lattice work on the bowsprit I can see the muscle pack shift under his dorsal. I would drive the dart right there. If I did it well, I would pierce his heart or main arteries. A mortal wound. But still he would fight me, and maybe he would be so wild I would have to cut him loose to face a slow death or mutilation by his equals. At best I would have to cut his throat and wrestle him aboard.

"Hey, can you eat these guys, steak 'em up and grill 'em like swordfish?" I ask the crew.

Brownell shakes his head. No way.

Borges says blue shark flesh tastes like tire rubber.

My stomach gorges up in my throat, and try as I might, I can no longer think of a reason to kill. The muscles across my shoulders feel pierced by some enormous weight. Black spots rise before my eyes.

"Forget it," I say and walk back to the bridge.

If this shark cannot feed people, then why should he die? Haven't we all been party to enough sacrifice; isn't even a shark our brother?

"Aaaallll riiiight!" smiles Brownell. He steers the boat clear of the shark. "You're starting to catch on."

It is 1500 hours and SHAN-LIN's diesel barks alive. We are heading home to Mattapoisett. Clark hands out beers. The pacing, shoulder rolling, and swaying from one foot to the other has stopped. We sit in silence and drink with the great fish at our feet. Each of us is thinking his own thoughts. Perhaps about young lions playing on the beach.

Thick fog sets in. The harpooner says he can smell the whales spouting out here; they are all around us. We just can't see them.

As I retreated from my memory of harpoon fishing, I found myself still standing in the companionway aboard SARAH ABBOT as the first streaks of sunrise broke through the fog. The purr of the stick boat's engine was long gone, but I stared southeast along the route she took. My legs felt stiff, my shoulders heavy.

"What are you looking for?" Jackie's voice gave me a start, and I flinched involuntarily when her arm suddenly looped around my waist.

"I don't know," I said lamely. "Maybe I just need to get off this schooner and go for a jog." How could I tell her that I was awash in images of young lions on the beach and long, charcoal-colored whales blowing clouds of spray with great sighs? They slid beneath the waves like submarines.

XVIII   SIPPICAN HARBOR

The morning came on with a clear-air, cold-front passage that brought a sharp wind shift to the northwest. The crisp Canadian air mass settling over southeastern Massachusetts dried up the fog, put a tang in the air, and gave us unlimited visibility. From our mooring in Mattapoisett, I saw the hills of Martha's Vineyard rising on the horizon more than 18 miles away. A truly spectacular day. But after waking in the darkness and reliving my dreams of harpoon fishing, I passed the rest of yesterday in a kind of personal haze. Maybe I was simply groggy from a lack of sleep, but I think something else nagged at me too. Not the old free floating *saudade*, but something else—a goal, a dream. The thing, or part of the thing, that I had been searching for in history books and around this bay for weeks. I could almost see where I was headed. Name the final acts of humility, expiation, and courage that lay ahead. But not quite. My mind was in the clouds and I was more than a little glad I could count on having two other responsible adults aboard.

Despite my personal preoccupations, the day was one of the highlights of the cruise for our teenage crew. Having passed the primary test to become Dead Pirates by sleeping on deck, the crew was now ready to take on a new challenge. For different crews the second phase of Dead Pirates initiation takes different shapes, but the challenge always requires teamwork. Some crews have had to fish, collect mollusks, and prepare a dinner out of whatever they can find in nature; other crews have had to make due for a night after being stranded on a deserted island with essential equipment, food, and a communications radio.

This crew with its reliable seafaring skills faced a different hurdle. In

XIX   OFFSHORE

I guess I had sensed that this was coming. But I could no longer deny the impulse. Now, as Ahab said in *Moby Dick*, "The deed is done." Here we were, a small boat on a gray sea sailing west toward the coast of Massachusetts—homeward bound from a bluewater adventure. The wind came in blustery puffs out of the southwest, but the eight-foot swells rolled in from the southeast. There was a storm brewing somewhere near Bermuda. SARAH ABBOT climbed and slid between waves like small houses. We could see ten or twelve miles beneath a low cotton-like overcast, but no land had been in sight for twelve hours. Two of the students had been seasick after breakfast. Eventually they shrugged it off, and this afternoon they stood their watches with the rest of the crew as we beat toward shelter before the weather turned truly dirty.

Yesterday, like a thousand Buzzards Bay captains before me, I had forsaken the familiar shores of southeastern Massachusetts and struck off into the cold Atlantic with a green crew on what Ishmael called "the high and mighty business of whaling."

Although in other years *Oceans* cruises had traditionally spent a few days searching for and studying the herds of whales that gather off Cape Cod to feed during the summer, whales were not in the plan for this year. We had decided to forego a trip offshore to look for whales to allow time for our mission, a deep and thorough survey of the Bay. Furthermore, a dramatic shrinkage in the whale population had made allotting significant time and effort to hunt for whales a questionable commitment. Recent years had found the once plentiful summer whales, especially the gregarious humpbacks, reduced to just a few scattered animals as the whales'

mid-morning Jackie, John, and I appointed one of the girls in the crew watch officer and showed her the chart of Buzzards Bay. We told her to draw her crew together to come up with a safe plan for getting SARAH ABBOT underway and sailing her safely to Sippican Harbor (Marion), seven miles to the north. If the crew could get us there, we would adhere to the tradition of Yankee schooner crews and whalers, ending our cruise where it had begun to measure how time and tides had changed us.

In short order the watch officer divided up the responsibilities for steering, navigating, dropping the mooring, and setting sail. Jackie, John, and I watched as our student crew got the schooner underway safely without any help from us, hoisted sails, and began a reach east from the harbor into the Bay. To fetch Sippican Harbor in this northerly breeze, SARAH ABBOT had to sail close by the wind, beating back and forth up the Bay— first on port tack, then starboard. As the vessel sailed to windward with her lee rail awash and the hiss of foam echoed astern, the watch officer coordinated her crew, consulting with her navigator, the deck watch, and the helmsperson to plot her course on the chart and steer clear of ledges. When the navigator and watch officer agreed that the moment had come to tack, all the crew stood by to adjust the sheets when the command came down, "Prepare to come about. Ready about. Hard a lee."

"Hard a lee," echoed the girl at the helm as she spun the schooner's wheel and rolled the bow of the vessel through 95 degrees on the compass. Then—for about 10 seconds—SARAH ABBOT stood upright in the water until the wind caught the other side of her sails, she heeled over under the pressure, and gathered way again. Rounding Converse Point and heading toward Ram Island at the entrance to Sippican Harbor, I watched some of the crew smiling to themselves while others trimmed sheets and encouraged their shipmate at the helm.

"Put the boots to this baby," urged one of the boys as he watched the digital speedometer hovering around 7.6 knots.

The helmsperson worked SARAH ABBOT about five more degrees off the wind and the speed climbed: 7.7, 7.8, 7.9, 8.0.

The crew cheered. Before we reached Ram Island everyone stood one last trick at the helm. Then we dropped the jib, clicked on the engine, and motored through the narrow gut between Nyes Wharf and Ram Island as the crew dropped and furled the fore and the main. Two minutes later, we had picked up the mooring float near the north beach off Ram Island. Our schooner fell back on her heavy chain and swung to a 10,000-pound block of granite buried in the mud of Sippican Harbor. From the wharf on Ram Island, a woman in shorts and a tank top waved. Her four young boys looked up from rigging a small sailboat at the island wharf and chorused, "Welcome back, SARAH ABBOT!" Such was our homecoming.

As it turned out, this moment was not the last we saw of this woman and her boys. Her name was Hannah Moore, and after we secured the schooner's sails and tidied up the halyards and sheets, Hannah motored out to SARAH ABBOT in her red skiff and asked us if we would like to come ashore on the island to see one of the Bay's real heroes at work. Even without my explaining the significance of Hannah's invitation, the crew knew that this was an extraordinary invitation. Anyone who has ever been to Sippican Harbor has wondered at Ram Island. About the size of Tom Sawyer's Island at Disney World, Ram is a throwback to the days in the eighteenth and nineteenth centuries when Bay islands were the individual homesteads of families. Today, most of those islands had succumbed to developers like Sippican Harbor's Planting Island or reverted to wilderness under the protection of conservation groups. But Ram Island remains a private domain where the old stone and shingle house stands tucked between saltmarshes and a knoll of hardwoods. Hannah grew up on this island, and now she and her scientist husband Michael, whom we had visited at his lab in Woods Hole, were raising their boys here, commuting back and forth to the mainland with skiffs and a lobster boat. Except for Ram Island's exceptional geography, and its single-family ownership, there was nothing exclusive here. Donkeys as well as shaggy Newfoundland sheepdogs and gawky Russian wolfhounds roamed free. Mammoth colonies of fiddler crabs ruled the tidal flats; clams and oysters grew in

abundance along
forms. When you
you saw the parei
searching for sci
hard, you heard
tween the mothe

It was thes
invite our crew
known locally as
the five-week-old
back ospreys to
of Ram Island,
ladder propped

His wrinkl
resting on a nos
so closely. Fine
rested on the u
zipped up all tl
trousers barely l
tangled and wo
with age so his

When he
osprey under on
from becoming
talons or ruffl
gestures. Inste
holding the lar

He spoke
ring to them b
who. . . ." He re
eral war woun
birds. He told u
he tried to cap

limbs with razor-sharp t
most seemed boastful
banded had turned up
then returned here thre
born, making a migrati n as fully-frocked Dead

After clasping a b the early morning with
Fernandez handed the b ar, and cleaning SARAH
girls in our crew to hold last eleven days. Every-
a handkerchief at talon to the town dock. Then
learned that mature ma the van and others fin-
and will return to the sai gning the Dead Pirates
years in a row. Here they ce of prominence in the
then breeds with the m dled under the pavilion
grow so fast that Fernan r names into the plank
fore they get too big a dents sat huddled there
against the attacks of ag st each other, talking in
his right eye where a mo rsations between cellos.
were all part of a day's w "Let's go." So the crew
or a little dicey, but he l up in front of the boat.
are now over 400 nesti nd me. You couldn't tell
Fernandez knows most ded the voyage.
strategies, and migratory minutes after the crew

After we had watch nd with pictures of John
band a second bird befo rch, Ishmael, and even
Ram Island lobster boat, He couldn't get his mind
was definitely cool." ht that I knew just abou

"Going into the nes
birds could have ripped I
They were like tiger claw

"He's a survivor," ju
"Just like the osprey
"It felt so strong,"
fledging still twinkling ir

food sources had moved northeast into the Gulf of Maine. This July, whale

achusetts coast for the first

ic answer to this question
nts the crew was currently
d to see whales in the wild.
that I really could not un-
sailing in the wake of its
rstand the powerful lure of

why we were out here was
had become a bit obsessed
rent reports of gloom and
husetts whale watching, I
find a whale or two.
in search of cetacea, after
everal species, I craved the
aybe I was just a throwback
whaling cruise spoke to my
o the whaling grounds, the
nd then came the hunt—
aves for a blow, a spout, a
l fin, and perhaps the wave
ded. Finally, there was the
nd if the chase was success-

ful, there was the whale—50 to 100 tons of hungry, breathing creature—
as large or larger than the schooner.

Like me, that animal sometimes yielded to an abiding curiosity. Then the whale approached SARAH ABBOT. For a few moments, time stopped: the vessel and the whale cruised a parallel course. Sometimes you were close enough to touch each other or look into a fathomless, lidded eye, and wonder what mysteries it had seen. When you parted company, you had the long passage home to reflect on how the trip had changed a green crew and their captain. Finally—just maybe after this trip—you slept the dreamless sleep of a child again.

So it was for Cruise Three. Yesterday we shipped out from Sippican Harbor in the wake of the nineteenth-century Marion whalers like the PO-CAHONTAS, DRYADE, LEXINGTON, INDIAN QUEEN, ANNAWAN, and MARY ANN. We followed humbly in the tradition of captains like George Blankenship, Charles Beale, and Stephen Luce whose houses still stand along Main and Front Streets ashore in Sippican's Marion village. But instead of harpoons we packed cameras. In lieu of filling barrels, we have tried to capture whales on rolls of film.

In the golden age of whaling, Sippican whalers, like Melville's crew on the PEQUOD, sailed across the Atlantic, around Africa, through the Indian Ocean to the Pacific whaling grounds. Such voyages took three years; ours will have lasted three days.

Our cruise took us to one of Cape Cod's oldest and richest whaling grounds, Stellwagen Bank. This bank is a 30-mile half moon of gravel on the sea floor. It rises about 100 feet above the bottom of the deep basin spanning the entrance to Massachusetts Bay north of Cape Cod. Generally, bait fish gather here, particularly the sand eels or sand lance. Filter-feeding baleen whales like minkes, fins, and humpbacks crave sand lance, and the whales congregate on Stellwagen to feed as long as the schools of sand lance remain. Several years ago, in recognition of its importance to the whales, the federal government declared Stellwagen a national marine sanctuary.

Yesterday, the new crew with scientist Margaret Brumsted met Jackie, me, and SARAH ABBOT at Island Wharf, Sippican Harbor, Marion. In spite of a dank, smothering fog, the new crew bagged aboard with laughter and energy. Then I heard all of them cheer when one of their number urged, "Let the Dead Piracy begin!" At that moment I knew that I had a crew alive with the spirit of carpe diem, a crew primed to do extraordinary things. I told them about my hunch that I could find us some whales, and I confessed to them that whales had become a bit of an obsession with me. I also told them all about the risk and discomfort attendant to the long days at sea that lay at the heart of a whaling cruise. Then I gave them the choice of staying in Buzzards Bay for their whole cruise, highlighting how much we had to explore in the Bay. What was their choice?

"Whales!" cheered the crew.

So in late afternoon we set out on what promised to log 125 miles of sailing before we return to Marion again. We left under jib, mainsail, and motor with no better than a quarter mile visibility in the fog. Rounding Bird Island near the entrance to Sippican Harbor, we veered northeast into the Hog Island Cut and the shipping lane leading to the Cape Cod Canal. With the help of spring tides, the fair current raced at more than five knots and rocketed us through the 7.5-mile canal crossing the Cape's "shoulder." Meanwhile each member of the new crew stood a trick at the helm. They steered carefully and kept sharp lookout, practicing for the responsibilities that would come. When we cleared the east end of the canal, and the fog shut in around us again, a four-hour trip across Cape Cod Bay still lay ahead before we could anchor overnight at Provincetown on the tip of the Cape. Provincetown made a convenient staging area to rest and regroup before heading out into the deep blue in search of whales.

As night settled and the radar helped us to dodge freighters and tugs with tows westbound for the canal, the crew swaddled themselves in sweaters or slickers, gathered shoulder to shoulder in the cockpit, and sang old camp songs. They seemed particularly fond of the theme song from the classic TV comedy *Gilligan's Island*.

We broke out of the fog just a half mile south of the breakwater that sheltered Provincetown's inner harbor. As we headed up into the wind and furled sails, we could hear the sound of bass speakers pounding out a disco beat from dance clubs on shore. From this distance, the music seemed out of place with the village reflected in the twinkling lights. Cupped in the fishhook tip of Cape Cod, Provincetown was a thickly-settled clutch of gray-shingled buildings, white churches, wharves, and wooden fishing trawlers. They huddled at the base of a wooded hill from which rose the stone Pilgrim's Monument like the tower for an enormous castle.

"Party?" asked scientist Margaret Brumsted, who seemed in a liberated mood ever since coming back aboard after her two weeks of teaching ashore in Andover.

"It's Provincetown's middle name," I confirmed.

Since the first night when I visited it almost 30 years ago, the town had struck me as a place swinging to the rhythms of a perpetual Mardi Gras. Once this spot was the barren New World cape where the Pilgrims made their landfall after crossing the Atlantic in November 1620. But over the centuries this village at land's end had developed as a free-wheeling port for whalers, wreckers, and pirates. In the early-twentieth century, Portuguese fishermen gravitated here to drag the inshore waters, and a significant artist colony began to develop in this town where a laissez faire attitude was as traditional as clam chowder. Before gay couples held hands in public enclaves like San Francisco and Key West, homosexual lovers came to Provincetown to embrace openly.

Today, gays own more than three-quarters of the town's businesses, and Provincetown attracts crowds of gay summer vacationers to miles of empty beaches, a host of quaint B&Bs, restaurants, and bars. Straight crowds come to gawk and feel like they've had a walk on the wild side. On the long, narrow strand of Commercial Street, shoppers find boutiques selling everything from fine art to sex toys. A constant parade of hippies, bikers, drag queens, gay/lesbian couples, and wide-eyed straight folk fill the street. Provincetown also has more than its share of men and women sporting head bandannas, wild pony tails, tattoos, limps, and eye patches. More than once I have imagined confronting Long John Silver with a saber swinging at his side and a parrot on his shoulder ducking out of one of the low dives on Commercial Street.

So it was the twinkling lights and music of this pirates' den that beckoned to our crew as we set the anchor just clear of a sunken fishing dragger off the wharves at the heart of town. Once we had secured the schooner, I shuttled the crew ashore in the dinghy. Clearly, Provincetown qualified as an exotic port of call for our crew. By the time the crew returned to the schooner two of the males sported new earrings. They all had temporary tattoos of skulls and crossed bones on their arms, and they were bubbling over with stories about drag queens they had seen looking like Whitney Houston, Madonna, and Barbara Streisand.

Meanwhile I paced the deck like Ahab. For some reason I thought of the scary children's book by Maurice Sendak *Where the Wild Things Are* and thought, "Let the wild rumpus start!"

The next morning when we headed offshore in search of whales at 4:00 a.m., Jackie, Margaret, and I let the crew sleep while we got the anchor up and motored out of the harbor in the wake of three fishing draggers. Shortly after rounding Long Point and setting a course for the southwest tip of Stellwagen Bank about 15 miles out to sea, we set the sails. But the breeze was light so we kept the engine ticking. Minutes later Province-town's lights disappeared and, except for the blips of the fishing boats on the radar screen, we were alone in the fog.

As we cleared Race Point on the tip of Cape Cod, long ocean swells began to roll under SARAH ABBOT. Hours passed. Jackie cycled off watch and went back to her berth to rest. Margaret and I took turns steering the boat, navigating, and watching for traffic on radar. Eventually, one of the girls in the crew appeared wide-eyed on deck and volunteered to take over the helm. Dressed for the cold and the fog in a heavy sweater, ball cap and slicker, she already looked like a seasoned mariner. So we beat on.

At seven o'clock I roused the rest of the crew. We needed them to steer and keep watch. Experience told me that we would be in the whales' territory within the hour. As the crew ate their cereal and took their turns at the helm, an eerie quiet settled over the vessel. All you could hear was the subtle thrum of the engine and the wind in the sails. At some point a new sound broke the desolation: Yankee roused herself from sleep under the table in the main saloon, came on deck and began to sniff at the air, snort, and pace—her claws clicking against the deck. She smelled whales.

As the fog began to thin, we spotted the silhouettes of a line of tuna-fishing boats that had been sitting out here all night in the seas on the edge of Stellwagen Bank. The fishermen were hoping that one of the schools of giant bluefin tuna would come afoul of the fleet's lures on their annual pilgrimage over the bank and into Cape Cod Bay to feed. If the tuna were here to feed, a whale would probably be too. So with the visibility improving to 200 yards we began to search, sailing a zigzag pattern as SARAH ABBOT worked her way to the northeast along the western edge of Stellwagen. Everyone was on deck—clinging to the halyards that run up and down the masts—looking for a cloud of vapor from a whale's blow, a dark back and dorsal fin breaking the surface, or the Wilson's storm petrels, small black and white birds that follow the whales and feed on the leftovers.

"Whale up, two o'clock, a half mile," called a girl from the bow— with the position and distance of the animal—just as I had instructed the crew. A few seconds later I saw a small minke, maybe 20 feet long, break the surface for a breath of air. The whale was the color of the gray ocean, and it was racing away from us to the east.

I had to make a drastic change of course to keep the minke in sight, and the commands went forward to the crew: "All hands, heads up. Stand by your sailhandling stations; prepare to jibe; jibe ho!"

I spun the wheel, The schooner veered east and then the sails jibed from one side of the vessel to the other. Amid the clatter and commotion of the jibe, we lost the minke in the fog. Up on the foredeck someone swore. He spoke for us all.

So the search began again. An hour or more passed. The crew sagged in the sweaters and slickers at their lookout stations. Then, suddenly, Yankee began to sniff the air and pace the deck again. Suddenly, a whale surfaced with a burst of air that sounded like steam rushing from a boiler. As the whale's V-shaped head started to submerge, its dark back arched slowly, and foot-by-foot a body that seemed as big as a submarine showed itself above the waves. Finally, the dorsal fin broke the surface and made a perfect triangle against the sky before sliding back beneath the waves. About eight feet beneath the surface, we could see a massive tail fanning the water into a boiling eddy—the whale's "foot print"—as it slid out of sight.

I gave the helm to Margaret and told her to hold her course as I climbed into the lower rigging of the mainmast to get a better view of the whale. From 15 feet up, I could see the dark form of the whale patrolling about 10 feet below the surface. With the magnification of the water the whale looked substantially longer and wider than SARAH ABBOT. At least 60 feet long. Focusing my eyes, I could see the white scythe marking on the whale's lower right jaw clearly identifying this animal as the so-called greyhound of the sea, balaenoptera physalus, known as the common rorqual or, most often, a fin whale, close cousin of the largest animal on the planet, the blue whale. I could see its dark right eye scanning our schooner.

The presence of this fin whale gave us a clue as to what bait fish were in the area to attract whales in light of a reported absence of sand lance. The most likely answer was herring, schools of herring. Fin whales love the critters, and we would probably find the remains of herring in the samples of orangish whale feces we scooped up to analyze. A whale this size needs more than a ton of herring a day to stay healthy, and usually the single-minded pursuit of such a banquet kept a fin swimming its search patterns much faster than most boats can follow. Clocked at speeds of over 25 knots, fin whales were not popular with nineteenth-century whalers who generally considered fins to be shy, elusive animals. An oft-spoken judgment of fin whales heard among whalers and whale researchers is "now you see one; now you don't." Only once before had I seen a fin at such close range, and she was a mother lingering close to the schooner to protect a slow-swimming calf dawdling nearby. Now, here we were with the second largest specie of animal in the world swimming in formation with us, barely 10 feet off our port rail. At 30-second intervals its head broke the surface to breath. The crew steadied themselves with their hands on the halyards and clicked away with their cameras.

Then, suddenly, I saw the whale make a sharp lunge as its body turned toward SARAH ABBOT and picked up speed.

"It's going to hit us," shouted one of the crew.

I saw one girl grasp the foremast. A boy looked like he was saying his prayers.

"Hold your course," I called to Margaret at the helm.

From my perch in the rigging, I saw the animal's dark body begin to slide under the schooner. Three seconds later the whale rose within 10 feet of the boat on the starboard side. Water poured off its back like rushing streams, and we could see the scars on its fin and sides where the animal had been bitten and slashed by killer whales. Suddenly, the animal rolled on its right side, and for two or three seconds its left eye broke the surface of the water and held SARAH ABBOT and the crew and me in its stare locking pictures of us in its memory. Then the whale dropped its head, arched its back a bit and exhaled. A cloud of fishy vapor settle over the schooner.

"Yes!!!" I shouted. And for several seconds I felt the long gasps of the fin's deep breaths wash through me like a geyser.

"This is it; this is what my whole summer of searching has been leading up to!" I thought.

But this was not the climax of some kind of Native American vision quest. There was no moment when the Wampanoags' manitous struck me with a lightning bolt. No curtain of surface reality peeled away to offer me a glimpse into the very soul of life or even New England history. No such luck. I saw no vision. Just a schooner drenched with about 20 gallons of whale snot. It took my breath away. And then I felt my whole face curling into a silly grin like a kid caught with his hand in the cookie jar. I just couldn't help it.

Meanwhile the creature accelerated to the west. You could hear its lungs working like slow, enormous bellows as it vanished into the fog. Nobody spoke.

One of the crew wrote in his journal:

"Now, after seeing my first whale, I can relate to the reasons why young boys have always gone to sea. I understood how they had a desire to seek their dreams and find themselves in the face of these waves and mighty monsters. I can make the connection to my forefathers because I felt nervous, a little afraid, and small when I confronted a whale and the wide green ocean for the first time."

Theodore Tripp, the last of the old whalemen of Sippican, had felt the same. He once said in an interview:

"You know, I'd never seen a whale until I was in the boat pullin' and one of the ugly critters come right up alongside me. I jumped and Jarvis sez—You know Jarvis Blankenship. He's the mate I told you weighed me and said I didn't weigh more than a dried codfish—Well, Jarvis sez, 'What's the matter Tripp? What you 'fraid of? Next time he comes up that way you spit in his eye!'"

In your dreams, Jarvis.

Now, with the whale gone and the schooner making slow progress back toward the coast of Massachusetts, I left Jackie in charge of the deck watch and retired to my berth to give my eyes a rest. But I could not sleep. I found myself wondering how far we were pushing the envelope of safety by being out here in the fog with creatures who could turn SARAH ABBOT into kindling in seconds. I had sailed among whales dozens of times and never felt particularly vulnerable even when large humpbacks brushed their noses against our trailing dinghies, swam under the schooner, or lay alongside waving a pectoral fin in the air. Close enough to touch. But, today, replaying the moment when that fin whale swam under the boat kind of took my breath away again. I wasn't grinning. I stood in awe of an animal that can swim the North Atlantic for a hundred years, stretch almost twice as long as most whales I've seen, and weigh 60 to 70 tons—almost four times as much as the schooner.

Like almost all the whales I have met, this fin was friendly, curious, and clearly conscious of avoiding a collision with our vessel. But whales have sometimes been the nemeses of those who pursue them. *Moby Dick* is not purely fiction. The novel's plot roots in the story of the whaler ESSEX that was deliberately rammed and sunk by a sperm whale in the South Pacific in 1820. And Melville's malevolent white whale has its origins in that real light-skinned sperm whale known as Mocha Dick. The animal allegedly sunk three ships and caused the death of 30 men before he died at the hands of Amos Smalley in 1859.

As my mind unraveled around the perils of a whaling voyage, I recalled a flood of tragedies. I remembered the story of the HECTOR that sailed from New Bedford in 1832. Ninety days out of port the crew sighted a sperm whale and lowered their whale boats for the chase. But hardly had the chase begun when the whale turned on the mate's boat and stove it just as the harpooner was planting his lance. The crew had to wrap a sail under the hull and bail to keep the boat afloat before continuing the chase. Meanwhile the captain's whale boat moved in for the kill, but the whale turned on the boat and snapped it to pieces in its jaws. Rescuing the captain's crew, the mate's boat gave chase again, but once again the whale turned on the boat and chased it for a half mile or more snapping its toothed jaws within six or eight inches of the boat. Finally, the whalers succeeded in driving a lance through the whale's vitals and killing it. Upon cutting into the carcass, the crew found two irons belonging to the ship BARCLAY whose first mate had lost his life in an encounter with this whale.

The story of the loss of ANN ALEXANDER from New Bedford in 1850 was even more terrifying. Launching the whale boats on a herd of sperm whales on the so-called Off-Shore Ground, the mate's boat was soon fast to a victim when the whale turned, rushed the boat, took it in its jaws, and smashed it to fragments. The chase continued with two other boats, and soon a second boat had been chewed to pieces like the first. After rescuing the crews of the wrecked boats, the third boat beat a retreat to the ship. The whale followed and so the crew continued its hunt from the ship, driving a lance into the sperm whale's head as it drew near. But this strike was not a killing blow, and the whale charged the ship. On the first charge, the vessel veered into the wind to escape a collision. On a second charge the whale struck the ANN ALEXANDER abeam the foremast and shook her like she had struck a rock. Water poured into the ship, and the crew abandoned her at night to drift in their fragile whale boats for days before rescue.

The crew of the UNION out of Nantucket was not so lucky. Just 12 days out of port en route to the Brazil Banks, the UNION accidentally struck on a sperm whale and smashed the timbers of her starboard bow. By the middle of the night the pumps would no longer hold and the water rose between decks. Ultimately, the crew of 16 abandoned ship in their whale boats. For the next eight nights they weathered gales, famine, and dehydration before reaching the Azores.

Could such a thing happen here and now? Who knew? In these very waters between Plymouth and Cape Ann a legendary sea serpent know as scoliophis atlanticus was twice sighted between 1815 and 1817. A report judged it "between 80 and 90 feet in length and about the size of a half-barrel" with a "head as large as the head of a horse." It had "50 distinct portions out of water at one time" and moved "at a rate of a mile in two or in at least three minutes. A tongue like a harpoon" flicked from its mouth.

I am no believer in sea serpents. Scoliophis atlanticus was probably a giant squid, a creature of the continental shelf that found itself blown in-shore by storms. But whether it was a serpent or a squid, images of its giant writhing body tormented me. Like that fin whale today and the stories of whalers' disasters I remembered, scoliophis atlanticus reminded me how much of a foreigner I was out here at sea. So why was I out here? Why did it feel so good even when I was dog-tired and a little scared?

Those were questions better not gotten into here and now. Sometimes a sailor's berth on an offshore passage can be a dangerous place to be alone with one's thoughts. A wise captain would do well to limit his hours below decks at sea. Better to spend one's time making sure we had a sharp watch on deck or passing out a bag of chocolate chip cookies to nourish the crew. We had miles to go before we slept.

XX MARION

SARAH ABBOT arrived back in Marion last evening after an overnight stop at Scituate in Cape Cod Bay. The crew spent yesterday catching up on the science reading and consulting about their cruise projects with Margaret as we made a long, slow sail to the east end of the Cape Cod Canal at Sandwich, a passage through the canal, and finally a six-mile bash to windward in Buzzards Bay before reaching home. As we turned north for the last leg of the trip back to Sippican Harbor, it occurred to me that a schooner's return to this harbor after a whaling cruise is nothing new to Marion Village.

Unlike the neighboring deep-water harbors of New Bedford and Mattapoisett, Sippican never depended on a large fleet of barks and brigs to circle the globe for whale oil and bring wealth to the village. From the early days of seafaring from this port, sailors recognized that Marion's shallow Sippican Harbor, less than eight feet deep in many places and with its narrow entrance between Ram Island and Nyes Wharf, is better suited to moderate-draft, nimble schooners than deep, lumbering offshore whalers. Many Sippican mariners have been schoonermen, and during the nineteenth century the harbor developed a tradition of sending their cargo schooners out on summer whaling voyages. A hundred and fifty years ago men like Captain Ben Handy, proprietor of Handy's Tavern on Front Street, made more money going summer whaling than he did at his thriving pub. In 1854 Ben Handy's schooner ADMIRAL BLAKE returned to Sippican and landed a cargo of blackfish (pilot whales) and sperm oil worth $11,000 after a two-month trip. The schooners ALTAMAHA and JAMES came home to Sippican Harbor with similar earnings.

As SARAH ABBOT worked her way around Bird Island, skirted Centerboard Shoal, and eased sheets for the final two miles of the trip yesterday evening, a thick low fog began to shroud us. We could see the blue evening sky overhead, but a white blanket, perhaps 30 feet deep, cut our lateral visibility to almost nothing. The radar scope showed a dozen vessels coming and going from Marion so prudence dictated that I call all hands on deck to keep a sharp eye out for traffic. At one point the bow watch sung out, and we saw the tops of another schooner's sails floating in the glow of the setting sun above the fog bank about 30 yards to port while the hull of the vessel remained totally invisible. Looking at the ghostly floating sails stirred thoughts in me of another two-master with Marion ties named the MARY CELESTE, the most famous ghost ship in American history.

The story of the MARY CELESTE had always raised questions among mariners who tell each other disaster tales as a way of schooling themselves in the whys and the wherefores of tragedies at sea. But here in Marion the story shimmered with the faces of the missing and the dead. Secluded among the pines and arborvitae on a knoll rising above Pleasant Street in the heart of the village stood perhaps one of the saddest places on all of Buzzards Bay. For at least a century this was the site of Captain Nathaniel Briggs' Rose Cottage before it burned. Five of the six children that Briggs and his wife raised here in the mid-1800s died at sea, taking spouses and a child with them.

Violent death stalked the family. Having survived a life at sea, Captain Nat died when lightning struck him as he stepped outdoors at Rose Cottage one June afternoon. Not only did the Captain's wife lose her husband to an act of nature, but she also lost her daughter on a whaling voyage with her captain spouse in 1859. Son Nathan succumbed to yellow fever on a ship in the Gulf of Mexico. Yet, despite these tragedies that might have persuaded another family to stay at home and avoid risks, two of Captain Nat's sons, Oliver and Ben, continued tempting fate as merchant captains.

In 1872, hoping to make money carrying Mediterranean fruit back to New York, the two brothers planned a cruise to Barcelona, Spain, with each man sailing a separate ship. Oliver started first from New York in early November aboard the family-owned JULIA A. HALLOCK and planned a stop in the Azores. Ben followed on November 7 with his wife Sarah and toddler daughter aboard a new ship in which he had an interest. The vessel was the MARY CELESTE, a 200-ton brigantine, a two-master rigged with square sails on her foremast instead of a fore-and-aft sail like SARAH ABBOT. The brigantine's cargo hold was full of barrels of alcohol worth $36,000. She carried a crew of eight men plus the woman and child.

Captain Ben's log found aboard the MARY CELESTE tells of a rough weather passage. But the ship made her way safely across the Atlantic, sighting the island of St. Mary's on November 25 as she passed south of the Azores into the Bay of Biscay. What happened aboard the MARY CELESTE during the next 10 days has been the subject of 125 years of speculation.

On December 5 the Nova Scotian ship DEI GRATIA came upon the MARY CELESTE in a curious state, sailing fitfully in rough seas 500 to 600 miles east of the Azores. The jib and foretopmast staysail were set. The lower foretopsail slatted from the yards. The upper foretopsail, the foresail, and some of the running rigging seemed to have been carried away. The main staysail had been hauled down and lay across the forward deck house. All of the rest of the sails were furled as you would expect in a vessel rigged for heavy weather sailing.

Concerned by the fitful progress and damaged look to the brigantine's sails, the master of the DEI GRATIA hauled up alongside and prepared to "speak the vessel" in order to render assistance. Hailing the vessel, the DEI GRATIA got no response, and sent the mate and his men to board the MARY CELESTE. Seen close up, the situation on the brigantine was even more unsettling. No one was aboard. The forward house which included the galley was awash with 9 to 12 inches of water, the ship had three and a half feet of water in her bilge, but the pumps were in good order, and the hull seemed new. The cargo was intact and well-stored in the hold. In Captain Ben Briggs' cabin the mate found the "clothing, furniture, etc.—the bed was just as they had left it." The seamen had left their oilskins, boots, and even their pipes. The log and charts were aboard, but the ship's register, chronometer, sextant, and navigation books were missing. The mate also noticed a child's toys and "the impression in the Captain's bed as of a child having lain there." Under the captain's bed, the mate found an Italian sword in its scabbard, but "there was nothing remarkable about it." Nevertheless, the MARY CELESTE had seen some violence: the compass binnacle had been stove in. There was also a sharp cut in the rail as if done by an ax. Why?

The mate, who ultimately sailed the derelict to Gibraltar with a crew of two from the DEI GRATIA to claim salvage rights, surmised that the MARY CELESTE "had been left in a great hurry" as the ship's boat was missing and so many personal belongings remained. He guessed that after weeks of heavy weather, the crew had sounded the pumps and found sufficient water in the bilge to make them think that they should abandon the ship before she sunk.

But in the admiralty court at Gibraltar where the DEI GRATIA claimed salvage rights, and on the docks of the world where the story was told, seasoned mariners were skeptical. Seamen argued that no sane captain and crew abandon a virtually new ship at sea. The first rule of seamanship is to stick with your vessel as long as possible for she will probably ride out a spell of rough weather better than the human body and spirit. And who would leave a ship with a valuable cargo and good pumps to risk a small open boat passage in the fierce conditions that are legendary on the Bay of Biscay in winter? Not a seasoned skipper and shrewd businessman like Marion's Ben Briggs, said the waterfront wags.

So the speculation began about what had caused the loss of the crew aboard the MARY CELESTE. Pirates. Mutiny. Sea serpents that can sweep the decks of humans. A captain grown crazy from dirty weather and the responsibility of his wife and child aboard. What had smashed the binnacle and chopped the gash in the rail? Was that blood or rust on the Italian sword found in the captain's cabin? Had there been a problem with the cargo? Had the alcohol given off vapors that had begun to rumble in the hold with the onset of the warm weather that you might get southeast of the Azores? Fear of explosion: that was a reason to abandon ship in a hurry . . . especially if a crew thinks they are within a day's smallboat journey of the Azores as the MARY CELESTE surely was when Ben Briggs made his last log entry.

Meanwhile, back in Marion Captain Ben's mother waited for word from her sons. Surely, Ben, Sarah, and the baby would turn up rescued or in the Azores and return to Marion on another ship. But no news came. And Captain Oliver and the JULIA A. HALLOCK were overdue in Barcelona as well.

At last word came from Europe. The second mate from the HALLOCK had been rescued from a floating deck hatch in the Bay of Biscay; for four days he had shared that hatch with Captain Oliver Briggs, but growing too weak, the captain had washed away just hours before help arrived. The mate said that the HALLOCK had met a storm after leaving the Azores with 50 tons of coal. The storm had set the ship to leaking, and the crew had not been able to keep up with the leaks because coal dust had clogged the pumps until the ship filled with water and foundered. Perhaps the same storm that claimed Oliver Briggs and the HALLOCK took the lives of Captain Ben, his family, and his crew. But after 125 years there is not a scrap of evidence.

There was a fanciful, illustrated map of Marion that was popular with visitors in the village gift shops these days. One of the curiosities on the map was a drawing of the MARY CELESTE anchored off Seal Rocks outside Sippican Harbor with a homecoming pennant flying. Passing Seal Rocks on a misty evening such as we had on our own homecoming, that map came to mind, and I pictured Captain Ben, his family, and his brigantine sailing home at last.

Well, isn't it pretty to think so?

Instead of tying SARAH ABBOT off her mooring at Ram Island at the head of the harbor, we made our homecoming in the style of Captain Ben Handy and his schooner the ADMIRAL BLAKE. We brought our vessel right into the small cove at the center of town between the arms of Island Wharf to the north and the Old Landing to the south where the figurehead from the AD-MIRAL BLAKE had decorated one of the granite piers for decades. As we picked up a mooring in the cove, the crew sang loudly. Once again we had choruses of the theme song from *Gilligan's Island*. No denying it, we were crowing. All of us felt the rush of adrenaline in our veins that accompanies a homecoming after a voyage made good.

While the crew charged ashore to use the public showers at Island Wharf and fill themselves with treats at Ginny's ice cream parlor, Jackie, Margaret, and I sat in the cockpit with mugs of tea and felt the press of history around us. During the last two centuries these wharves around the cove had unloaded untold barrels of whale oil and, even more important for the local economy, shipped thousands, perhaps millions, of tons of salt. As a part of the Wampanoags' lands of Sippican and colonial old Rochester, Marion shares its early history with Mattapoisett, but while Mattapoisett distinguished itself during the late eighteenth and early nineteenth century as a shipbuilding center, Marion made its mark with salt.

Probably old Rochester's early colonists made salt for personal consumption and preserving meat and fish by boiling off Bay water: from 300 gallons of Bay water, you can produce a bushel of fine seasoning. But salt making grew from a cottage industry to a business after the British trade embargoes against the colonies on the eve of the American Revolution. Not able or willing to import salt from the British West Indies or Europe, America searched for its own sources for the all-important preservative and found the resources and skills on the north shore of Buzzards Bay. Initially, local salt makers followed in the tradition of their ancestors, cutting wood and burning fires around the clock to boil off Bay water. But with a large demand for salt, firewood soon became scarce. So colonists studied the West Indies and French salt industries. In the West Indies, salt came from damming up sea water on sand flats and letting the sun evaporate the water. Such a technique was efficient in a tropical environment where the sun shone virtually every day. But in temperate New England where only half the days are sunny, the evaporation process needed technological help to make it efficient. In consideration of this problem, Captain John Sears noted that the French—with a climate similar to New England's—made salt using a series of vats for decanting the brine, and

Sears suggested that the French method might be modified to work on the shores of Buzzards Bay.

Enters the windmill. Mattapoisett and Marion salt makers realized that Buzzards Bay's windy weather could be harnessed to drive windmills that would in turn pump water through hollow logs to vats about 15 feet square. Salt makers accelerated the evaporation process by pumping liquid through a series of four vats. In each vat the denser brine settled to the bottom, and the water was drained off the top before pumping the ever-thickening brine to a new vat. When the brine reached the fourth vat, pure salt precipitated from the solution and settled to the bottom of the vat to be collected when the liquid was drained off. To protect the drying vats from nightly dew and inclement weather, salt makers constructed tall wooden cranes to swing roofs over the salt works. Such structures mingled with fields of windmills that sprouted all along the peninsulas, coves, and harbors that stretched from the western edge of Mattapoisett to Marion during the first three decades of the nineteenth century. Some years more than 20,000 bushels of salt rolled aboard local schooners in hogshead barrels for shipping up and down the East Coast. But the industry collapsed as ice became the preferred means to preserve foods.

With the demise of the salt market, some of the salt works on the shores of Sippican Harbor evolved into boatyards for the building of coasting schooners, brigantines, and small craft. Barden's Boat Yard on the cove where SARAH ABBOT now swung to a mooring is one the last survivors from the days when virtually every family in Marion Village could claim a captain and a boatwright as kin. While the yard's proprietor Fred Colson now makes much of his revenue hauling yachts to distant places on semi-trailers, the yard still supports craftsmen like Paul White and Paul Zychowicz who pursue the traditional Bay livelihood of boat carpenter. Wooden boats like SARAH ABBOT are rare here today so Barden's craftsmen have turned their woodworking skills on the interiors of fiberglass yachts. Now, instead of scraping, sanding, fairing, and painting wooden hulls, the boat mechanics work in climate-controlled sheds repairing and repainting fiberglass boats with exotic polymers like Awlgrip. Nevertheless,

Barden's Boat Yard and the cove retain strong visual echoes from the days in 1852 when the village on Sippican Harbor separated from old Rochester and renamed itself Marion after the revolutionary hero Francis Marion, the Swamp Fox.

Savoring the peace on the schooner that came with the crew at liberty ashore, Margaret, Jackie, and I felt surrounded by an earlier century. Dominated by Barden's gray-shingled office that recalls a counting house at an old packet landing, the grass-covered marine railway, and the wooden rigging crane, the cove began to look like an anachronism to us, especially when our eyes turned to the houses to the south. Lining the irregular twists and turns of the seawall stretching from the boatyard to the wharves of the Old Landing, stood a clutch of shingled, barn-like houses that ooze New England seaport ambiance.

One of these old treasures was a rambling, red cedar affair raised on a pale-colored granite foundation and pilings which give the house the appearance of floating in the air when the evening shadows obscure the lower supports. Not so long ago, the house rested on the ground next to its neighbors, but the owners raised the house after Hurricane Bob inundated Marion's lowlands, the boatyard, and the house with a tidal surge more than seven feet above the high tide line. Now looking at the raised old house always reminded me of that hurricane that destroyed millions of dollars of property in Buzzards Bay and drove hundreds of moored boats ashore in Sippican Harbor in 1991.

But this house also reminded me of something more. It was the primary setting in *A Storm Without Rain*. Bearing the name Carter & Son Boatworks in the novel, this house was both the home and boatshop for three generations of the central character's family. It was from this house in contemporary Marion that 15-year old Jack Carter left before a storm without rain hit Buzzards Bay like Hurricane Bob and whirled Jack backwards in time until he found himself adrift in the Bay world of 1904. And it was to this house that Jack returned to meet his grandfather and grandmother as contemporaries, live the life of an apprentice boatbuilder, and plot his return to the present.

When the crew came back aboard SARAH ABBOT, I pointed out the shadowy house and told them about its place in Adkins' novel about time travel. For several minutes the crew sat silently, and I found myself wondering what elbows in time they were visiting in their dreams. Finally, one girl disappeared below deck. Returning topside with her sleeping bag and a copy of *A Storm Without Rain*, she headed for the broad plane of the foredeck. In short order her shipmates followed with their own sleeping bags and copies of the book. Soon they huddled together on the foredeck like a litter of puppies, and by the beam of a flashlight the crew began to read aloud to each other: "All this I am about to tell you happened a long time ago, but sometimes I think it was only last August. . . ." Boy, did I know that feeling!

Our own storm hit about 2:30 in the morning. I woke to the rumble of thunder and flashes of lightning that lit the inside of the schooner like strobe lights. Then I heard the stampede of the crew as they hustled themselves and their gear below decks, before the wind began driving the rain against the deck and hull like machine gun fire. Generally free of deck leaks, the schooner soon yielded to the pressure of 50-knot winds driving the rain *under* the canvas boots cinched around the bases of the masts to keep out the weather. Soon, water began running down the masts to torment the girls trying to get back to sleep on the lower berths in the forecastle. As the storm shook the schooner and set her sawing back and forth on her mooring, we stretched garbage bags over threatened areas of the girls' sleeping bags. But between the rumble of thunder and lightning zapping nearby trees and boats in the harbor, I heard the girls groaning, and I knew that they were getting wet. All of us were beginning to feel like we lived on the bottom of the harbor. As the air grew saturated with moisture, water began condensing on our skin and everywhere else. I pulled on a pair of oil skins over my shorts, and scrambled topside. First, I checked the mooring. Then, I rigged a spare shroud trailing into the water to back up the boat's built-in grounding system and protect us from a lightning strike. The air reeked of ozone. Later, I sat in the shelter of the companionway with the hatch closed and watched the lightning and wind white-washing the harbor.

Finally, I squeezed into my wife's berth and wrapped her in my arms. When we awoke, the gray light of sunrise was in my eyes. Wet hair plastered over my face as if I had been swimming with whales in my dreams.

Now, I realized that going whaling had not been enough for me: not even sailing in the wake of Ishmael and my great great uncle, keeper of the family harpoon, could permanently calm my restlessness this summer. But if my restlessness was not simply leading me toward a whaling adventure, then what? I still had no clue. But I knew that the trip offshore to find whales and this homecoming had marked some essential passage for me. Like windjamming to Hideaway Cove. Another turning point.

Damp skin and itchy clothing had been part of this crew's existence since we had set off after whales days ago. After a crew lives this soggy life on a boat for long enough—no matter how adventurous their spirit—they eventually crave the land, a warm freshwater shower, and a dry roof. So, as fast as we could, Jackie, Margaret, and I got the crew ashore to the Beverly Yacht Club which opened its showers and a corner of the warm, dry clubhouse on Water Street to our crew. Here, the crew cleaned themselves, changed into dry clothing, and had a biology class with Margaret while Jackie and I toted bags of soggy clothes, towels, and sleeping bags to the local Laundromat for drying. By the time Jackie and I returned to the club with steam still rising from the rejuvenated gear, the students were taking a study break, teasing, and laughing with each other as they sipped cups of tea and milkshakes purchased at the club's snack bar.

Hardly had Jackie and I had a chance to drop our bags of gear, when one of the boys in the crew said, "This place doesn't feel anything like the town we read about last night in *A Storm Without Rain*."

The remark knocked me off balance. First, it seemed apropos of nothing to do with dry laundry—the focus of everyone's attention. And, second, during the last 12 hours I thought all of the crew had begun to feel as if we had somehow slipped into the past, into the world of the novel. Where was this guy coming from?

Then I looked out the club window and began to understand. Seated at a table ordering lunch in his tennis whites sat Geraldo Rivera and his wife. At the table next to the TV celebrity, sat the actor James Spader and two men who had "$500-an-hour-Boston-lawyer" written all over their pinstriped shirts. Across the harbor, long green lawns stretched between the water and monumental houses in a pastiche of styles ranging from Tudor and Victorian to contemporary and Southwest ranchero.

"Well," I drew in my breath preparing to respond. "Fashion and money have come to Marion."

The crew grew interested as I began explaining how Marion became a haven for the rich and famous. It all started more than 100 years ago. Following the Civil War and the decline of whaling and salt making, Marion went into economic decline. Grass grew on the wharves, houses went unpainted, and families moved away. Retired captains killed time telling sea stories at the Old Landing and casting a critical eye on everything. This was the town Elizabeth Pitcher Taber found when she returned to her native village in 1872 after a half century of life in New Bedford. A widow grown rich on family investments in ships, whaling, cotton mills, and bank stock, Taber found herself with no heirs. Suddenly, her heart felt moved by the shabbiness settling on her town. Finding she had the desire and means to bring a snap of culture to her home village, Taber began donating money for public institutions. First, she built a library and museum of natural history, then a private school, and finally a town hall.

Now, 125 years later, it is the school which she named Tabor Academy—spelling her name with an "o" for Mt. Tabor in Palestine—which has done most to add a sophisticated tone to Marion. Once a single building, Tabor Academy dominates the western shore of the inner harbor and its adjacent lands with academic buildings, dormitories, dining hall, chapel, athletic fields, and facilities for a first-class smallboat sailing program. In addition, the school's 92-foot sail-training schooner TABOR BOY calls the harbor home, while the shore facilities serve more than 500 high school students and faculty.

But polish, prestige, and wealth have accrued slowly to Tabor Academy. More than a century ago factors other than this prep school had more to do with Marion's entry into the world of fashion and celebrity. Simply put, Marion was discovered around 1880 by some of the most prominent people in the realms of American literature, art, and politics. First, the celebrated New York City poet/editor Richard Watson Gilder came to Marion looking for a place to rusticate and hide from the madding crowd. He fell in love with the landscape and the serenity. Gilder and his wife bought an old whale oil factory and turned it into a studio where great painters of the day like Augustus Saint-Gaudens could work and the literary crowd, including Henry James, could trade *bon mots*. Then Henry James added to the village's mystique when he made Marion the site of a romantic getaway in his novel *The Bostonians* (1886).

James celebrated Marion as "a little straggling, loosely clustered town [that] lay along the edge of a blue inlet, on the other side of which was a low wooded shore, with a gleam of white sand where it touched the water. The narrow bay carried a vision outward to a picture that seemed at once bright and dim—a shining slumbering summer sea, and a far-off circling line of coast which, under the August sun, was hazy and delicate. It was a town where you smelt the breath of the hay in the streets and you might gather blackberries in the principal square."

But one event trumped even Henry James' romantic description of Marion, when it came to putting the village in the national eye. In the summer of 1887 the young, attractive wife of President Grover Cleveland came to Marion by train to vacation at the Old Landing home of the famous Arctic explorer General Adolphus Greely. Suddenly, Marion swarmed with media, and the spotlight continued for each successive summer of the President's term as Mrs. Cleveland returned to hobnob with local society and the Gilders' summer crowd of artists and literati. Then after losing his bid for reelection, Grover Cleveland rented a house on Water Street and retired to the Bay for four years to fish and plot his second successful bid for the White House. The rich and famous from New York and Boston followed. Real estate prices ballooned, and summer mansions began sprouting all along what had been the deserted shores of the eastern side of the harbor. The old seaport had changed forever.

Despite the strong presence of wealth and celebrity, Marion has not evolved into a village of boutiques and restaurants for the leisure class like many of the old ports on Cape Cod. Marion remains a working town, and a place where marine tinkers, inventors, and explorers still feel at home. To draw such a conclusion our crew might have visited sailmakers at work in a loft by the Old Landing or hiked along Benson Brook Road to see boatwrights at David Knott's Inshore Boatshop rebuilding classic wooden sailboats from the keel up. Near the boat shop we could have discovered the cutting edge of maritime tinkering and invention at the sprawling labs of Sippican Inc., where engineers work on twenty-first century technology for the U.S. Department of Defense.

When the weather cleared, the crew found vital evidence of serious marine endeavors in the Marion townhall. The crew met Joe Costa, Executive Director of the Buzzards Bay Project, at his organization's offices and came face to face with an environmental scientist making a career of exploring Buzzards Bay and fighting pollution. Before meeting Costa, I think all of us imagined that keeping track of the health of the Bay involved a host of sophisticated monitoring techniques, space-age gadgetry, and feats of daring. None of us was prepared for the simple reality of an environmentalist whose dark features, agile body, and quick smile reminded some of us of the actor John Travolta.

Costa explained that the essence of his job is to chart the location of eel grass beds along the 228 miles of the Buzzards Bay coast. He said that he and his colleagues gauge the health of the Bay by documenting the presence of this grass that is the basis for a estuarine ecological system. The eel grass provides cover and habitats for many species of marine animals such as the scallop, mud crabs, small fish, and worms. The grass also absorbs some of the impact of waves, protecting smaller species of animals and prevents nutrient-rich soil from eroding.

So Costa has built a career on eel grass. During the 80s he made a map of all the eel grass beds in the Bay as part of his masters' thesis. In making his map of the eel grass beds, Costa had to interview a host of local people, scavenge for old aerial pictures of the Bay, and ask a lot of volunteers as well as professionals to put on pairs of deep waders and walk the coast and survey the eel grass. Now he is making another map of the perennial eel grass beds. This map is to study the changes between the 1980s and the turn of the twenty-first century. Sites lacking eel grass usually marked polluted areas from agricultural run-off and weeping septic systems. Places where the eel grass beds have increased in size show improved water quality.

"Well, how is the eel grass—and the Bay—doing?" one of our crew asked Costa.

"Things have turned around," he said and offered us this historical perspective. In 1984 the federal government started the Buzzards Bay Project to explore the health of the estuary and shortly thereafter designated the Bay as "an estuary of national significance." During the first six years of the study, scientists found the eel grass beds and water quality declining in coastal embayments around Buzzards Bay because of increasing fecal coliform contamination. To reverse this trend, the Buzzards Bay Project has been working side by side with a citizens group called The Coalition for Buzzards Bay. They are now working with 17 municipalities to reduce pollution by offering pump out stations for boat toilets, improving sewage treatment facilities, reducing lawn fertilizers in sensitive areas, and employing stormwater catchment facilities (like the one near Silver Shell Beach in Marion) to inhibit the flow of contaminants into the Bay. As a result of such efforts, Bay communities have opened up more than 300 acres of contaminated shellfish beds since 1992 and drawn thousands of Bay area residents into a grass roots commitment to the environment.

Maybe Joe Costa was not exactly Superman, and perhaps his career as an environmentalist was not as flashy as the celebrity scientists who work at Woods Hole Oceanographic Institute, but in his own way Costa showed us what it takes to save a bay if not our planet.

By the time we finished our visit with Joe Costa, the sky had turned blue, and we motored SARAH ABBOT out to her mooring at Ram Island where we could sunbathe and swim off the boat. But while most of us played like sea otters, one of the girls in the crew took our skiff out for a row and some exercise and found herself drawn like a magnet to Ram Island. Pretty soon I saw her deep in conversation on the beach with Hannah Moore. The island mistress looked confident and at ease in a simple T-shirt, shorts, and worn hiking boots while a baseball cap shaded her suntanned face. Donkeys, dogs, fiddler crabs, herring gulls, and four energetic young sons swirled around her.

A half hour later our shipmate returned to the boat proud to report that she had found her idol. Not only had Hannah Moore's strength, independence, and serenity charmed our shipmate, but her range of talents and accomplishments had surprised and inspired the teenager.

"She's not just a mother, wife, caretaker of about a dozen domestic animals and a whole island loaded with wildlife," boasted our shipmate, "but Hannah also teaches music in the elementary school, is involved in town conservation issues, and serves as the head of the Island Foundation."

True enough. The Island Foundation which Hannah Moore's late father started was an angel of support for local environmental initiatives like the Coalition for Buzzards Bay, scientific research, Marion's wastewater management projects, and a community sailing program in New Bedford. Our shipmate said that she saw Hannah Moore following in the same tradition as the town's great benefactor Elizabeth Taber. I had to agree: Hannah was the real thing, a Bay lady like so many other women on this coast during the past centuries who "made things happen ashore" while their men were off at sea. Dynamos. Yet these Bay ladies always seemed so serene.

Well, maybe calm, collected women like Hannah Moore were stirring things up in Marion village or on Ram Island, but very little of their energy disturbed the weary whalers aboard SARAH ABBOT. With the sun beating down, the winds light and fluky, and the temperature and humidity in the high eighties, the crew stretched out on the foredeck in bathing suits, nibbling on chocolate chip cookies and consuming mugs of lemonade. The scene could not have looked more lazy, but I sensed something stirred beneath the surface. You could see it in the way one boy unconsciously beat out a quiet rhythm on the deck with his hand, another boy sketched a picture of Ram Island furiously in his journal, and a girl fiddled with the braid in her hair.

"We're leaving, aren't we?" sighed one of the crew when I walked forward and sat down on the deck among the teenagers.

"It's a fair wind coming on," judged one of the crew who had fallen into the sailor's life and mariner's jargon as if he had been born to it. "Right, Captain?"

I nodded. The cold front that had brought the thunderstorms and rain had cleared out to the southeast and left us with a building north-wind. On this breeze we could sail to anywhere in Buzzards Bay in comfort and without the help of the auxiliary diesel. I knew that in the carpe diem spirit of Dead Pirates, we *should* set sail. But like many of the crew around me, I welcomed this warm, do-nothing moment in Marion. The crew deserved the chance to just vegetate; they had a long, hard passage behind them. Jackie, the schooner, and I had even more miles under our belt: we had been sailing now for more than a month. To me, right now, just staying in Marion to taste the pleasures of the harbor had the lure that stopping at Circe's Island must have had for Odysseus. Maybe the crew wouldn't mind if we just lay in Marion for another day or two.

In the midst of these reveries, I heard the Beverly Yacht Club launch rumble alongside and saw John Rogers climb aboard SARAH ABBOT. Back in the cockpit, Margaret had her sleeping bag, backpack, and crate of research books ready to hand down to the launch driver. Today was change day for the scientists; I had almost forgotten. Margaret and John split the duties on this third cruise, and this was the time and place for the passing of the torch. Suddenly, we were all on our feet hugging Margaret goodbye and briefing John with stories of our whaling cruise.

"So where to now?" asked John bouncing from one foot to another the way a man does who can't wait to put miles between himself and the land. "What an evening for a sail!"

The crew sniffed the warm northwind, looked at the old gibbous moon hanging in the bright blue sky, and exchanged glances. Slowly smiles began to bloom across their faces.

"Who is on deck watch?" asked one boy.

Five minutes later, SARAH ABBOT ran south out of the harbor with main, foresail, and jib drawing. Clearing Ram Island, we gathered in the cockpit and someone began to generate impressions of Marion. Soon everyone had something to contribute as if we wanted to catalogue the images of a place we could call "home":

keyhole entrance between Ram Island and Nyes Wharf

calm waters

well-protected harbor

a thousand sailing yachts on moorings

large summer cottages

Tabor Academy

tall swamp maples, oaks, and firs dominating the shore

a mix of sand, gravel, and rocky coast

many granite sea walls

oysters/mussels/quahogs

giant colonies of fiddler crabs

warm, murky water

lots of plankton

minnows

baby striped bass

gulls/osprey/cormorants/roseate and common terns

No doubt the captain of the MARY CELESTE had carried a similar set of memorabilia as a hedge against the unknown. And maybe he too felt an itching restlessness as he set sail on yet another trip.

XXI QUISSETT

Rarely have I been as undirected as when leaving Marion. As we glided south past Centerboard Shoal and sailed into the open Bay, I had but one clear purpose—to sail with the warm wind at our backs. Let's just explore the Bay like Gosnold did, I thought: we'll follow the water to the distant shore and see what turns up. While John Rogers enjoyed his first trick at the helm after a week ashore, quiet overtook the schooner. All you could hear were the sounds of chopping and dicing as the two students on galley watch worked at the table in the main saloon preparing a salad and garlic bread to go with our spaghetti dinner. Like seasoned mariners no longer ripe with the excitement of going to sea, the rest of the students retreated to their berths and lost themselves in reading, journal keeping, and naps. Meanwhile SARAH ABBOT coasted into the Bay with the swish of a magic carpet. Standing near the bows of the schooner, I hugged Jackie from behind with the force of a man in the full blush of romance, and I imagined what it was like to be a lover in Henry James's *The Bostonians*, gazing across the Bay where "the hazy shore on the other side of the water . . . seemed powdered with silver, a sort of midsummer light."

An hour before dark we passed Cleveland Ledge Lighthouse, looking like a white castle floating above the evening mist and shoal in the center of the Bay where President Grover Cleveland loved to fish. As we closed with Henry James' land of dreams on the Bay's southeast shore, the oblique angle of the sun reflected its fire in the windows of beach houses like the glow of a hundred Wampanoag camp fires. Then keeping clear of near-shore rocks and shoals, we veered southwest and searched the coast for a harbor. Collectively known as West Falmouth, the eight miles of coast stretching from Scraggy Neck to Penzance Point at the entrance to Woods Hole Passage are actually a pastiche of separate summer colonies that began to grow around small, local harbors at the turn of the century. First, we passed Megansett with its harbor like a small bay. On shore, thick pine forests covered bluffs and obscured rambling, cedar-shingled Victorian cottages. In the right conditions, the head of the harbor in Megansett could be a great site for students to work on cruise projects aimed at studying the relationship between tidal marshes and rocky coast. But with the wind backing to the west, Megansett would prove a rough anchorage and a difficult place for scientists to collect data.

We sailed south past Wild Harbor and Old Silver Beach which growing seas made unwelcoming to SARAH ABBOT. Probably Wild Harbor took its name from its exposure to the rough surge that pummels this anchorage in the Bay's strong, prevailing southwesterlies. And no doubt these same waves gave Old Silver Beach the fine sand that had been a magnet for the development of a beach club and tightly packed beach houses reminiscent of what you see in places like Malibu, California. Another mile to the south West Falmouth Harbor might have been a snug anchorage for our schooner, but a close look at the chart showed only four feet of water over the bar at the inlet and even less water throughout most of the harbor. Here was a place we could only enter on a high tide and in good light to avoid running aground.

We kept sailing. As the sun set, the crew gathered in the cockpit wearing jeans and sweaters to stand their watches, tell John more of their sea stories, and wonder aloud if we would find a harbor before dusk turned to dark. This was a question worth pondering as our schooner jogged south a half mile off Sippiwisset Marsh and then passed along an unbroken line of wooded bluffs. Fetching Gunning Point, we changed course several times to avoid submerged ledges.

Finally, one of the crew spotted a flashing red light ahead at the entrance to Quissett Harbor. Ten minutes later we turned eastward, jibed the sails across the vessel for a port tack, and sailed through a narrow cleft between two steep points as if entering a winding fjord. With Jackie at the wheel, John and I guided the crew in dousing the jib underway while the schooner followed the shadowy shorelines curve to the northeast. The green glow of our starboard running light illuminated three separate pockets of sailboats moored to the right side of the channel where several mansions kept watch from high bluffs. To the left steep cliffs stood overgrown with brambles and forest.

Just as the harbor entrance went out of sight around the bend in the shore astern, the wind all but died, and we found ourselves ghosting into a basin surrounded by a ring of hills and tightly-packed with two dozen moored boats. The digital depth sounder read 16 feet. Next to a wooden catboat that looked like something out of A *Storm Without Rain*, John Rogers spotted a float for a mooring pickup line, the only vacancy in a place too small and tightly-packed for anchoring. Without hesitation, Jackie swung SARAH ABBOT into a sharp left turn. For the next minute the schooner's momentum kept her creeping forward between moored boats until John hauled the pickup float and mooring rode aboard, the schooner stopped, and the crew and I lowered the foresail and—finally—the main. Nothing stirred except the occasional ripples from feeding fish and a chorus of crickets. The moon shown like a pale glow through the trees to the west. Without design, we had ended up in my favorite hurricane hole on Buzzards Bay. If there was one place where time seemed almost perfectly stopped on the Bay, it was here in Quissett.

Sleep claimed us early, and maybe that was why I found myself with the energy to rise at about 6:00 a.m. this morning and row Yankee ashore for a run. Yankee loves Quissett as much as I do because the entire north shore of the harbor is a wilderness of trails called the Cornelia Carey Reservation. Here a maze of trails lead through the woods to overlooks above Bay and harbor cliffs. Small secluded beaches abound. Since her puppyhood more than twelve years ago, Yankee has found the Carey Reservation prime territory for chasing, but never catching, rabbits. And after she gets thoroughly overheated she always descends to the small beach next to the mooring basin and wades in for a long swim. When I am sweating from jogging the trails with my dog, I join in the swim as well.

So Yankee and I had just finished our jog and swim when we met a sailing instructor at the harbor's edge waiting for her sailing students to arrive. A 19-year-old student at Harvard, Putney Cloos grew up in Quissett, and she talked to me about her home as Yankee and I dried ourselves in the sun. She said that her parents who are both local physicians have lived on the harbor for almost 20 years but still feel like "intruders on some ancient past that we're not a part of." According to Cloos, the harbor at Quissett had changed very little since the days almost a century ago when the Harbor House (on the Carey Reservation) was a seaside inn where chamber pots were the height of luxury for the guests. Those were the days before World War I when the family of Lilly Pharmaceutical heirs arrived at their summer mansion on the harbor with a parade of carriages, and the beautiful young women from the Marshall estate (now summer home for the National Academy of Sciences) rode around Quissett's shady lanes sidesaddle in long, white cotton dresses.

Putney told me that remnants of those days persisted in Quissett's rituals like raise-the-flagpole day, put-up-the-awning day, burn-the-brush day, paint-the-skiff day, and the yacht club ball. But she had heard residents around the harbor expressing concern for the future as the older generation of estate owners die off and their families can't afford to maintain the old summer mansions. Maybe a new breed of land owners was coming to Quissett. Perhaps, people would no longer believe—as the Marshall matriarchs had—that you could find God in Quissett sunsets and that Buzzards Bay life should be decorous and traditional. The day might come when a squadron of fiberglass motorboats would replace the fleet of classic gaff-rigged sloops that had been racing from the harbor for a hundred years.

"But not yet," said Cloos. The old houses still reigned, people still rowed or sculled their skiffs in the harbor instead of using motors, and the boatyard—the raggedy, little Quissett Harbor Boat Yard—still had a love affair with the care and feeding of wooden boats.

As if on cue, I saw a small wooden sailboat set out from the boat-yard wharf across the basin from us and sail slowly toward SARAH ABBOT. Aboard were a young man with a puckish grin, a woman with a long tangle of white-blonde hair, and two children in life vests. As they sailed by the schooner in the light air, the mother of the little girls reached out and put something on SARAH ABBOT's deck. Clearly, this family had business with me so I excused myself from Putney Cloos' company. By the time Yankee and I rowed out to the schooner, the small-boat sailors were more than a hundred yards down the harbor. Climbing aboard, I found a neatly folded sheet of paper with a penciled note written on it:

SARAH ABBOT—

You are welcome to the mooring until mid-afternoon when we expect the owner's boat to return. Please leave $25 dollars for mooring rental in the tin can on the dock. We've gone on a picnic.
Weatherly, Rick, Charlotte and Lily

"What's that?" asked Jackie as she came on deck and saw me reading the note.

Without speaking, I handed the note to my wife.

"From the boatyard?"

I nodded.

"Are they running a business or a hobby?" smiled Jackie.

Her question was rhetorical. To my wife, this note had a civilized, trusting, genteel tone that seemed lost on suspicious, harried America at the turn of the twenty-first century.

When I rowed ashore for a block of ice before lunch, I found the ice machine unlocked, a tin can inside for money, and the honor system at work there too. From a barn-like woodshop and office built onto the side of a hill next to the boatyard's marine railway, came the laughter of little girls, and I realized that the yard's first family had returned from their picnic. Drawn up the hill by the laughter and the sweet scent of mahogany sawdust, I entered the shop and found the girls playing hide and seek in a shed full of glittering, varnished speedboats with names like JACQUELINE and BABY BOOTLEGGER. As I began to get the impression that this tiny boatyard had become a haven for restoring exotic relics of the Roaring Twenties, I stumbled upon the girls' mother lounging at a dusty desk and dividing her attention between a pair of Canada geese in the harbor, her daughters, and an invoice in her hand.

Suddenly, I just had to ask: how does a person get a name like Weatherly? I knew a Stormy and several people called Spike; those were nicknames. Had this slender, blonde mother gained Weatherly as a nickname from some nautical exploit in the dim past?

"Nope," she smiled. "I was born in 1962, and my father named me for the twelve-meter wooden sailboat defending the America's Cup."

Do names like Weatherly seal a person's fate, I wondered, having named my own son Noah.

Weatherly Doris smiled.

"Look around you," she said. "My life is boats. Wooden boats. This is a family business—my father's yard; he builds and restores wooden boats. My husband Rick does, too. I wouldn't sail in anything else. Why change a good thing?"

When she said this, I gathered that she was speaking about traditions in her life beyond just wooden boats, but before I could pursue my inference, Weatherly's husband Rick bounced into the office slapping sawdust from the legs of his shorts.

"We change things here sometimes. We *got rid* of the gas pumps. *That* made things a whole lot more peaceful around here. We tell the customers who come looking for fuel, a travel lift, and launch service they just wouldn't be happy here. We got water, ice, rice, and advice. Some shellfish beds have reopened in the harbor. There are lobsters out there and a half dozen different kinds of ducks. In the shop we hate using the power tools; you can listen to birdsongs all day long in Quissett. They're hypnotic."

After my meeting with Weatherly's family, I heard the birdsongs as I rowed back to SARAH ABBOT with the ice. I guess that I really should not have been surprised to find the entire crew sleeping in their bathing suits on the foredeck as if they had come to Quissett on a yachting holiday. I joined them, and as I recorded these impressions in my log, the birdsongs swelled around me until my eyelids grew heavy. All I wanted to do was lie back and listen, but I should have guessed that the Bay was not finished with me yet.

XXII POCASSET

I woke to a memory of a foul weather forecast and an overwhelming sense of duty. A strong cold front loomed to the west, and if we didn't get moving, we would be weathered in by stiff northwest winds at Quissett for two days. We couldn't afford such a delay. This student crew still needed to survey several more harbors near the head of the Bay for their cruise projects before the end of our trip. Pocasset, nine miles to the northeast of Quissett, topped the list of primary stops for project work that John had given me after he came aboard and surveyed the students' projects and research needs. Feeling the pressure to be off for Pocasset, I roused the crew by blasting a tape of humpback whale squeals, groans, and moos over the stereo system.

My wife sat up, rubbed the sleep from her eyes, and mumbled, "You're risking mutiny, Captain Bligh!" I think she was only half teasing.

Thirty minutes later the crew had come alive and cleared the decks of personal gear before SARAH ABBOT departed Quissett's fjord harbor to meet a stiff southwest wind that felt like it blew from the mouth of hell. To the west on the other side of the Bay, the towering anvil-shaped cumulonimbus clouds that mark thunderstorms looked like a phalanx of pillars holding up the heavens. You could hear distant thunder.

Recalling a line from a Robert McCloskie children's book, I thought, "It's a comin'; she's a gonna blow!"

In preparation for the downwind run before us, I had the crew haul up only two of our three sails—the fore and the main—that would set best running before the wind. But just minutes after we cleared the harbor's headlands and began rolling from one beam end to the other in a foaming sea, I knew that the shelter of Quissett's inner harbor had lulled me into misjudging the force of the wind: even these two sails were too much for the schooner to carry in such a breeze. The 450-square-foot mainsail had to come down before we over-strained the rig. But for our crew, who did not have the experience to anticipate the movement of the vessel and gear in such rough conditions, dousing the main was an invitation for injuring someone with a flailing boom or losing a shipmate overboard from the pitching deck. Still, the sail had to come down *immediately*. I could hear the shrouds straining and see the center of the mainmast pumping back and forth from the surge of the waves. Seas crested above the schooner's stern, and the boat began to surf at 11 knots down the face of waves then stall in the troughs with a shudder. At the helm, Jackie spun the wheel at lightning speed first port, then starboard, then port again to keep the rudder alive and the boat tracking straight. For a second she shot me a look that begged, "Do something: I can't keep this up forever!"

Returning to the shelter of Quissett made the most sense, but we were already a half mile downwind from the harbor entrance and beating back upwind with these steep five- to seven-foot seas trying to stop us dead—even with the engine cranking at full power—would be really rough. The crew would likely be sick and the rigging would be tested to its limits. What a time for a lesson in how complacency aboard ship courts disaster.

As calmly as I could, I briefed the crew. Jackie would turn on the engine and steer the boat into the wind for no more than ten seconds while John and I doused the main. Craig, our Billy-Budd muscle man, would sit next to Jackie and trim in the main sheet to keep the boom from swinging dangerously over the cockpit when we turned into the wind. The rest of the crew could help by staying seated in the cockpit, holding sail ties ready to wrap around the main before the wind could play havoc with the loose sail when it fell. We had no time for a neat harbor furl; the crew should just keep both feet in the cockpit, heads clear of the main boom, and tie down the sail with a reefing knot asap. I told the students to practice tying the knot now around their legs before trying to do it on the swaying boom. This was going to be a rough ride. Was everybody ready?

As the crew tied their practice knots, I went below and secured all of the deck hatches: no doubt we were going to take green water over the bows when Jackie swung SARAH ABBOT into the waves. Finally, John and I defined our roles. He would brace himself between the main shrouds and the mainmast ready to release the main halyard when Jackie turned the boat. I would stand by Jackie in the cockpit in case she needed help. When the boat had made its turn to windward, I would join John at the mainmast to tug down the sail and get sail ties on the forward end of the sail.

Ready? Everyone nodded. I could feel my own heart pounding against my ribs, but as I looked at the crew no one looked scared. They looked focused. Several of the crew gave me a thumbs up.

"We can do this!" I thought.

So we did. After Jackie swung the schooner quickly into the wind before a wave could catch us broadside and knock us down, the whole operation took just six seconds. Only once did SARAH ABBOT bury her bows in the waves and let a cascade of green water race down the decks. Then as the wave of water spilled astern, we had the mainsail down, sheeted home, and tied. As Jackie rolled the wheel to her right, and the schooner turned back toward her downwind course, a wave crashed against our quarter and showered the crew. Some crews might have howled in dismay, but these guys cheered.

The rest of the run up the Bay to Pocasset was a sleigh ride with the foresail driving us along in excess of 7.5 knots. The crew sang, making up new verses to the theme song for TV's *Gilligan's Island*. Meanwhile the pillars of cumulonimbus had merged into a dark wall on the northwest side of the Bay. We could see lightning strikes in the vicinity of Mattapoisett and Marion. Thunder rumbled in great drum rolls with just four seconds between the lightning flashes and the thunder. Since sound travels more slowly than light, the rule of thumb is that every second measured between the flash of lightning and the sound of thunder is equivalent to a mile distance between the observer and the storm. By this measure the squall line lay four miles off and closing. Checking the National Weather Service storm bulletin on the VHF radio, I learned that this squall line was heading our direction at 15 miles an hour, covering a mile every four minutes. With our boat speed about half of the storm's, I knew we needed to cut the distance between us and our anchorage in Pocasset to less than two miles if we were to be secured on a mooring when the squalls hit.

From where we were in the Bay, following the dog leg of channel buoys to Pocasset would be a 2.5-mile trip. Probably too much water to cover before the squall line hit. To beat the storm we would have to veer out of the channel and sail a straight line that threaded a needle over a nasty reef called Southwest Ledge that extends from a headland known as Scraggy Neck. I'd made this inside passage before in settled weather paying close attention to my bearings and eyeballing the ripples, eddies, and dark patches beneath the surface that are the telltale signs of shadowy ledges. But on this trip conditions were too rough for me to see the subtle signs of the ledges. The pitching and rolling of the schooner would make getting accurate bearings off the land difficult. And due to the rough seas, there would be no turning back once we had committed ourselves. Yet here lay the route that would assure our beating the squall line to Pocasset, and I wanted to beat that storm. It packed blinding rain and probably winds gusting over 60 knots. Common sense dictated that SARAH ABBOT be safely moored behind Bassetts Island, protected from the waves and wind when the storm struck.

So as we hurtled north, I scrambled below to plot a careful course through this inside passage that followed a 10- to 15-foot-deep trough between the submerged boulders on Southwest Ledge. Then after I came back on deck to gain my bearings, and prepared to issue a course change to the girl at the helm, I shivered—maybe from the force of the wind but maybe from something else. Then, as I stood there hugging myself for warmth, I heard a voice inside my head.

"Trying to race the weather has killed a lot of good mariners and pilots, Mister."

The voice was my late father's, and he had spoken these words to me ten years ago as he tried to dissuade me from steering SARAH ABBOT on a short cut through the Thimble Islands in Connecticut to beat a thunderstorm to our anchorage at Stoney Creek. But I had ignored his advice that came from 27 years of beating the odds against catastrophe as a Navy seaplane pilot and submarine hunter. In the end I had run the schooner hard aground. Had a local lobsterman not been nearby to tow SARAH ABBOT back into deep water, the boat could have pounded herself to pieces in the swells.

No, no way! I was not repeating that scenario. Trying to beat the weather to Pocasset had caused me to make a questionable decision today about putting to sea from Quissett and setting too much sail; I was not going to compound the problem by taking a risky shortcut over Southwest Ledge. Even if the squall hit before we made harbor we could survive by staying in the channel, dropping the foresail, and steaming into the wind. We could use the radar, Loran and GPS to help us hold a safe position if a downpour cut off our visibility. Yes, it would be rocky, rolly, and miserable, but we would survive, no question. If something went wrong and we struck on Southwest Ledge, we were lost. No short cuts, no more racing the weather. Time to listen to the wisdom of the man I had often thought of as an old pelican.

So SARAH ABBOT stuck to the channel, and as the squall line fumed to within two miles of us, I rigged a ground cable to trail off the leeward main shroud to safeguard us from a lightning strike. Then I briefed the crew on everyone's duties if the squall hit, and reassured them that the schooner's wire rigging created a cone of protection to shield us from a lightning strike. Finally, I had everyone put on their slickers and life vests and review abandon ship procedures. We were ready for the worst. An old pelican would have been proud.

As it turned out, the squall line just grazed Pocasset, and SARAH ABBOT flew before 30-knot gusts right into a fork behind Bassetts Island which sits like a wooded keystone between the long arms of Scraggy Neck and Wings Neck. We snagged a mooring in virtually still water. Furling the foresail and brushing the spitting rain from my eyes, I found myself smiling.

"What's so funny?" asked Jackie.

"I just was thinking about some lines from Hamlet," I confessed.

"Well . . . ?"

" 'If it be now, 'tis not to come; if it be not to come, it will be now; if it be not now, yet it will come. The readiness is all.' "

"You're one weird old pirate," judged my wife.

After the squalls cleared, a rainbow hovered in the eastern sky while we ate a late dinner of macaroni and cheese in the cockpit. The air and the water grew stiller than still. As the sun set we watched a pair of large owls begin circling on swift, dark wings over the marsh in the heart of Bassetts Island. A great blue heron sailed past us at deck level, looking like a shadowy pterodactyl. The woods on the island and to the north on Wings Neck hummed with locusts. Yellow lights from a few exclusive summer homes filtered through the dense growth of oak and maple.

This anchorage among a dozen unattended cruising sailboats was one of my secret places on the Bay. Unless you came here on weekends when there was a steady parade of recreational boats plying the channel, you almost always had this spot to yourself. With a sturdy dinghy and an engine full of gas, you could spend hours exploring the channel that looped around the north side of Bassetts Island and connected a half dozen coves carved into the coastline east of the island. No place except Westport at the other end of the Bay had such an expansive network of waterways that formed a distinct estuary unto themselves, a perfect nursery for all manner of fish. Two years ago an *Oceans* crew pulling our 100-foot seine net along the shores of Bassetts Island found the water full of baby striped bass, a discovery that surprised and delighted scientists at Woods Hole Oceanographic who had scant evidence that the famous game fish spawned in the Bay.

Now, feeling the urge to explore, I coaxed Jackie into joining me for a long dinghy ride under the stars on the pretext of trekking to Pocasset Village to buy ice cream for the crew.

"Start your homework," I counseled before Jackie and I left John in command and jumped ship. "The ice cream store is miles away: see you in an hour and a half."

In truth, we could have made the round trip for ice cream in 35 minutes. But after such a hectic afternoon, I felt like getting out alone with Jackie in a small boat and following the trails of star shine on the water. I don't know why, but such trips have a way of unlocking my mind, especially when I share these moments with my wife.

With the four horsepower Suzuki purring, our skiff soon put a half mile between us and the schooner. The night opened up around us. I slowed the boat. Now, Jackie and I sat side-by-side on the middle seat of the skiff and watched the purple shadows of the low hills standout against a sky of diamonds. Coasting along like this, we rounded the northeast tip of Bassetts Island. Here, the waters stretched out before us into Hen Cove, Red Brook Harbor, and Hospital Cove, and we found it easy to understand why the Wampanoags had named this place Pocasset——"where the waters widen."

Decades after the Pilgrims had settled in Plymouth, Pocasset remained Indian territory. Twelve miles north was a large winter community of the Wampanoags called Manomet. During the summer the Indians from the village trekked south to plant corn on the rolling hills overlooking Bassetts Island and to fish the adjacent waters of Pocasset. The trail the Indians followed was known as the Megansett Way; it ran south along the east side of Buzzards Bay. Richard Bourne, an early colonial explorer of the Megansett Way, found "eight Indian Families of about thirty persons in Pokesit." During the next four decades, Bourne established a colonial outpost at Sandwich and endeavored to "civilize" the Wampanoags by introducing them to Christianity. After these efforts, he boasted "40 praying Indians" in the village just south of Pocasset which had been named Cataumet after a local Wampanoag sachem.

No doubt the cooling southwesterly Bay winds that blow into the face of Pocasset and Cataumet were an attraction to the Wampanoags, but so was the abundance of fresh water that they could get from Hope Spring. In addition, hunting was good in the Pocasset estuary. The now-extinct Great Auk, a huge penguin, used to congregate at a tide pool that became known as Penguin Hole. Easy to kill, the auks provided excellent down feathers for insulation, tasty flesh which the Indians smoked and stored for the winter, and significant amounts of oil that could be rendered from the bird's fat. The Indians harvested the auks at a subsistence level, and the animal thrived. But after the Indians introduced Europeans to the wonders of the Great Auk, market gunners hunted the creature into oblivion by the mid-nineteenth century.

White settlers were slow to intrude upon the Indian territory of Pocasset/Cataumet. The Plymouth Colony had been developing for about 50 years before five white families purchased local lands from the Wampanoags in the 1690s. The early settlers were not simply subsistence farmers like those who had first settled Dartmouth and Rochester on the other side of the Bay. They grew wheat to mill and sell as flour, tapped pine trees for making turpentine and pitch to sell to shipyards, and raised sheep.

Jackie and I could imagine those sheep farming days as we motored along the sandy beaches on the east side of Bassetts. While a few vacation homes dotted the island woods near SARAH ABBOT's anchorage, at least two thirds of the island remains undeveloped with the old sheep paths still leading through a mix of forest, marsh, and—especially—low dunes overgrown with beach plums and poison ivy. But looking to the mainland shore across the water, the host of lights winking from houses brought to mind more recent times. During the eighteenth century, the five original households at Pocasset expanded to 29. In addition, once-migratory Wampanoags settled permanently. They formed the second largest Indian community, after Mashpee in Southeastern Massachusetts, which after 1765 enjoyed the so-called Indian Church, a Methodist congregation with services in both Algonquin and English. During these years a packet sloop carried Indian goods like fox skins, raccoon skins, deer skins, beeswax, and oysters from Pocasset to the Boston markets.

Taking a turn through the broad cove known as Red Brook Harbor—now dominated by Parkers Boat Yard, Kingman Marine, and slips or moorings for hundreds of pleasure boats—Jackie and I could see the shadow of rigging cranes looming above the skyline. Cranes have been a part of this landscape for almost 200 years. Following the American Revolution Captain William Handy who had prospered as a whaling skipper began building vessels on the shores of Red Brook Harbor. During the first quarter of the nineteenth century a string of large sloops and schooners like the LOVE, SOPHRONIA, NANCY, RESOLUTION, and the ACHSAH PARKER slid down the ways. Gangs of boat carpenters swarmed over the yard, framing up ships like the brig FAME in 1806 and heading up the road to the Dimmick Tavern for a glass of stout or "flip" after work.

During the colonial era, settlers discovered that the fresh water bogs of Southeastern Massachusetts were rich in limonite, bog iron which could be mixed with readily available seashells (for lime) and smelted over a charcoal fire to produce pig iron. So the skills of iron making were well developed in coastal Massachusetts when iron master Hercules Weston arrived at Pocasset in 1822 to set up Cape Cod's only cold air blast furnace on the north shore of the Pocasset River.

At first the Pocasset furnace limited its market to the shipyard and local blacksmiths. But as decades passed, the shipyard declined, and the demand for iron ware of all sorts accompanied a wave of national property fueled by the industrial revolution; the old furnace became an ironworks and foundry producing kettles, pots, pans, and stoves. This business grew so prosperous that one of the incarnations of the company, Blackball and Burr, had their own trading schooner and warehouse on the end of the wharf at Barlow's Landing.

The iron business went defunct in 1891, but the wharf remains. This is where Jackie and I tied up our skiff to fulfill our promise to buy ice cream for the crew. Walking from the landing to a convenience store at the crossroads which marks the village center, we found it hard to picture this town as an industrial enclave: our walk passed amid tall shade trees and a thickly-settled community of summer homes built in the late-nineteenth and early-twentieth centuries. But now, from deep in the village woods, came the blast of a train's horn, and the sound reminded me why and how Pocasset had changed almost overnight from an industrial village to a summer place.

XXIII WAREHAM

After four and a half weeks of sailing, I admitted being weary.

"I turned 50 this summer," I thought. "Maybe I'm just getting too old to go dashing around the deck of this schooner like a bucaneer, heading out to the banks to search for whales, glueing myself to a radar screen for hours, or trying to outrun storms." Maybe it was time for this old seadog to hand over the helm to a younger generation like John Rogers and my son Noah who was just finishing college.

All I wanted to do was vegetate here at Bassetts Island and play out the last few days of this final *Oceans* cruise of the summer. But back on the boat, the crew buzzed about completing their own research as well as the scientific and cultural survey of Buzzards Bay. The crew wanted to check on the harbors at the head of the Bay where hearsay claimed the environment was at risk because of development and urban decay.

To be frank, the rumors of pollution and communities gone to seed had always kept me away from exploring the harbors at the northeast end of Buzzards Bay. In fact, my knowledge limited itself to my many transits of the Cape Cod Canal connecting the head of Buzzards Bay at the west end to Cape Cod Bay at the east. Not once in more than 20 years of passing through the canal had I taken a side trip into one of the harbors that lay nearby. I just had no interest.

But now the crew reminded me of our mission to make a complete and thorough survey of the Bay.

"You have to finish what you began," Jackie counseled. This sounded like fortune cookie advice.

Nevertheless, I once again called the crew to raise sails; then we

During the summer of 1872 a new rail line opened connecting Pocasset (and the other communities on the southeast coast of Buzzards Bay, including Woods Hole) with the Old Colony rail line that ran from Bourne to Boston. With the new rail service, the cool winds and clean water of Buzzards Bay lay just a half-day's train ride from the heat, crowds, malaria, and yellow fever that plagued Boston during the summers of the late-nineteenth century. Trains with names like *The Flying Dude* ran ten or fifteen trips a day from Boston to the Pocasset station carrying hordes of affluent summer people in search of Eden. Boarding houses, fine hotels, summer cottage developments, fishing clubs, and yacht clubs followed.

Pocasset's old families had a name for these sophisticated folk who arrived on *The Flying Dude* to buy up the shorefront property, build or rent summer cottages, sunbathe on the beaches, race their yachts, and "rusticate with a boat and a good book or two for the season." The summer people became known as "downers" as in "down from Boston" or "down on vacation," "down for the beaches." Now downers own the bulk of Pocasset property. They *are* a local tradition.

Years ago SARAH ABBOT's crews had obtained permission from the majority owners of Bassetts Island to carry on non-invasive scientific studies on the north beach, but rarely had our crews seen anyone on the island or glimpsed the life of downers who rusticated in a compound at the center of the island. But this morning, when our crew went ashore to work on a capture/release study of island fiddler crabs the crew found themselves shaking hands with a man who reminded some of them of Ronald Reagan. This was Stuart Chase, master of the island, and in the tradition of genteel downer society he invited us "up the path through the woods" for coffee and muffins with him and his wife Moni.

After this greeting, Stuart Chase led our crew to seats on a porch looking west over the Bay and told us that in "real life" he had been head master for almost thirty years at Eaglebrook, an exclusive pre-prep boarding academy in Deerfield, Massachusetts.

dropped the mooring, and headed out into Buzzards Bay. A stiff northwesterly breeze blew in the wake of the cold front that had cleared the coast with the squall line last night. We motorsailed to windward with the sails acting more to steady the vessel than as motive power against the foamy chop on the deep blue water. Our destination was the mouth of the Agawam River east of Marion. If we could follow the channel along the sharp twists of the river for four miles, we would sail SARAH ABBOT right into the Narrows at the heart of the town of Wareham, historically one of the commercial centers on the Bay. Having heard stories for years about this river's tendency for unexpected shoaling with sand and mud did nothing to stir my enthusiasm for this passage. My only hedge against a potentially dangerous grounding was timing the trip to ride the last hour of a 4.5-foot flood tide up the river, giving the schooner a reasonable chance to make the passage without striking the bottom.

As we passed Bird Island to its east and closed on the mouth of the river, the surface winds backed 90 degrees to the southeast. The breeze sometimes shifts like this when air over the land on shore heats up and sucks the cooler air off the Bay into the vacuum. Visually, this was a disconcerting phenomenon because you could see by the clouds overhead that the wind was still honking from the northwest right out of Canada, yet down here on the Bay it flowed from another direction entirely. But odd as this situation looked to my eye, I welcomed the wind shift because it gave the crew a chance to silence the motor, ease the sheets, and ride the breeze up the river. We could do a bit of windjamming again.

During the trip from Pocasset, a student had been busy reading about the history of Wareham from two books in the vessel's library. Now, passing Bird Island, she asked, "Isn't this the place where the NIMROD launched its famous attack on Wareham?"

True enough. I had read the story, too. When war broke out again between the States and England in 1812, the English tried to blockade Buzzards Bay. To this end, during the spring of 1814 the British brig NIMROD and a 74-gun ship of the line named the SUPERB patrolled Buzzards Bay. Local mariners played cat and mouse games with British warships throughout the conflict, but the villages of the Bay declared themselves neutral in an attempt to prevent an English attack like the one that had destroyed New Bedford in 1778.

As warm weather crept over the Bay in 1814, Falmouth natives antagonized the English by refusing to give up the Nantucket packet which the British believed to be engaged in smuggling. In response, the NIMROD bombarded Woods Hole from noon until night and then began sailing up the Bay in search of targets of opportunity. Wareham, near the head of the Bay, was perfect. The town enjoyed a reputation for manufacturing leather, cotton, and iron, as well as shipbuilding, but unlike the Bay's other commercial center New Bedford, Wareham had no fortifications to protect it. So, on June 13, 1814 the NIMROD with six barges rounded Bird Island and dropped anchor somewhere in the vicinity of Wings Cove. Two hundred and twenty soldiers boarded the barges, rigged lateen sails, and paraded up the river.

Aboard SARAH ABBOT we had several accounts of the subsequent events of the raid that cost Wareham 12 vessels and $20,000, but the one that captures my imagination most was penned to Commodore Perry, the American naval hero of the day, by eight of Wareham's leading citizens who hoped for an American reprisal for their losses. They wrote:

"We saw the British with six barges approaching this village with a white flag hoisted in one of them at which time our flag was not hoisted, but Thomas Young was carrying it down the street towards the wharf, where it was afterwards hoisted . . . On the landing of the commanding officer from the barge where our flag was hoisted, the officer did agree that if he was not fired on by the inhabitants he would not destroy any private property belonging to the inhabitants; but he would destroy public property which did not belong to the town, and requested one of us to point out the Falmouth property or vessels, which we agreed to do, and one of us went into the barge with the second in command, and then they took down their flag of truce and proceeded to set fire to the Falmouth vessels. They then landed a part of their men, and in violation of their agreement set fire to private property, by setting fire to a vessel on the stocks and five others that were at anchor and a Plymouth vessel. They were reminded of their agreement, and that they had taken advantage of us by false promises, but they threatened to set fire to the village and put the inhabitants to the sword if any resistance or any attempts were made to put out the fires, for they did not care about any promises they had made; also they landed a party of men and set fire to a cotton manufactory. They then returned to their barges, took 12 of the inhabitants with them on board their barges, and said if they were fired upon by the inhabitants they would put them to death. The commanding officer ordered the flag of truce to be hoisted, and the second in command swore it was a damned shame and disgrace to any nation to enter a village under a flag of truce and commit the greatest outrage and depredations possible, and then return under a flag of truce, but on orders being again given by the commanding officer the flag of truce was hoisted. Our men were landed about three miles below the village, and the barges proceeded on board the brigantine NIMROD, then lying in the bay."

The part of the story that I really liked was that while Commodore Perry never extracted revenge from the NIMROD, Buzzards Bay did, almost instantly. While getting underway again, the NIMROD ran aground east of Bird Island. Local legends had long asserted that the crew jettisoned the ship's top deck cannons overboard in order to lighten the vessel and float her free and that local scallop fishermen, even in modern times, had been known to snag their drags on these cannons. Over the centuries, most citizens dismissed these tales as romantic fantasies. But several years ago the Bay gave up some of its secrets: divers uncovered a clutch of the NIMROD's cannons during a search mounted by the Kendall Whaling Museum of Sharon, Massachusetts. Buzzards Bay had trimmed the NIMROD's claws so that she never had the courage to strike here again.

Gliding past the Stone estate and its château looming through the evergreen woods at the foot of Great Round Hill, the crew of SARAH ABBOT had different vistas than the British soldiers navigating the river's shoals and meanders nearly 200 years ago. In the marines' day, the peninsula of Sippican Neck to our west, now dominated by exclusive homes and the Stone estate, was an outlandish place—a pirate's den—where local lore claimed, "There existed . . . a huge mass of rocks behind which . . . was a cave, the entrance to which was not noticeable to those who passed along the shore. If anyone had landed at the exact spot, it might have seemed a narrow hole entering the crags . . . fitted up with many relics of wrecked vessels and a pile of shells that rose high against one of its walls."

Wilderness still dominates the eastern side of the river, but once we passed the Stone estate, and the river began to branch and meander, we found hundreds of vacation cottages built side-by-side on tiny lots, each with a septic system. This was the part of the Bay I did not want to see. Not since Cruise Two had visited New Bedford had the specter of human pollution been so tangible, and I wondered aloud about whether these waters could still support a healthy ecosystem. When we rounded a bend in the river, we discovered the water turning as thick and green as the local Portuguese kale soup. I found myself wishing for the cool relief of a swim. But not here, not now, not in this cesspool.

So we doused sail without fanfare and began to ease toward a berth at Cape Cod Shipbuilding's float at the Narrows, a spot where the river shrinks to a channel between the yard's marsh shore and ancient granite wharves. With several tall brick chimneys breaking the skyline, the Narrows had a nineteenth-century industrial look even though the factory buildings on the wharves had been converted into condos with private boat slips. On our side of the channel, the shipyard sprawled.

The scene reflected the town's history. Known as Agawam, meaning "place where fish are caught," the settlement developed in parallel with its neighbor colonial Rochester in the late seventeenth century following King Philip's War. The early years of Agawam's colonization mirrored the real estate speculation and the farming homesteads typical of the north shore of Buzzards Bay. But Agawam had a different topography from neighboring settlements—steeper hills, abundant lakes, and several rivers that fell 50 feet between their head waters and the Bay. Colonists quickly realized that their fortunes lay in harnessing the water power from the Agawam, Wankinco, and Weweantic Rivers. Eventually, nine dams were in place, and by 1739 the village had incorporated as the town of Wareham.

Grist mills were the first industries to use the water, but tanneries, cotton fulling mills, a paper factory, iron furnaces, and rolling mills for making nails followed as America gained its independence and the Industrial Revolution spread. Of course, shipbuilding bloomed here just as it did on neighboring harbors. Looking across the channel as we eased along the dock in a foul current on this hot, sticky afternoon, I could picture life here a century ago when the chimneys of the iron furnaces were smoking. Rafts of cargo schooners lay to the wharves unloading coal to fuel the furnaces and iron ingots from Poland for conversion into hollow ware and nails. The smell of oak sawdust filled the air as carpenters sawed planks for a whaler at the shipyard.

"You just missed all the excitement," grinned a shipyard worker as he broke my daydream and offered to take our lines while we docked. "We had a whale in here just the other day!"

He had to be kidding. A whale—rare even in the crystal water of Buzzards Bay—had navigated this soupy river? No way!

But a copy of a local newspaper brought down to us from the shipyard's office proved the truth of the dockman's tale. Complete with a picture of the 15-foot minke whale, the article explained how this juvenile baleen whale had been discovered snorting and blowing just north of the Narrows in the salt pond behind the Cumberland Farms convenience store on Main Street. The animal seemed disoriented and unwilling to swim under a highway bridge and through the Narrows to the broader waters of the river and Bay to the south. As a crowd of over 400 people gathered, harbor master Bill Ellis and our old friend Dr. Michael Moore got in an outboard and teamed up with helicopters from local TV stations and neighboring cranberry plantations. With the helicopters working as spotters, Ellis and Moore were able to shepherd the minke out of the pond and down the river to safety.

"The minke must have come up the river to feed," guessed one of our crew. "But what in the world could it find to eat in these scummy waters?"

My sentiments exactly. Just the sweet, rotting stench of these waters sent shudders through my shoulders. But, of course, SARAH ABBOT is a research boat and this was a scientific cruise so I should not have been surprised by what happened next.

"Let's go see!" proposed John Rogers. Within minutes he had three students armed with plankton and seine nets out in the big dinghy to evaluate the health of marine life in the upper river. The results surprised us all: Here at the head of the river we found slightly lower salinity and warmer temperatures than we had found in the fish nursery that was Pocasset. And most surprising, the murky river water—which we had imagined to be oxygen starved by fecal coliforms leeching from a host of septic systems—turned out to register dissolved oxygen readings as good or better than we had found in Pocasset. According to John Rogers, we had found all the key ingredients for a fertile estuary in the midst of Wareham's urban center. Life on planet Earth had probably begun in a place like this. The water was not soupy with death; it was soupy with a half dozen kinds of plankton. A banquet for schools of small fish like herring which are, in turn, a staple food source for whales. The minke may not have been lost or disoriented at all as it puffed and splashed around the salt pond, speculated John; the whale might have been wild with the excitement of finding itself overwhelmed in the presence of its favorite food—like the crew of SARAH ABBOT when they get near an ice cream parlor.

Two of the girls sighed at the thought of ice cream. A boy began licking his lips unconsciously. I knew how they felt, so I handed one of the teenagers $10 from SARAH ABBOT's "war chest" and told the crew to go wild. Within two minutes they had abandoned ship and were literally racing each other to the ice cream coolers at the Cumberland Farms store up the street in town. John, Jackie, and I weren't far behind. Later, when the crew collapsed in their berths, we tried to read *A Storm Without Rain* aloud, but we hadn't read four pages before I heard a girl softly snoring against her pillow. Three pages later, a boy snored in harmony; another shipmate lay in his berth with his forearm over his eyes like a dead man. One drooled. Two others leaned together against a bulkhead at the head of a berth like a pair of rag dolls. I blew out the oil lamps and found my own sleeping bag and pillow where I dreamed of pods of whales singing their cello-like songs as they fed.

This morning we met Gordy Goodwin, the president of Cape Cod Shipbuilding. We came across him standing in the shipyard's office lobby looking hot from an excursion into the old gray and red storage buildings in the shipyard. In fact, one of the crew noted that Goodwin looked like his shipyard—simple and well-used, but at the same time enduring.

After inviting the crew into his office and offering us seats on an old couch, he began to unfold some of the shipyard's history. Gordy Goodwin sighed as he told us that he was the third generation owner, born in 1944 here in Wareham. As our conversation developed, he got louder and more excited. The crew was picking his brain with their questions, and he seemed to enjoy it. Totally without guile, Goodwin admitted to us that in the past couple of years his boatbuilding business had been struggling.

"Fiberglass sailboats last longer than wooden boats, so people don't buy them as often," he said. "Which is great if you are a boat owner, but a little rough if you are a boatbuilder."

When the crew's questions steered Gordy Godwin back to the past, he continually spoke with reverence for his father who had run the business for most of the twentieth century. It seemed that Goodwin always felt his father's presence and competition when speaking about the past successes of the company. By way of contrast, he pointed out that during his father's heyday the yard built a boat a day; today the yard's craftsmen build a boat a week.

According to Goodwin, his company had been evolving for more than 100 years. Cape Cod Shipbuilding Company started as a wagon wheel building factory in 1880, but with the invention of rubber tires and steel wheels the company decided to make wooden sailboats instead. Then, in 1951 the company began making fiberglass boats and employing hundreds of workers from Wareham. Some of their more popular models were the Bullseye, Mercer 44', and the Herreshoff 12½. But, during the past few years, the demand for new boats had dropped, so the Cape Cod Shipbuilding Company had to release many of its employees.

Maybe this was the end of an era, but Gordy Goodwin didn't think so. Today, he was keeping his yard alive as a repair and storage facility, as well as a spar-building shop. But maybe better times lay ahead because the company had just added new, popular models to their line of small sailing craft. Goodwin beamed with smiles as he told our crew that his daughter Wendy had come to work for the company. He had hired her just like his father hired him to help in the office. I got the sense that family businesses like Cape Cod Shipbuilding were a way of life in Wareham, and they had always been struggling to evolve and survive. Maybe this port no longer produces ships like the 415-ton whaler KUTUSOFF, launched from these shores more than 150 years ago, but boatbuilding continued at the Narrows. Something told me that being part of this tradition helped Gordy Goodwin sleep like a baby at night in spite of the struggles and evolution of his business, as if being locked into Bay traditions by birth and circumstance was all this man needed.

Finast kind, Gordy.

XIV   ONSET BAY

As foreign and uneasy as Wareham made me feel, it was becoming a known quantity. But my stomach positively curdled when I contemplated heading out to visit our last scheduled port of call and complete our survey of Buzzards Bay. The place is called Onset. Its harbor lies only about five miles from the Narrows and overlooks the meeting point between Buzzards Bay and the Cape Cod Canal. For years I had avoided Onset village, actually a district on the eastern border of Wareham, because this resort community that stood on the bluff overlooking the head of Buzzards Bay carried a reputation for crime, drugs, unsavory people, and filth. Around Buzzards Bay, people said that seasonal laborers drawn to work in the massive cranberry bogs of Wareham had found cheap off-season housing in Onset's summer cottages and out of poverty and desperation turned Onset into a crumbling coastal slum. I could hardly think of a worse place to bring SARAH ABBOT's exploration of the Bay to a close. But as Jackie had reminded me the other day, I needed to finish what I had started. In my brain I heard the voices of the explorers and dead pirates chorusing, "carpe diem—stir it up!"

So an hour before the tide crested in Wareham, I made good on what I had started and asked the crew to cast off the lines.

"Lines away," they echoed.

Two minutes later we had all three sails set, and SARAH ABBOT rode the first of the ebb tide out of the Wareham River with no British barges or minke whale in sight. As the schooner jogged along at five knots I devoured six oranges as if to fortify myself against the prospects ahead.

An hour and a half later, we were sailing into Onset Bay before a warm, late-afternoon southwesterly when my eyes did a double take. Instead of an urban war zone, I saw a village that had the spit-and-polished look of classic Victorian resorts like Cape May, New Jersey, and Oak Bluffs on Martha's Vineyard. Turreted, gingerbread homes dressed in pastel yellows and blues, as well as the rich colors of a flurry of American flags, swelled the landscape on the steep slopes above the town pier and along the beaches near the Point Independence Yacht Club. Mellow reggae and Jimmy Buffet ballads drifted from the pool bar at the Onset Bay Inn and Boat Club. Families with healthy, tan children waded in the shallows.

"Cool!" said a couple of the kids.

"Pizza party," proposed some others.

Suddenly, I felt like I could breathe a little deeper.

So it was that as dinner time loomed, I declared a cooks' holiday. As soon as we had secured the vessel, we motored to the beach in our big dinghy and headed into town. As the sun set, the facades of the inns and B&Bs came alive with strings of white lights accenting historic architecture that reminded several of our crew of Disney World's "Main Street, USA." Families strolled the walks along the edge of the park and the crest of the bluff facing the harbor, wooded Wicketts Island, and the breeze. Couples stopped for ice cream in shops glowing with Gay Nineties ambiance. Popcorn and cotton candy vendors drew a crowd to the pier where passengers lined up to board a steel cruise boat for a trip up and down the Cape Cod Canal. Entering Marc Anthony's Pizza, we found the proprietor offering a litany of comic commentary on his life and business. Two dozen customers waiting in take-out lines in the restaurant chuckled the way people used to when summer meant hanging around the neighborhood Italian bakery and buying slices of pizza, not just because it was tasty, but because this was entertainment.

Where were the crime, drugs, and bombed-out buildings that I had been hearing about for decades? We asked Marie Oliva, Director of the Onset Bay Association, when we ran into her after dinner outside the Point Independence Yacht Club. The question energized this 30-year-old woman with short dark hair. As she talked with us about Onset's boom, decline, and renaissance, she paced back and forth like an athlete before a competition.

Oliva told us how Onset began to develop as a resort with the coming of the Old Colony Railroad to Wareham in 1848. Developers brought the rail line from Boston to Buzzards Bay with hopes of reducing the cost and time of shipping Wareham's industrial goods which had always depended on long, dangerous packet voyages to reach population centers like Boston and New York. But the railroad had the additional effect of exposing tens of thousands of Boston's growing middle class to the cool winds, warm waters, good fishing, and pristine coast of Buzzards Bay. For 24 years, before the railroad extended through Pocasset to Woods Hole, Wareham was the only area on the Bay easily accessible to tourists. And they came in droves. Not to explore industrial Wareham, but to lull around on the beaches, bluffs, and islands of dramatic Onset Bay, a two-mile trip from the rail depot by carriage and, later, narrow gauge and electric rail service.

Seeing a market, developers quickly subdivided the breeze-cooled terrain on the bluffs above Onset Bay into minuscule lots and sold these properties with miniature Victorian cottages whose main features were airy front porches and huge windows to ventilate the summer heat. Called the Onset Bay Association, the community grew—like so many other camp towns across America—on the Chataqua concept which emphasized retreating to nature for spiritual contemplation. Outdoor religious services provided entertainment and community glue, and Onset also attracted a host of fortune-telling spiritualists like the On-I-Set Wigwam Workers who revered mystical aspects of Native American culture.

By the beginning of the twentieth century, Onset had become a small-time Coney Island overbuilt with hotels, dance halls, and casinos. The railroad and packet steamers brought tourists by the thousands. The spiritualists fled for quieter climes, and Onset got the reputation for being a low, populous resort. Vacationers with more money could now take the extended rail lines to less-developed enclaves around the Bay like Pocasset, Quissett, Marion, and Mattapoisett.

According to Oliva, Onset went into a serious decline in the 1940s as gambling regulations closed the casinos and other seasonal businesses began to wither and die. The cost of summer rentals fell, and landlords began letting their properties year round to anyone who could come up with the modest rent. Property values fell. Then, between 1965 and 1975, drugs moved in, and urban-style youth gangs began to appear.

"Onset hit rock bottom," she said.

Since those days the Onset Bay Association of property and business owners had been trying to revitalize their community. But signs of their success were slim until a 1993 grass-roots initiative to revive Onset won a half-million-dollar grant to support historic preservation, small business loans, and a significant increase in police presence. The result has been the disappearance of the crack houses and gangs, a complete facelift on the village's quaint, historic housing stock, a host of wholesome public events like concerts and fairs, and the return of families in the mood for an old time, light-hearted outing by the Bay.

"We had to fight a lot of apathy in the beginning," recalled Oliva as she remembered the beginning of this bootstraps operation.

"You would never know it now," judged one of our crew nodding his head toward the thunder of applause rising from the village green as a band concert began. "This place is dope."

Maybe he could have found a better metaphor, but I knew what my young shipmate meant. Walking the streets, I could not resist sucking in the scent of cotton candy and gobbling a box of popcorn from a street vendor like the kid I was more than 40 years ago on a family vacation to Virginia Beach.

Later, back on the schooner, our crew carried their sleeping bags on deck to stretch out and listen to a medley of show tunes like *Summertime* from Porgy and Bess drifting over the water from the band concert on the village green. Jackie, John, and I grabbed our own sleeping bags and joined our shipmates. As the brass section of the orchestra swelled to the last bars of the song, we saw the first flare of a skyrocket go up, followed by four more. Two seconds later the music ended. The rockets burst with heavy thuds and lit the sky like strobe lights. Even before the popping had stopped, five—no, ten—more rockets zipped into the sky. Fireworks bloomed directly overhead, and for a half hour the night sky rained red, white, and blue stars. In the dark Jackie and I gave each other back rubs until my whole torso felt wrapped in silk for awhile.

After the last shower, from somewhere off in the distance came the sound of people singing. The song was the old Beatles' classic *Sgt. Pepper's Lonely Hearts Club Band*. At first, the tune seemed totally out of context with the scene—but then again—maybe not.

When the singing ended, the night was so still you could hear the clang of a bell buoy more than a mile away in the Cape Cod Canal. After this evening the crew only had one night left aboard SARAH ABBOT. But they were in no way ready to leave the Bay, this vessel, and these shipmates. How could they? In spite of all the things this crew had been through together, they weren't truly Dead Pirates yet.

XXV CASTAWAY ISLAND

I awoke to find Jackie sitting at the table in the main saloon doodling in a notebook. When she had finished her drawing she tore it out of the notebook and handed it to me. It was a pencil sketch of a skull and crossed bones.

"I was thinking the same thing," I confessed.

Stumbling into the galley with toothbrush in hand, John looked at Jackie's sketch on the table and smiled.

"Castaway Island?" he asked.

"One last adventure," I said.

"I think it's time," said Jackie.

She meant that this crew had become so comfortable aboard SARAH ABBOT that they needed one final challenge to keep growing. We all needed a new adventure to free us from the blues that come with the end of a voyage.

"I heard them talking last night," said John. "They're expecting something: they heard about Cruise Two's treasure hunt in Marion, but they have no clue about the island."

I flicked on the VHF radio and picked up the National Weather Service's marine forecast "from Chatham, Massachusetts, to Watch Hill, Rhode Island, out to 25 nautical miles."

"Today—fair weather," stated the announcer. "Southwest winds 12-15 knots, visibility 5 miles in haze."

"It's safe," I judged. "The weather's good! Let's go."

"Now?" asked Jackie.

"We could be at sea before they wake up," mused John as he looked out the saloon window. "They'll never know where they are; the haze will block out the shoreline."

I pulled the *Eldridge's Tide and Pilot Guide* off the bookshelf, opened it to the section on Cape Cod Canal tides, and told Jackie and John what I had suspected. According to the tables, we only had an hour and a half before the tide turned against us in Hog Island Channel. If we wanted to break out of Onset Bay and escape treacherous foul currents funneling into the canal through Hog Island Channel, we had no time to lose.

"I'll make the tea," said Jackie, "if you guys get us underway!"

As I climbed topside to start the engine, I felt the rush of adrenaline pulse through my body that always came with a sudden decision to put to sea. This was something like what I had felt when Crew Two had brought SARAH ABBOT into Woods Hole safely through fog and stormy weather. Something like what I felt when the fin whale had swum beneath the schooner and rose again to stare our little ship in the eye.

A second after the Volvo perked to life, John walked forward in soft barefoot steps so as not to awake the sleeping crew and cast us free of the mooring pennant. Seconds later we were gliding east through a layer of ground fog toward a fiery sunrise and the place where Onset Bay meets the Cape Cod Canal and Hog Island Cut. Once this area marked the quiet head waters where the Monument River spilled into Buzzards Bay, Indians fished for eels, sport fishermen cast they lines, and clammers worked the sand bars. But everything changed with the digging of the Cape Cod Canal.

Shovels first broke ground in 1907, but the canal's origins root in the seventeenth century and the Plymouth Colony. In 1623 Miles Standish undertook a small boat exploration of Cape Cod Bay and discovered the Scusset River which flowed into the southwest corner at Sandwich. After sailing inland on the 9-foot tide to the head of the river, Standish and crew dragged their boat three miles through a valley until they reached the Monument River which could carry them downstream to Buzzards Bay. Standish returned to Plymouth and proposed that a canal be dug through the valley, connecting the two bays. If the Pilgrims had undertaken the task, the canal would have been the first public works project in America.

The venture was too costly for the fledgling colony, but the idea for a canal surfaced like clockwork every 30 to 40 years thereafter for the next two and a half centuries. Yet no actual construction took place until the 1880s when a dredge arrived to begin cutting a channel at Scusset Beach on Cape Cod Bay. After 7,000 feet of initial dredging, the effort foundered and was not revived until 1904 when August Perry Belmont entered the picture.

Belmont was the son of a wealthy financier and heir to a Bourne family that included Commander Matthew Calbraith Perry (grandfather) who "opened Japan," and Oliver Hazard Perry (uncle), hero of the 1813 Battle of Lake Erie. He had the right financial and social credentials to draw together a pool of investors to build a canal across the isthmus of Cape Cod. In addition, Belmont was known as a winner capable of building New York City's first subway, raising thoroughbreds like Man O' War, and sponsoring America's Cup victors. Within three years of taking on the project, he had raised the capital and executed the necessary engineering studies to build a canal that would free America's coastwise shipping from making the dangerous trip around the outside of Cape Cod. Financial studies estimated that if half the 30,000 vessels carrying cargo around the Cape each year used the canal, the ditch could earn about a half million dollars a year by charging tolls.

Anticipating such a bonanza, Belmont and Company built mammoth dredges, laid railroads, employed steam shovels, and attracted crowds of the curious. After repeated setbacks, the canal finally opened for commercial traffic in July 1914. Not including the entrance channel in Buzzards Bay, the canal measured 7.5 miles in length, 100 feet wide, and 25 feet deep. But while the canal shortened the sea trip from New York to Boston by 70 miles, only 5,000 vessels took advantage of the canal during its first year of operation. The canal's tolls and reputation for wicked currents in excess of five knots deterred many mariners, and Belmont and his investors lost money. Accidents and debts plagued the canal, and the federal government finally took over control of the troubled enterprise in 1928, handing the day-to-day operations of the ditch over to the Army Corps of Engineers who removed all tolls. In 1935 the Corps broadened the channel to 480 feet to permit two-way traffic, increased the depth to 32 feet, and dredged a new straightforward approach to the western end of the canal via Cleveland Ledge Channel and Hog Island Cut. Traffic and tonnage in the canal soared during World War II when Buzzards Bay became a staging ground for North Atlantic convoys. Today, the canal handles more than 30,000 vessels annually, at least 6,000 of which are cargo ships. Many of the larger vessels are coastal tankers or tugs and barges carrying petroleum products up and down the coast to refineries or storage depots.

On our way to Castaway Island, SARAH ABBOT had to slow to a crawl and give way to one such tug and tow as we poised on the threshold between Onset Bay and Hog Island Channel. Fully loaded, the barge passed in front of us looking like a black submarine on the verge of a dive with only a few feet of her 25-foot deep hull showing above the water. After the barge had passed, the vacuum created by its wake sucked our schooner right out into the channel like a helpless piece of flotsam, and I knew the fear of a vessel gone out of control that the canal inspired in every captain bringing a boat into these turbulent currents. While I revved the engine and spun the wheel furiously to compensate for the eddies and whirlpools, John kept watch for other traffic that might materialize out of the ground fog which had thickened to the east.

"Ship," he barked, pointing astern toward the canal's eastern entrance. "It looks like it's gone out of the channel and aground."

With one eye still on the tug and tow westbound ahead of us, I turned to see what John was pointing to. He was right: less than a mile behind us I saw the silhouette of a 500-foot freighter that looked to have made a detour from the canal and entered shallow Buttermilk Bay. But I knew this ship: the PATRIOT STATE was not lost or aground. She was tied to a pier at the Massachusetts Maritime Academy's campus in the town of Buzzards Bay. As a school ship for the academy, the PATRIOT STATE made this pier her berth when not on her winter training cruises.

Jackie came up for a look while I was explaining to John what I knew about the PATRIOT STATE and her mission to train merchant marine officers.

"It kind of puts our little schooner and program in perspective, doesn't it?" she said. "What a Goliath!"

She had a point. Our 55-foot schooner and 18-student *Oceans* program looked puny compared to the PATRIOT STATE and the college it sails for. Over the years, I had worked with a number of the Academy's graduates, attended several safety seminars at Mass Maritime, and come to respect this small college of 800 students for its high standards and hands-on education. Begun in 1891, the Academy is not only the oldest maritime academy in continuous operation in the United States, but its graduates have been consistently first in the nation in passing the Coast Guard licensing exams for deck and engineering officers. Part of the school's success is due to the training it provides in computer-driven simulators that recreate handling a large tanker or tug and tow under a multitude of weather and sea conditions. The Academy's Oil Spill Response Simulator and the Slow Speed Diesel Training Simulator (for ship's engineers) trains working professionals as well as cadets.

"Pretty impressive," admitted John after listening to my little sketch of Mass Maritime.

"But we've got something they don't," I bragged.

"Like what?"

I reached into the pocket of my fleece sweater, pulled out the black eye patch I carry for moments requiring a sense of high drama, and positioned the patch over my right eye.

"*The Dead Pirates Society*!" I proclaimed.

"Sometimes I think you're way too deep into this buccaneer make-believe," said the love of my life, shaking her head and rolling her eyes.

"You love it!"

"I can't help it: I'm a sucker for men who don't shave regularly."

"Do you have a sister?" asked John stroking his chin stubble.

We all laughed. An extremely eligible bachelor, John had turned his search for the perfect woman into something of an epic during the years we had been shipmates.

"What a crazy life we lead out here," chuckled Jackie.

So true. I knew the Dead Pirates Society smacked of some rowdy fraternity invented by a group of Jimmy Buffett fans after far too many boat drinks, but everything about it brought a smile to my face. The eight-year-old in me loved pulling on the eye patch, striking the Stars and Stripes, and hoisting the Jolly Roger when we were in close quarters with a boat loaded with young kids. And the latent camp counselor in me got a rush from surprising a crew with an unexpected treasure hunt or the challenge of being marooned for a night on Castaway Island. But most of all, I liked the way the Dead Pirates Society brought focus to the *Oceans* experience for our students. I firmly believed that on a cruise such as ours, shipmates came to feel what Joseph Conrad had called "the strong bond of the sea, and also the fellowship of the craft." For me the Dead Pirates Society gave a name to the spirit that our students discovered in themselves, their shipmates, and the challenges that came from hands-on learning about the sea. Now, I might add Buzzards Bay to that list of challenges as well.

After SARAH ABBOT broke free of Hog Island Cut, the breeze came up at 12 knots out of the south. The clocked chimed six bells: 7:00 a.m. While Jackie steered the schooner, John and I hoisted all three sails. Then Jackie spun the wheel to the right, and the schooner caught the breeze over her port side, heeled under the force of the wind, and took off like a rocket for the center of Buzzards Bay. With the seas still calm, a plume of foam raced along the lee side of the vessel as the knotmeter climbed through 6.5 knots of boat speed. The coastline faded away in the mist, and soon we were alone—a painted ship on a painted sea. Standing near the bows and bracing myself between the foremast shrouds and the jib halyard, I heard stirring in the forecastle beneath my feet. Girls' voices rose from the forward hatch, and I knew that the sudden heeling of the vessel had disturbed our youthful sleepers.

"Well, good," I thought, taking off my eye patch and stowing it in my pocket for future acts of piracy. The crew should be up here witnessing this spectacular morning and SARAH ABBOT running out to sea with all the grace David Stevens could build into a schooner.

I wanted the crew to relish the sights, sounds, and smells of these moments, but try as I did, standing alone here on the foredeck, I couldn't keep focused on the here and now. My mind kept looping back to the Dead Pirates Society and our plan to maroon the crew on Castaway Island. Tucked in the back of the ship's log next to the radar in the nav station was a dog-eared photocopy of *Youth* by Joseph Conrad. On the backs of a few pages, my ragged handwriting had recorded the founding principles of buccaneer worship in fading, blue ink. Almost a decade ago, one of our research crews had gathered in the main saloon one night in Provincetown after a successful trip offshore to find humpback whales. We had been full of the fire that came with having traveled among whales, and we wanted to celebrate our kinship across time and space with legendary adventurers who lived life by the motto carpe diem. So it had been in this spirit that I had served as secretary to the ship's company and recorded their collective wisdom:

THE DEAD PIRATES SOCIETY
Articles of Faith
Purpose:
>   *to suck the marrow of the sea*
>   *to woo, to waste time, to go a whaling(wailing?)*
>   *to continue the traditions of self-reliance and*
>   *adventure*
>   *exemplified by THE IMMORTALS*
>   *Bert O'Neil (the ghost on SARAH ABBOT)*
>   *Captain Kidd*
>   *Jean Lafitte*
>   *Blackbeard*
>   *Long John Silver*

antennas among nearby rocks. Striped bass moved like ghosts ng the shadows cast in the water by clouds. Sea robins, flounder, and es tried to make themselves invisible against the sandy bottom.

It was not until early evening, after stuffing ourselves on chicken w over rice, that John coaxed his students into the dinghy. I ferried them hore for a field trip on Castaway to study the bird colonies at the other le of the island. Once the crew had disappeared over the island hills, ckie and I scurried around SARAH ABBOT preparing the gear that would be sential to the students after we marooned them. First, I checked the VHF adio for the National Weather Service Broadcast to make sure we had set-led weather to insure a safe night for the students on the island and SARAH ABBOT in this tiny anchorage. Satisfied by the forecast, Jackie and I took a large garbage bag and filled it with sweatshirts, jackets, and jeans. We stuffed four sleeping bags in a second garbage bag, a flashlight, a cache of snack food, two gallons of lemonade, bug spray, and a handheld VHF radio to communicate with SARAH ABBOT in case of an emergency. Then Jackie wrote a note on a paper plate giving safety instructions and explaining that the crew had been cast away, *pirated*, for a night on the island as a final test of their worthiness to become Dead Pirates. Finally, we carried the gear ashore, picked up John, and retreated to the schooner where I once again pulled on my eye patch. Then I hoisted the Jolly Roger, and the three officers of this brigand schooner gathered in the cockpit to clink steaming mugs of spiced tea to let the good times roll. Ashore, all hell broke loose among the crew. One of the teenager's journals picks up the story from the crew's perspective:

"On the island, John said he had to go back to get the binoculars and that he would meet us on the other side of the island where the birds were. Before he left, he told us to come back to the beach when the boat's horn was blown because the skiff couldn't land on the other side of the island. I thought his last instructions were strange because he was going to be back with the binoculars, but I didn't think too much about it.

"We didn't start our assignment of watching birds until we had wasted some time taking pictures of the sunset and scaring the seagulls by

Calypso
Circe
Medusa
Charles Darwin
and . . .
Bob Marley

Who Shall Be Members:
all those who dream of reclaiming the coastal wilderness that belongs equally to all creatures; all those who dare to reject vanity, privacy, showers, fresh running water, and real milk in favor of the free flow of natural bodily essences, the development and appreciation of inner beauty, the fellowship of the craft, the cleansing nectar of salt spray, and the nutrients inherent in Crystal Light lemonade, Carnation Instant Milk, and—of course—the sacred PB&J.

Where Meetings Shall Be Held:
on the beaches that are the rightful property of all creatures, OR the saloon of the schooner SARAH ABBOT, depending on the weather.

When:
when the evils of privilege, class, money, racism, sexism, and spiritual intolerance threaten the strong bond of the sea, the fellowship of the craft, and the pursuit of life itself, OR any time we want to party (i.e. eat cookies).

How:
meetings shall be founded in readings from the sacred texts—Youth, Moby Dick and A Storm Without

Rain—especially when rendered in the indigenous accents of the members. In addition, meetings shall be a forum for the presentation and discussion of plans for sucking the marrow of the sea.

Here we were beyond the sight of land, alone with the hush of the wind in the sails and, unknown to the student crew, heading for their rendezvous with Dead Pirates' destiny on Castaway Island. One of a handful of deserted islands on the Bay, Castaway's name did not appear on any chart except those aboard SARAH ABBOT, nor did the charts offer any hint that a vessel might find a protected, deep anchorage among the reefs that surround the island. Simply put, the location of Castaway Island— and the approach route through a reef of submerged boulders that could tear the bottom out of a boat—was a secret. The uninitiated would never venture this way: Dead Pirates tell no tales! But like Hideaway Cove the anchorage existed, Castaway thrived, a daughter of Buzzards Bay lost in time and space.

Time moved like the mola mola, a giant ocean sunfish the size of a queen-size bed, that we saw drifting with the current and waving a pectoral fin skyward in a lazy act of surrender to the elements. Meanwhile, with quiet jabbering that respected the privacy of others, the crew meandered through their morning rituals of dressing, washing, and eating before settling into independent reading in their science texts, journal keeping, or conferring with John and me about their cruise projects and writing. With just a hint from Jackie, the crew set up a watch schedule of their own device.

I was down below checking the radar for ship traffic and plotting our course to Castaway when I heard the girl at the helm ask John where we were headed.

"It's probably my favorite place on the Bay," he began. "Castaway Island is a paradise for wild things. The captain says we have the right weather to make the trip so I thought you guys would like to see it."

"It's sort of a secret or—well—sacred place f[...] Society," added Jackie.

"What's it like?" probed one of our teenagers.

"There are five different bird rookeries on the islan[...] weave through the shallows; sometimes you see fox, rac[...] loads of wild berries to eat," rhapsodized John.

"But what does it look like? How will we know it wh[...] asked a shipmate.

"Did you ever see Walt Disney's *Peter Pan*?" asked Jack[...]

"Cool!" gushed a boy as an image of Neverland must ha[...] his head.

"Really?" asked another boy with a skeptical edge.

"You'll see," said Jackie.

Four hours later we did. Rising like a mirage amid the [...] water that sparkled like a billion drops of mercury, the purple sil[...] of hills materialized off the starboard bow less than a mile away.

"Holy shit," gasped one of the crew, picking up his sketch boo[...] beginning to draw furiously to capture the image.

"Welcome to Castaway Island," I said imitating Ricardo Monta[...] in *Fantasy Island*.

Several students brought cameras on deck and began clicki[...] pictures.

"You have no idea how much you're going to love this place,[...] smirked John as he winked at Jackie and me.

Even at this distance, I could hear the blackbacks and herring gulls laugh.

Fifteen minutes later, we had struck and furled sails, and threaded our way through a field of submerged boulders into a tiny, sand-bottomed basin with eight feet of water directly off a small beach. We set two anchors to hold our position clear of the rocks, and the crew dove overboard en masse. The water temperature felt tropical, and had a clarity three or four times greater than any place we had seen on this cruise. Wearing one of the schooner's snorkeling masks, students could watch lobsters waving

throwing rocks. By the time the horn blew, we had been settled and working for only ten minutes. Straggling back around to the other side of the island, we were faced by an empty beach. The only thing present was a mound of plastic bags. The skiff was off the stern of SARAH ABBOT.

"I was the last one to reach the pile of bags, but I had already figured out what happened. We had been deserted or *pirated* as the paper plate attached to the bags said in its instructions and explanation. To initiate us into the Dead Pirates Society, we had to rough it for a night on the island and write a song about our voyage on the SARAH ABBOT. Our first reactions were ones of anger and denial that they had left us on the island.

"Once we got over the initial shock, we took an inventory of what the adults had given us to survive. The ingredients for s'mores and stove were good, but, once we counted the sleeping bags, we were not so optimistic. There were only four for the six of us, and one was a mummy bag that didn't unzip all the way. We began grumbling again, but we soon accepted our fate. We were stuck on an island overrun with birds for the night.

"We sat down with the one flashlight that was provided and began our song. A couple guys wanted to compose a rap, but the idea was soon nixed for the tune of *Gilligan's Island*. It actually seemed relatively easy to create the words, although we often became stuck on a rhyming sound. We laughed at our escapades and tried to include them all. After a few verses, which covered our trip to the point when we were coming back from whale watching, we grew tired of composing. The best thing about the song was that it put everyone in better moods so we began to really enjoy ourselves. Before, we were angry at our adults for *pirating* us on Castaway Island, but after our songwriting and singing we were savoring our forced isolation.

"Because we had experienced many memorable events such as the trip offshore for whales, watching each other puke over the side, and exploring Provincetown, we were already close. But somehow, being stuck on an island in the dark with nasty bugs invading our personal space, we got even closer to each other than we had living on the boat for nine days. Through the night we talked about everything. Conversations describing our ideal mates led to each person's vision of love and a discussion of beliefs about afterlife. It was the first time I had ever slept beneath the stars without any shelter (or covers for that matter). Every one of us saw shooting stars."

As the crew sorted out the dilemma of being cast away and began to make their peace with the Bay, the island, and the night, Jackie, John, and I sipped our hot tea and watched through binoculars. Eventually, all we could see were shadows that seemed to dance around the low flame of the camp stove, collide, and merge into a low, many-headed creature. A melancholy Tom Waits song called *Sailin' Away* was playing on the tape player when we heard the first singing from the shore. Even though we couldn't make out the words of the crew's song, we turned off the tape player and listened. The song echoed over the Bay. The sound of Dead Pirates burying treasure.

Later, I could still hear the singing after I crawled into my berth for the night. For some reason, the music reminded me of the singing of the whalers aboard the PEQUOD in *Moby Dick* while Ahab brooded in his cabin—torn between the chase of the white whale and longing to see his wife and only child back in Massachusetts.

The next morning the crew came back aboard the schooner, and six sandy, smiling faces huddled together under the fluttering Jolly Roger and belted out their opus for all the natural world to acknowledge that this crew aboard SARAH ABBOT had now earned the right to call themselves Dead Pirates. John, Jackie, and I snapped pictures of the Pirates with a collection of cameras as they sang their own words to their beloved theme song from *Gilligan's Island*.

The singing went on for about twenty verses, but I can't remember them: I was laughing too hard.

EPILOGUE   **THE STORM**

The sound of distant thunder cut short our euphoria. Yankee began to bay as she does when she hears a siren. Pillars of cumulonimbus grew like billowing anvils to the west. On the VHF the National Weather Service was broadcasting a "severe weather statement" for the south coast of Massachussets and Rhode Island.

"Winds in the vicinity of strong thunderstorms could exceed speeds of 60 miles an hour," advised the radio. "All mariners in the vicinity of the coast should seek immediate shelter."

"That's us, guys," I said. "We're out of here. You know the drill." So began the final passage for Crew Three.

Three minutes later we had the engine humming, all the electronics up and running, and both anchors aboard and stowed. John and three students pulled the small dinghy on deck and rigged a second safety tow line on the big dinghy as three other students stood in the bow and gave me directions in navigating clear of the boulders cluttering the reef off Castaway Island. Then we set the foresail and ran before the wind in a breeze that had built from a zephyr to over 20 knots in just 10 minutes. A half hour later the sun vanished, and the sky to the west loomed black as coal. Rain began to spit from the sky. When I set the watch, I warned the deck crew to wear slickers, and told the rest of the ship's company to hit their berths and rest up; we might need all hands if these thunderstorms struck before we made it home to Marion. All you could hear aboard the schooner was the mechanical sweep of the radar scope and the creaking of the lanyard rigging as the vessel rolled before the building waves. I switched the watch every half hour so as not to wear down the crew's energy.

Four miles out of Marion, I was down below tracking the storms on the radar screen when I saw a yellowish green cloud of radiated particles bloom on the scope over Marion until the town disappeared from the radar like a science-fiction image of the apocalypse. As I clambered on deck, John was already pointing to something off the port bow; a white wall of rain raced toward us with the sound of an express train. While the girl at the helm turned the schooner to meet the squall, John and I doused the foresail and revved the engine just seconds before the storm hit. In an instant it was as dark as night on the schooner until lightning bolts began to illuminate the coast as they snapped at targets on shore. Twice bolts zapped the hilltop water tower in Mattapoisett; three strikes, accompanied with deafening bangs, lit up the radio tower at the head of Sippican Harbor.

Meanwhile rain came aboard in buckets and sheets. Below deck the rain made the sound of an endless drum roll on a timpani. In the cockpit our helmsperson pulled the draw strings tight on the hood of her foul weather jacket as she sat straddling the wheelbox, gripping it with her knees like a jockey. John sat beside her with his face muffled in his hood in similar fashion. He held his hands cupped over the compass so that the girl at the helm could see the numbers to steer by in the rain. Down at the nav station, the radar screen remained a blizzard of clutter no matter how I tuned it. But with the scope on the six-mile range, I could tell from the intensity of the clutter that the worst of the storm was tracking right over Sippican Harbor with no fewer than three distinct squalls lined up to hit our home port. We were just on the edge of these storms, and still we were picking up gale-force gusts.

"Thank God for radar," I thought. Without it, I might have been tempted to run for the shelter of Sippican Harbor—just as the severe weather statement had advised—and steer us right into the heart of the fury. But now the scope showed me where to steer to avoid the worst of this. To be safe all we needed was the time and space that mariners call sea room to sit out here in a holding pattern until the squalls passed.

"Alter course 90 degrees to the left; head two five zero; slow the boat to two knots." I shouted to the deck watch from the companionway.

"Ninety degrees left," echoed our helmsperson as she hunched over and squinted at the compass. "Two five zero."

"Slow to two knots," called John as he eased back on the throttle.

Bracing myself against the cabinetry in the nav station, I swung my head back and forth trying to assess both the image on the radar scope and the wild scene on deck. I wanted to be up there; I thought I should be at the helm in case of an emergency. But watching this scope was critical to a survival strategy, and I couldn't be in two places at once.

Suddenly, I heard a voice in my head. It was the soft Virginia accent of Pocasset's Moni Chase.

"You can't fight this old Bay. Just try to work with it. Try to keep your balance as things change."

The next thing I knew, I was poking my head out into the storm.

"Are you guys all right up there? Do you want relief?" I asked.

John shot me a thumbs up. He was OK.

"You need me on deck!"

The girl at the wheel shook her head.

"No! We got this covered."

I felt something shift in my chest. Then, for what seemed a long time, I held my breath.

"It's your boat," I shouted at last, "Stir it up!"

All of a sudden a smile broke over our helmsperson's rain-streaked face.

After a few seconds her mouth opened as if to release a balloon.

"I was just thinking about the book," she spit into the hiss of the wind and rain.

"Say that again?"

"About *A Storm Without Rain*," she laughed giddily.

"What do you mean?" I barked.

"The end. This storm is like the end when. . . ."

I lost her words in the howl of the wind and the symbol crash of thunder, but I knew what she meant. I knew that after this storm passed, we would have sailed through a time warp like Jack Carter had at the end of the novel. We would be returning to a world of e-mail, cloning, and space shuttles—a place where Wampanoags, whalers, and Dead Pirates were merely food for dreams. Everything—the whales, the night passages, the fog, Castaway Island, even Provincetown—would seem like things that happened to other people in another country a long time ago. With these thoughts came the hammer blows of my pulse against my arms and shoulders and temples.

Then, watching my young shipmate at the helm and her mentor John struggling together like comrades to insure the safety of our schooner and crew, I heard lines from *Storm* replaying in my head; they were sentences about friendships transcending time and space. Something like a shock crackled through my body. And I remembered what Jack Carter had said at the end of the novel when he tallied up what he had to show after his adventure:

"I've got the Bay, which I know in a new way. In some ways it doesn't change, though all the people have tried to change it. Or maybe they haven't tried hard enough to change it. It is part of some big natural magic, a force, a power, a sustainer."

I felt myself gasp for air.

In the cockpit rain lashed across the helmsperson's freckled, sunburned cheeks and plastered her red hair to her face. But as her eyes squinted into the storm, her hands moved rhythmically, automatically correcting the schooner's yaw in the gusts and sticking to her course—two five zero. A broad grin still spread across her face.

Lightning flashed in staccato bursts across the horizon.

Suddenly, a tangle of lines from Joseph Conrad rumbled through my mind as I remembered my own youth aboard the skipjack RUBY G. FORD with Captain Bart Murphy and "the feeling that I could last forever, outlast the sea, the earth and all men." Conrad had wondered, "Wasn't that the best time, that time when we were young and at sea; young and had nothing on the sea that gives nothing, except hard knocks?"

Thunder rumbled again, but its drum roll sounded slightly fainter as the squall began slipping away to the northeast. Little by little a cool breeze like the breathing of whales began sewing through my mind.

OK, the Dead Pirate and the story teller in me would like to imagine that when my eyes drifted back to the girl at the helm I saw the ghost of my youth standing watch behind her. His face poked out of his muddy, orange slicker with a half-cocked, silly grin on his face. The stubble of a post-adolescent beard was just coming on. And behind that young man stood the rain-soaked, shrouded figures of my father in a gold Navy pilot's hard-hat, skipjack Captain Bart Murphy, my great great uncle with his harpoon, Captain John Smith, and SARAH ABBOT's first skipper Bert O'Neil.

Some mystical part of me wants to claim that when I looked back into the darkness below decks, the faces of the crew in their berths changed. One second they were the people I had been sailing with for the last 10 days. Then they were the faces of Bartholomew Gosnold, Awashonks squaw sachem of the Sakonnets, John Paul Jones, Captain William Kidd, Herman Melville's Ishmael, one of the gray ladies of Woods Hole or Mattapoisett, and Marion's Elizabeth Taber. An instant later those same faces looked like Cuttyhunk's sea dog Donna Hunter, scallop angel Wayne Turner, catboat builder Skip Marshall, Naushon's youthful Eric Wish, Hannah Moore of Ram Island, and Quissett's Boat Yard's Weatherly Doris. Pirates. Dead Pirates all.

But this is no made-for-TV movie . . .

What is true and honest is that among the shadows beyond the glow of the radar scope, I found the real and welcoming face of my wife as she reached out from her berth with her arm and took my hand. And somehow I knew that soon she would be telling me she was pregnant with our son Jacob.

Finast kind! I could hardly wait until we introduced him to SARAH ABBOT, his big brother Noah, and all of us could start fresh exploring this place all over again through his young eyes.

So, for me Buzzards Bay truly has turned out to be an elbow in time. But I suspect that almost any place you sail can be. On the coast, the past is constantly reaching out to touch the present. And—as I found out—the future. Or maybe it is the other way around. To explore slowly—as under a press of sail—is sometimes to feel the *saudade* for all the rituals and people you thought that you and this land had somehow lost. And at the same time you discover how those traditions and friends endure. Whales vanish; but they don't vanish. Shipmates leave us, but they never really leave. Youth fades, but it returns in new shapes. Like this Bay—one day a millpond, the next day a tempest. But always here.

Looking ahead again through the rain, I could see the shadow of Ram Island taking shape at the entrance to Sippican Harbor. So we beat on; the squalls were passing off to the east. Somewhere whales slid beneath the waves like submarines, and young lions played on the beach. We were almost home with our Jolly Roger popping in the gusts.

FURTHER READING

Adkins, Jan. *A Storm Without Rain*. 1983

Allen, Everett S. *Children of the Light*. 1973

Bliss, William Root. *Colonial Times on Buzzards Bay*. 1888

Bourne, Russell. *The Red King's Rebellion*. 1990

Cadwalader, George. *Castaways, The Penikese Island Experiment*.
1988

Comiskey, Kathleen Ryan. *Secrets of Old Dartmouth*. 1963

Costa, Joseph. *The Buzzards Bay Project*. 1991

Cuttyhunk Historical Society. *Cuttyhunk and the Elizabeth Islands*.
1993

Drake, James D. *King Philip's War: Civil War in New England
1675-1676*. 2000

Ellis, Leonard B. *History of New Bedford*. 1892

Emerson, Amelia Forbes. *Early History of Naushon Island*. 1935

Farson. Robert H. *The Cape Cod Canal*. 1977

Geoffrey, Theodate. *Suckanessett, A History of Falmouth*. 1928

Landers, Elmer Watson. *From Pocasset to Cataumet*. 1988

Lewis, Arthur. *The Day They Shook the Plum Tree*. 1963

Maiocco, Carmen. *The Westport Point Bridge*. 1992

Mattapoisett Historical Society. *Mattapoisett & Old Rochester*. 1907

Melville, Herman. *Moby Dick*. 1851

Mendell, Charles S. *Shipbuilders of Mattapoisett*. 1937

Peters, Russell M. *The Wampanoags of Mashpee*. 1989

Rider, Raymond A. *Life and Times in Wareham Over 200 Years
1739-1939*. 1989

Sippican Historical Society. *Lands of Sippican*. 1934

Smith, Mary Lou. *Woods Hole Reflections*. 1983

Tucker, Donald F. *A Coastal Schooner Life on Southern New England Waters*. 1999

BALTIC MISSION
A NATHANIEL DRINKWATER NOVEL
by Richard Woodman
Captain Nathaniel Drinkwater and his frigate HMS ANTIGONE are ordered to the Baltic on an urgent and delicate mission. As Napoleon's forces push on towards Russia, Drinkwater faces his oldest enemy and is pushed to the brink of death.

IN DISTANT WATERS
A NATHANIEL DRINKWATER NOVEL
by Richard Woodman
Captain Nathaniel Drinkwater confronts formidable enemies, mutiny and a beautiful and mysterious ally. Off the coast of San Francisco, he is struck with an extraordinary twist of fate.

A PRIVATE REVENGE
A NATHANIEL DRINKWATER NOVEL
by Richard Woodman
Assigned to escort a mysterious convoy with a single passenger along the China coast, Captain Drinkwater is drawn into a vicious web of treachery, perversity and greed, culminating in a climactic rendezvous in the remote tropical rainforests of Borneo.

UNDER FALSE COLOURS
A NATHANIEL DRINKWATER NOVEL
by Richard Woodman
Acting for the Admiralty's Secret Department in the dregs of London's docklands, Captain Nathaniel Drinkwater advertises his cargo of Russian military supplies, thus embarking on a scheme to flout Napoleon's Continental System and antagonize the French Emperor's new ally, Tsar Alexander.

THE FLYING SQUADRON
A NATHANIEL DRINKWATER NOVEL
by Richard Woodman
Amid the internationally acrimonious atmosphere of 1811, Captain Nathaniel Drinkwater stumbles upon a bold conspiracy by which the U.S. could defeat the Royal Navy, collapse the British government and utterly destroy the British cause.

America's Favorite Sailing Books
www.sheridanhouse.com